JESUS

Jesus

apocalyptic prophet of the new millennium

Bart D. Ehrman

OXFORD
UNIVERSITY PRESS

OXFORD
UNIVERSITY PRESS

Oxford   New York
Athens   Auckland   Bangkok   Bogotá   Buenos Aires   Calcutta
Cape Town   Chennai   Dar es Salaam   Delhi   Florence   Hong Kong   Istanbul
Karachi   Kuala Lumpur   Madrid   Melbourne   Mexico City   Mumbai
Nairobi   Paris   São Paulo   Shanghai   Singapore   Taipei   Tokyo   Toronto   Warsaw

and associated companies in
Berlin   Ibadan

Copyright © 1999 by Oxford University Press, Inc.

First published by Oxford University Press, Inc., 1999
198 Madison Avenue, New York, New York 10016

First issued as an Oxford University Press paperback, 2001

Oxford is a registered trademark of Oxford University Press

Library of Congress Cataloging-in-Publication Data
Ehrman, Bart D.
Jesus : apocalyptic prophet of the new millennium / Bart D. Ehrman.
p. cm.
Includes bibliographical references and index.
ISBN 0-19-512473-1 (Cloth)
ISBN 0-19-512474-x (Pbk.)
1. Jesus Christ--Historicity.
2. Jesus Christ--Prophetic office.
3. Millennialism--Palestine--History. I. Title.
BT303.2 .E37 1999
232.9'08--dc21
98-31586

1 3 5 7 9 10 8 6 4 2
Printed in the United States of America

To Kelly and Derek

contents

preface

Scholars have written hundreds of books about Jesus (not to mention the thousands of books written by non-scholars). A good number of these books, mainly the lesser-known ones, have been written by scholars for scholars to promote scholarship; others have been written by scholars to popularize scholarly views. The present book is one of the latter kind. I really don't have a lot to say to scholars who have already spent a good portion of their lives delving into the complex world of first-century Palestine and the place that Jesus of Nazareth occupied within it. And frankly, having read scores of the books written by scholars for scholars, I don't think anyone else has much more to say either. This is a well-beaten and much-trod path.

There does seem, though, to be room for another book for popular (i.e., general-reading) audiences. It's not that there aren't *enough* books about Jesus out there. It's that there aren't enough of the right *kind* of book. Very, very few, in fact.

For one thing, most popular treatments are inexcusably dull and/or idiosyncratic. I've worked hard to make this one neither. You'll have to decide for yourself whether it's dull. But I would like to say a word about idiosyncrasy.

It's true that some rather unusual views of Jesus sell well: "Jesus Was a Marxist!" "Jesus Was a Feminist!" "Jesus Was a Gay Magician!" After all, if any of these views should be *right*, it might be worth knowing. What has struck me over the years, though, is that the view shared probably by the majority of scholars over the course of this century, at least in Germany and America, is equally shocking for most nonspecialist readers. And yet it is scarcely known to the general reading public. This is the view that is embraced in this book. In a nutshell, it's a view first advanced most persuasively by none other than the great twentieth-century humanitarian Albert Schweitzer. It claims that Jesus is best understood as a first-century Jewish apocalypticist. This is a shorthand way of saying that Jesus fully expected that the history of the world as we know it (well, as he knew it) was going to come to a screeching halt, that God was soon going to intervene in the affairs of this world, overthrow the forces of evil in a cosmic act of judgment, destroy huge masses of humanity, and abolish existing human political and religious institutions. All this would be a prelude to the arrival of a new order on earth, the Kingdom of God. Moreover, Jesus expected that this cataclysmic end of history would come in his own generation, at least during the lifetime of his disciples.

It's pretty shocking stuff, really. And the evidence that Jesus believed and taught it is fairly impressive. Odd that scholars haven't gone out of their way to share that evidence with everyone else. Maybe they've had reasons of their own.

The evidence itself plays a major role in this book. Most other popular treatments of Jesus rarely discuss evidence. That's a particularly useful move—to avoid mentioning the evidence—if you're going to present a case that's hard to defend. Maybe if you just tell someone what you think, they'll take your word for it. In my opinion, though, a reader has the right to know not only what scholars think about Jesus (or about any other person or event from the past), but also *why* they think what they think. That is, readers have the right to know what the evidence is.

I think that the process of understanding history is analogous to taking a long trip by car. If you know your driver well, you can simply say, "Take me to Pensacola," and assume that when you're there, he'll let you know. If your driver is a complete stranger, though, you're probably better off getting a map and figuring out the route yourself, just in case. The scholars who write books about Jesus are probably strangers to you. If they are going to take you on a trip through history, you have the right to know which map they've decided to use and which route they've opted to follow. The reality is that a lot of drivers along this particular road take shortcuts that end up going nowhere, and others find themselves revving their engines (for effect) in dead ends. More commonly, they end up in California, when you wanted to go to Florida. But they tell you it *is* Florida, and since you haven't been shown a map, you pretty much have to take their word for it.

For this book, I want not only to state my views of the historical Jesus but also to show *why* they are my views. As it turns out, the map itself is interesting. Pity that it's so unfamiliar to the people who would be most fascinated by it. In any event, I plan to use this book not only to map out a consensus view of the historical Jesus, a strange new land for many first-time travelers, but also to trace the route through the intriguing twists and turns of history, showing what the surviving evidence is and how it can be used. Anyone who doesn't like where the journey takes us will, therefore, be able to retrace his or her steps, figure out where I've gone astray, and take a different path that leads elsewhere.

For all those who stay with me to the point of destination, both those who decide to stay there and those who choose to explore some other routes, I'd like to say that I'm glad you're along for the ride and hope you enjoy the trip.

Let me end these brief prefatory remarks by acknowledging some of my debts. I'd like to thank my editor at Oxford University Press, Robert Miller, who urged me to take on this project and guided me along the way with uncommon skill. Once it was finished, I asked several people to read the manuscript and found their comments enormously helpful. First was my incisive graduate student at the University of North Carolina at Chapel Hill, Diane Wudel, one of the few people on the face of the planet who actually seems busier than me. Then came three relatively young (we keep hoping this) but seasoned (this one is assured) scholars in the field, friends with incisive minds, quick pens, and the good sense to agree with me on lots of interpretive issues: Dale Allison of Pittsburgh Theological Seminary, a prolific and learned scholar; Susan Garrett of Louisville Theological Seminary, one of the most sensible exegetes in the business; and Dale Martin of Duke University, the smartest New Testament scholar I know. Last and (with apologies to the others) best (for reasons unrelated to the manuscript) was my partner, Sarah Beckwith, a brilliant medievalist in the English Department at Duke, whose mind is something to behold.

I am dedicating this book to Kelly and Derek, my kids—so different from one another (and luckily for them, from me), yet both so terrific and so much a part of who I am. They mean far more to me than they will ever know. I would give them the world, but since I'm a bit constrained in my resources just now, they'll have to settle for this book.

Translations of the Greek New Testament and the Coptic writings of the Nag Hammadi Library are my own; for the Hebrew Bible, I've used the NRSV.

JESUS

the end of history as we know it

FOR NEARLY TWO THOUSAND YEARS THERE HAVE BEEN CHRISTIANS WHO HAVE THOUGHT THAT THE WORLD WAS GO-ING TO END IN THEIR OWN LIFETIMES. THE THESIS OF THIS BOOK IS THAT this belief is as ancient as the Christian religion itself, that it can be traced all the way back to the beginning, to the teachings of Jesus of Nazareth. Jesus thought that the history of the world would come to a screeching halt, that God would intervene in the affairs of this planet, overthrow the forces of evil in a cosmic act of judgment, and establish his utopian Kingdom here on earth. And this was to happen within Jesus' own generation.

It is a bold thesis, and I will need some time to develop it properly. I'd like to start not at the beginning of Christianity, with the life of Jesus, but closer to our own time, with views that continue to be found among some of Jesus' followers, contemporary visionaries who still maintain that the end of all things is imminent. From there we can move back-ward in time to the views proclaimed by the founder of Christianity. The question underlying this survey can be expressed simply: Is it possi-ble that modern-day (and nineteenth-century, and medieval, and early Christian) doomsayers who have proclaimed the imminent end of their world have actually subscribed to the views of Jesus, who proclaimed the imminent end of his?[1]

Starting Near the End

Future historians looking back on the twentieth century will not consider 1988 an exceptionally significant year. It *was* a time of large-scale natural disasters—a hurricane that left half a million Jamaicans homeless and an earthquake in Armenia that savaged entire cities and left forty thousand dead. Somewhat less earthshattering was the national news here in the States: in 1988 the federal government bailed out the country's savings and loans institutions and George Bush trounced an ill-fated presidential bid by Michael Dukakis. More significant politically were the developments on the international scene, in particular an uncommon number of international peace initiatives—the end of a six-year war in Nicaragua, the Soviet withdrawal of troops from Afghanistan, the Ayatollah Khomeini's proclamation ending Iran's war with Iraq, the first meeting between representatives of the United States and the PLO. But from a historical perspective, these developments pale in comparison with the cataclysms of the year to follow—1989, the year of Tiananamen Square, the fall of the Berlin Wall, the first free election in the Soviet Union, the execution of the communist dictator of Romania, Nicolae Ceausescu, the victory of Lech Walesa's Solidarity Party in Poland. By way of contrast, the most intriguing events on the American scene in 1988 were human interest stories that made little long-term impact on the history of the world: this was the year that Leona Helmsley was indicted for income tax invasion, that Sonny Bono was elected mayor of Palm Springs, that the Chicago Cubs played their first game in Wrigley Field under lights, and that evangelist Jimmy Swaggart staged a tearful confession before millions for taking a prostitute by the hand for purposes other than evangelism.

But it was not supposed to be that way. 1988 was *supposed* to be the year of the century—in fact, the year of all time. 1988 was to be the year the world ended.

The Peculiar Case of Edgar Whisenant

Proof was given in a widely distributed and remarkably influential booklet entitled *88 Reasons Why the Rapture Will Be in 1988.*[2] Written by Edgar Whisenant, a former NASA rocket engineer—who presumably, therefore, was a pretty smart fellow—the book, true to its title, enumerated biblical and logical reasons why 1988 would be the year that history would begin to end. Sometime during the Jewish festival of Rosh Hashanah, September 11–13, Jesus Christ would return from heaven to remove his followers from earth (the "rapture"), before a seven-year period of cataclysmic disaster on the earth (the "tribulation"). The tribulation would begin at "sunset 3 October 1988," when the Soviet Union invaded Israel and so inaugurated World War III (p. 47). The crises that ensued would lead to the rise of a personal agent of Satan, the Antichrist, who would lead millions away from God, and, in the midst of worldwide ruin and despair, declare himself to be divine. He would then try to take over the world's government, leading to a thermonuclear war on October 4, 1995, which would devastate the United States ("you can walk from Little Rock to Dallas over ashes only"), throwing it into nuclear winter (temperatures would never rise above -150° F), and eliminating its food and water supply. It wouldn't be a pretty picture.

The book may sound like a bit of science fiction, but it was read as Gospel Truth by a surprising number of sincere and devout Christians and sent untold numbers of others scurrying to their Bibles to see if these things could be so. Within months of its production, over 2 million copies were in circulation.

Numerous Christians, of course, pointed out that the Bible itself indicates that no one can know when the end will come. As Jesus states in the Gospel of Matthew: "But of that day and hour no one knows, not even the angels of heaven, nor the Son, but the Father only" (Matt. 24:36). Whisenant himself, though, was unfazed by Jesus' words. He, after all, had *not* predicted "the day and hour" of the end, just the week: "We just cannot know the day nor the hour. But I'm still just as happy knowing the week. I do not need to know the day and the hour" (p. 8).

The "88 reasons" that Whisenant provides for his readers are presented, for the most part, as biblically certain prophecies that many co-literalists had difficulty disputing. For example, from the same chapter of Matthew, after detailing the cosmic disasters that would happen at the end of time before the arrival of the Kingdom, Jesus said:

> From the fig tree learn its lesson: as soon as its branch becomes tender and puts forth its leaves, you know that summer is near. So also, when you see all these things, you know that he is near, at the very gates. Truly I say to you, this generation will not pass away until all these things take place (Matt. 24:32–34).

What, though, does this mean? Whisenant points out that in the Bible, the "fig tree" is often used for the nation of Israel. The fig tree "putting forth its leaves" is obviously a reference, then, to Israel coming back to life after a long hiatus. Thus, the end will come within a generation of the reestablishment of Israel as a nation. Since the modern state of Israel was established in 1948, and since a generation in the Bible comprises forty years—voilà! 1988 must be the year.

Whisenant claimed that dozens of other biblical predictions all pointed to exactly the same time. Most of them are highly complicated. As one of the simpler examples: in Leviticus 26:28 God tells the people of Israel that if they are disobedient, they will be punished "sevenfold" for their sins. Whisenant takes this to mean a punishment lasting seven "years," and he notes that in the Jewish lunar calendar, a year consists of 360 days. Moreover, in a number of biblical texts (i.e., Num.14:34), God reckons one day as a year. This means, then, that the punishment of Israel, before it can inherit its reward, was to last 7 x 360 years, or 2,520 years in all. According to the book of Daniel, Israel's punishment was to begin with the seventy-year oppression of Israel by the Babylonians, which started, according to Whisenant, with the reign of the monarch Nebuchadnezzar in 602 BCE and ended, therefore, in 532 BCE.3 If the time of Israel's punishment is to last an additional 2,520 years, that happens to bring us up to...surprise!...1988.

Despite the massive and detailed argumentation—it goes on for page after interminable page—not everyone, even among Whisenant's closest followers, was convinced. A letter written by Norvell L. Olive, executive director of the World Bible Society, the group responsible for circulating the book, serves as its foreword and, somewhat oddly, provides a kind of rearguard protection: "If for some reason these events do not happen, I cannot see how any honest person could say anything but good about someone who would sound the alarm when they smell smoke."

Mr. Whisenant himself, of course, was far more confident. Of his eighty-eight reasons "why 1988 looks like the year of the rapture" (p. 3), he points out that "Reason #17, added to reasons #10 and #11 plus reason #4, provides four witnesses of God that 1988 through 1995 is the 70th week of Daniel [i.e., the period of the great tribulation following the return of Jesus for all his true followers]. It all fits together a little too neatly to be discarded completely. I could not have faked it, had I wanted to" (p. 2).

Many readers agreed. Throughout the South, especially in parts of Appalachia, there were readers who took Mr. Whisenant's book with the utmost seriousness. Newspaper and TV accounts reported people quitting their jobs, selling their homes, and devoting themselves completely to prayer immediately prior to the fated week of September 11.

When the end didn't come, they had to pick up the pieces as best they could.

Mr. Whisenant, however, remained true to his convictions. When time continued on merrily after his projected date, he published another booklet, *The Final Shout Rapture Report: 1989*, explaining his slight miscalculation.4 By an oversight, he had neglected to observe that when the Gregorian calendar that we use today was first created in the sixth century, it started the first decade of the new era as AD 1. There was no year zero. But as a result, the first decade AD had only nine years. And so, all of his earlier calculations had been off by one year. But the end was sure, now, to come on September 11–13, 1989!

In places, though, the bravado of this second edition begins to ring hollow, as the author gives some statistical probabilities: "Jesus is coming, and I would give it at least a 50% chance in 1989; if not then, an abundance of Scriptures point to 1992. However, if the birth date of Christ is off one or two years, then it could be 1990 or 1991. There seems to be a lot more evidence for '89 or '92 than any other time for the Rapture" (p. iii).

Taking the World by Storm:
Hal Lindsey's Late Great Planet Earth

The end never did come, however, and the millions of copies of Mr. Whisenant's booklets have been relegated to the trash heaps of historical curiosities.

And there they reside next to scores of others, no less curious. The predicting of the time of the end has a long and noble history; and even though every attempt to pinpoint the end since the beginning has proved to be incontrovertibly wrong, the enterprise continues alive and well among us. Prophecy books that predict the cataclysms of our immediate future, based on readings of the Bible no more or less bizarre than Mr. Whisenant's, are among the best-selling religious literature today. In fact, probably the single most read author of religion in modern times is a writer who, while somewhat more guarded than Mr. Whisenant, predicted in 1970 that a thermonuclear holocaust would engulf the planet by the late 1980s. The author is Hal Lindsey, and his book, *The Late Great Planet Earth* was *the* best-selling work of nonfiction (using the term loosely) of the 1970s. Today there are over 28 million copies in print.5

Lindsey was no number cruncher like Whisenant. He was a savvy observer of the times with an unusual knack for relating to, even mesmerizing, the average mildly interested reader—especially college students. His book reads like a detective novel (where we know whodunnit—or better, who'lldoit—but want to find out when and how) and is packed with anecdotes, plausible historical scenarios, and predictions of mass destruction and misery tailor-made for audiences soon (this was 1970) to enjoy such apocalyptic cinematic thrillers as *The Exorcist* and *The Omen*. Lindsey sees the world as the stage of God's historical activities and the Bible as the blueprint. He begins by insisting that the Bible has a track record: just as the ancient prophecies of the Messiah came true in the coming of Jesus, so too the prophecies of the end will be fulfilled in his second coming. These prophecies are not straightforward predictions per se, since the ancient prophets could not have possibly realized what God was showing to them: their revelations presupposed advanced military technologies unimaginable to the world of spears and swords. And so, when the prophet Zechariah said that when God wages war against his enemies, "their flesh shall rot while they are still on their feet; their eyes shall rot in their sockets, and their tongues shall rot in their mouths" (Zech. 14:12) this, according to Lindsey, is "exactly what happens in a thermonuclear blast." The prophet wrote what he saw; he just didn't realize what that was.

Particularly striking is Lindsey's precise calculation of what will happen at the end of world history. The major players in the prophetic scenario are the restored nation of Israel; oil-thirsty and power-hungry Russia and its eastern bloc allies; an alliance of Arab states, headed by Egypt and intent on reestablishing Palestinian control of the Holy Land; China, with its standing army of 200 million; and a ten-nation European commonwealth (with whom the United States may be vaguely aligned, although Lindsey thinks the United States may already have been destroyed by nuclear war or taken over by Communists by then) headed by a charismatic and widely adored statesman who, unbeknownst to the world at large, is in fact the Antichrist.

The cataclysmic events portrayed by the ancient prophets begin sometime in the 1980s. Israel, having acquired control of Jerusalem, rebuilds the Temple (which had lain in ruins since the Romans destroyed it in 70 CE),[6] creating enormous tensions with the surrounding Arab states. Concerned about its growing sense of isolation in an age of nuclear threat, Israel signs a peace treaty with the leader of the European commonwealth, who through uncanny skills of diplomacy is able to keep the peace. But after three and a half years, he reveals his true colors: entering the Jerusalem Temple, he declares himself to be God and institutes a bloody reign of terror intent on making the world bow to him as the one who holds all economic power. In response, the Arab-African confederacy invades Israel from the south. Russia, driven by its need of the natural resources of the Middle East, uses the occasion to launch an amphibious and ground invasion from the north, over-throwing Israel and crushing the southern alliance as well. It then moves on to take Egypt. In response, the European commonwealth launches a tactical nuclear attack against the Russian army, destroying it, and the Russian homeland, in toto. This leaves, then, two major world forces—the European commonwealth headed by the Antichrist and China, whose 200-million-man army will converge on the Holy Land and engage the Europeans in the final battle. Nuclear arsenals will be unleashed; the major cities of earth will be destroyed. And then, when there appears to be absolutely no hope, God will intervene once and for all. Christ will appear from heaven to overthrow the forces of evil and to set up his good Kingdom on earth.

Lindsey repeatedly tells his reader that these events are described in precise detail by the ancient prophets, who, of course, must be believed. And he repeatedly affirms that all the pieces are already in place, so that the world does not have long to wait. China (by 1970) had boasted that it could field a 200-million-man army, the European common-wealth had nearly all ten members, the Soviet Union was flexing its expansionistic muscles, Israeli-Palestinian tensions were at an all-time high. And, although no one could know *exactly* when the Antichrist would make his move, anyone who could read the Bible could know *pretty nearly* when. Appealing to Matthew 24, as Edgar Whisenant was to do with more extensive numerical proofs some years later, Lindsey tells his readers that it would be sometime "within forty years or so of 1948." He assures them that "many scholars who have studied Bible prophecy all their lives believe that this is so."

Indeed, they did. For decades, John Walvoord, professor (and president) at Lindsey's alma mater, Dallas Theological Seminary, has made a career (and a very nice one) of writing books about the imminent end of the age. Some of Lindsey's fellow students have claimed that *The Late Great Planet Earth* was little more than cribbed lecture notes.[7]

What, though, happened when the time drew near and historical events called the details of Lindsey's predictions in doubt? As might be expected, he wrote another book, *The 1980s: Countdown to Armaged-don*, arguing that everything was going according to plan.[8] And clearly some things were: the book stayed on the *New York Times* best-seller list for twenty-one weeks.

Problems *did* arise, of course, with the demise of communism—since so much of Lindsey's reconstruction was built on the expansionistic tendencies of the now-defunct Soviet Union and on American fears of the spread of communism. His first reaction revealed Lindsey's true conspiratorial colors: "the reality," he argued, "is that the 'collapse' of

Communism is part of a masterful game of deceit engineered by Mikhail Gorbachev and the Soviet KGB. It is part of an elaborate strategy to secure Western aid and technology, buy time, persuade the West to unilaterally disarm and, at the same time, continue a covert but nevertheless dramatic military buildup of its own."[9] When this became too implausible even for Lindsey to believe, he changed his views again, seeing the final battle of Armageddon as precipitated, not by a Soviet communist takeover, but by insurgencies caused by Muslim fundamentalists.

And so it goes—alterations based on the changing tides of historical events, whisps of smoke scattered to the wind but still taken to signify impending doom. Evidently Lindsey's reputation has not been tarnished a whit either by his failed interpretations or his more recent claims that UFOs are deceptive ruses by demons, who will soon stage a massive UFO landing to mislead earthlings into believing in life on other planets.[10] His books and videos continue to be enormously popular.

And the End Keeps Comin'

The failure of these past predictions to materialize has done little to stall the cottage industry of prophecy books. In fact, if millions of the Bible-believing faithful in America thought the time was ripe at the end of the 1980s for the fulfilment of the ancient prophecies, the end of the 1990s has created even more worldwide interest in the possible end of the age, even outside of the evangelical ranks. The end of the millennium itself is the chief culprit, a moment still future for me now as I write these words, but past for many of you who are reading them (unless, in fact, the End has come!). Oddly enough, people have been interested in this particular period—the time of the year 2000—for centuries. And the interest, again, has biblical roots.

Traditionally, the calculus has worked something like this.[11] The story of creation found in the book of Genesis indicates that God created the world in six days and then rested on the seventh. Moreover, in the New Testament book of 2 Peter we are told that "with the Lord, a day is as a thousand years and a thousand years as a day" (2 Pet. 3:8, cf. Ps. 90:4). In an ancient Christian writing called the Epistle of Barnabas (which some early Christians included among the books of the New Testament; it now may be found in the collection of works known as the Apostolic Fathers), produced around the year 130 CE, we find the first instance of a Christian maintaining the corollary that has been picked up by Christian date-setters for centuries: God's creation is to last six thousand years, followed by a thousand-year period of rest—the so-called millennium.

What, though, does this have to do with the year 2000? Well, for purists, nothing. As I noted, when the calendar used today was invented in the sixth century—by a monk named Dionysius Exiguus (whose name is translated "Dennis the Short" by the witty and fellow short fellow Stephen Jay Gould)—it began the new era with the year 1. There was no year zero. This means, technically, either that the first decade of the Common Era had only nine years rather than ten (Edgar Whisenant's temporary fallback position), or that every new decade, century, and millennium begins, like the first, with years ending with a 1 (1981, 1991, 2001, etc.). If so, then every old decade and century ends with a year ending with 0 rather than 9 (so that the last year of the 1980s, oddly enough, would be 1990, and the end of the second millennium would be 2000, etc.). Calendrical purists tend to prefer this second option, since mathematically a "decade"—even the first—does indeed require ten years, so that the year 2000 marks the end of the second millennium, not the beginning of the third.

But to return to the question. What does the year 2001 (or 2000, for those who just prefer keeping things simple) have to do with the calculus of the age-old Christian belief that the world was to last six thousand years? Since the seventeenth century, many Christians have believed that the world was created around the year 4000 BCE.

Actually, the date can be made more precise. In 1650 CE, an Irish archbishop and scholar, James Ussher, engaged in a detailed study of when the world began. Ussher based his calculations on the genealogies of the Bible (which state not only who begat whom, but also indicate, in many instances, how long each of the people thus begotten lived) and a detailed study of other ancient sources, such as Babylonian and Roman history. On these grounds, he argued that the world was created in 4004 BCE—in fact, at noon on October 23. This chronology became dominant throughout Western Christendom. It was printed widely in King James Bibles and continues to be believed by nonevolutionarily minded Christians today.

Why, though, did Archbishop Ussher not simply round things off a bit and opt for the year 4000 BCE, say, sometime in late afternoon? It was because he realized full well that in addition to failing to start the era with the year 0—a failing for which he can scarcely be faulted, since the concept of zero was not mathematically worked out yet in the sixth century—Dionysius Exiguus miscalculated the date of Jesus' birth, from which the era had its beginning. For if Jesus was in fact an infant during the reign of King Herod—as related by both Matthew and Luke in the

New Testament—then he must have been born no later than 4 BCE, the year of Herod's death. This creates a problem, of course, for those who continue to work with the abbreviations AD (anno Domini: Latin for The Year of our Lord) and BC (Before Christ)—since, as sometimes noted, according to the calendar we use Jesus was actually born four years Before Christ!

The larger problem, though, is that if the world were to exist for exactly six thousand years—as many readers of the Bible have maintained since practically the inception of the Christian religion—it should have ended already, by noon on October 23, 1997. But the world keeps on tickin'.

I obviously won't be able to pinpoint every moment that every Christian has thought the world was going to end. That would require a book of about two thousand chapters. But I do want to show that this isn't just a recent phenomenon. And so, I would like to say a few words about several of the highlights (or, depending on one's take, lowlights) of the tradition, moving back in time now to the nineteenth century, then the Middle Ages, and then the early Christian church.

William Miller's Great Disappointment

Probably the best-known date-setter of American history is William Miller, a kind of nineteenth-century Edgar Whisenant.[12] Unlike his fated successor, Miller never published anything like 2 million copies of his writings; but the splash he made in American history was far greater. He wasn't as precise as Whisenant in knowing the particular week in which Jesus would come, but he did know the year. Based on a careful study of biblical prophecies, Miller maintained that Jesus would return to earth in a cosmic blaze of glory in the year 1843.

A simple and uneducated farmer from up-state New York, Miller had been raised in a religious home but rebelled from his Christian heritage as a soldier fighting in the American War of 1812. After the war, burdened by his doubts and troubled by his irreligious ways, he turned to the Bible to find the Truth. And find it he did, in clear and certain terms: not only the truth of the existence of God and of the importance of faith in Christ, but also of the end of the world. For two years Miller studied in detail the texts of the prophets. In particular he was engrossed with the book of Daniel, which states that "unto two thousand and three hundred days, then shall the sanctuary be cleansed" (Dan. 8:14). His interpretation of the passage was based on several (for him) fairly obvious assumptions: (1) that the "sanctuary" referred to

God's holy creation, (2) that its being cleansed referred to the purging of the creation at the end of time, (3) that, as elsewhere in the Bible, a day of God's time refers to a human year, and (4) that the terminus a quo—the time from which the clock would start ticking—was the beginning of the reconstruction of the earthly Jewish sanctuary, the Temple in Jerusalem, in 457 BCE. Miller then drew the inevitable conclusion: 2,300 years after 457 BCE would be 1843 CE. In his own words: "I was thus brought, in 1818, at the close of my two years' study of the Scriptures, to the solemn conclusion, that in about twenty-five years from that time all the affairs of our present state would be wound up."[13]

It was a conclusion he stuck to for the rest of his life, even after the twenty-five-year period had expired.

At first Miller had no converts at all; in fact, he scarcely told anyone of his discovery. But eventually—after five more years of study devoted to ensuring that he had not made a mistake—he began to tell neighbors and friends, and eventually ministers. By 1831 he began receiving invitations to speak to small congregations in rural New England, then to ministers' conferences, then, as he won more and more adherents, to massive rallies in major cities in the Northeast. Some of his converts were, unlike Miller himself, organizationally and entrepreneurially inclined (though, unlike some of his latter-day successors, none of them made any money off their involvement). As the fated date approached, huge tent meetings and camps were arranged; thousands of people came to hear the good news, and many of them converted. Soon the movement, with eloquent ministerial converts who attracted the hoards, began to take on a life of its own. Even though Miller himself remained a humble Baptist to the end, there was talk (and some allegations) of creating a new denomination.

Miller himself had never set any specific date for the end—apart from the somewhat vague claim that it would come "sometime around 1843." In January of that year, he made one clarification—that the date needed to be calculated according to "ancient Jewish reckoning," so that it actually extended from March 21, 1843, to March 21, 1844. Those who had expected Christ's return by the last day of 1843 were disappointed when the new year appeared, but they placed their hopes on the revised terminus ante quem in the spring. The movement continued to thrive, picking up thousands of converts, until that date, too, came and went.

One might have expected this failure to have ended the movement. But as with Whisenant and Lindsey and their countless thousands of followers in our day, so too then. It was noised about that a brief delay was all part of the divine plan; among other things, it allowed more converts to join the fold and so escape the coming wrath of God. The movement picked up steam and reached a fevered pitch when one of its more articulate members insisted that the final date was to be October 22 of that year. Miller and his closest colleagues resisted the date, but the groundswell of support made it impossible to ignore. By October 6, 1844, they conceded that in fact the world had just over two weeks to live.

This time the failure of the end to appear created particular hardship. Their fervent hopes completely dashed, Millerite believers were subject to abject ridicule and, in some cases, real physical hardship: some of the faithful had quit their jobs to devote themselves to the mission of spreading the word; some farmers had left their crops in the field unharvested; some people had given away all their possessions (at least one of whom went to court afterward in an effort to win some of them back).[14] Some never recovered from the non-event that historians have come to call "The Great Disappointment." It was enough to keep most Christians from ever predicting the day and the hour of Jesus' return: apart from the occasional Edgar Whisenant, most have been content to talk about what will happen in "our generation."

But the Millerite movement was not itself without long historical precedent. Move the clock back six centuries, and mutatis mutandis, you can find a similar movement sweeping across the continent of Europe.

Joachim of Fiore's New Era of the Spirit

Joachim of Fiore is scarcely a household name, but it used to be.[15] For centuries. Joachim was born in Calabria (the toe of Italy) in 1135 CE. As a young man, he served as an official in Silicia, in the court of Palermo. But in 1171 he entered the Benedictine monastery of Corazzo and soon thereafter became the abbot. While on a trip to another monastery south of Rome in 1183, Joachim had a series of visions in which he learned, directly from God, he claimed, the mysteries that would unlock the meaning of the Bible and the course of human history. Over a period of eighteen years, he wrote and discussed these mysteries, while remaining actively involved in political affairs as a kind of liaison between secular and church officials.

Joachim believed that when God, the Holy Trinity, created the world, he put something of his own essence into it. The world, therefore, must be understood in a trinitarian way as moving through a sequence of three ages or eras. The first was the era of God the Father, in which humans were under the harsh and restrictive, but just, Law of God. This era lasted from the time of the call of Abraham, the father of the Jews, up to Jesus. Jesus brought in a new period, the era of the Son, in which humans were given the gospel of God and freed from their bondage to the Law. At the end of this, the second era of the world, the Antichrist would arise, acquire as an ally a leading political figure (probably a Muslim infidel), and be opposed by a holy and powerful pope along with two groups of Christian "spiritual men." This would lead, then, to the third and most glorious era of all—the era of the Spirit, in which people would be liberated from the human restraints of this relatively evil age and freed to worship God fully in lives completely devoted to contemplative meditation. This might not sound like utopia for people today, but for a twelfth-century monk, it would be paradise.

Joachim was clear that the end of the age would come soon: "This [crisis of the second era] will not take place in the days of your grandchildren or in the old age of your children, but in your own days, few and evil."[16] He observed that the time of the first era, that of the Father, from Abraham to Jesus, lasted, according to Matthew 1:17, for forty-two generations. Since Joachim believed that events of each era are foreshadowed in the ones that preceded, he claimed that the second era would also last for forty-two generations; moreover, since for him a generation was an average of thirty years, he maintained that the forty-first generation had begun in the year 1201. When, then, would the history of this age draw to a final close? You do the math.

Still, Joachim refused to name the specific time of the end, and was able to fudge a bit by claiming that unlike the preceding generations, the forty-first and forty-second might take a bit longer. But as so often happens, his followers found his vague and general predictions somewhat less than satisfying and worked to tighten up the timetable. A couple of decades after Joachim's death, some Franciscan monks disinterred his writings (they had not made much of a splash in his own day), forged a number of other writings in his name, claimed divine authorization for their teachings (since they allegedly derived from revelation from on high), and insisted that the world as they knew it was certainly going to come to an end in the year 1260.

Of course, it didn't. But for centuries afterward, church people reinterpreted Joachim's teachings, believing that the antichrist was soon to appear here at the end of the second era of the world, before the new age of peace, harmony, and freedom arrived.

Montanus and the New Jerusalem

We have moved, rather quickly, from the twentieth century to the middle of the nineteenth to the end of the twelfth. But our hop, skip, and jump through the history of Christian apocalyptic doomsayers has not yet come close to its point of origin. If we now choose to skip back an entire thousand years to the end of the second century, we continue to find prominent Christian groups proclaiming the imminent end of history as we know it. While several groups of this ilk are known from this time, I will mention just one. It is a group of Christians who followed a self-proclaimed prophet named Montanus and who were known, therefore, as the Montanists.[17]

One of the reasons the Montanists have been seen as so important historically is that one of the most prominent theologians in the history of the church joined their ranks at the height of his career. This was the fiery and prolific North African author Tertullian, commonly regarded as the father of Latin theology. Tertullian wrote most of his surviving works after the turn of the third century. Montanus had been active some thirty years earlier.

As with most ancient figures, we don't know as much about Montanus as we would like. According to later reports, he came from the town of Pepuza, a small and rather insignificant place in the province of Phrygia, in what is now west-central Turkey. He understood himself to be a prophet inspired by God to proclaim his divine truth directly to believers in Jesus. Early on Montanus acquired two female prophetesses as followers, Maximilla and Prisca. Several of their prophetic utterances have survived for us in the writings of other early Christians.

Some of the Montanists' proclamations were moral in character. As a group, they were ethically quite strict—insisting, for example, that a Christian should not remarry after the death of a spouse but should be completely devoted to the church instead (Tertullian liked this idea, and in fact wrote a letter to his own wife forbidding her to remarry should he leave this mortal coil before her). These strict ethics may have derived from their view of the end of time—that it was near and that people needed to prepare for it. In particular, Montanus believed that the new Jerusalem, to replace the old one characterized by the unbelief of the Jews, was to descend from heaven to Pepuza. That is where the Kingdom of God would arrive and Christ would then reign. Christians should devote themselves to its coming, standing up for their faith, even to the point of being martyred if necessary.

When, though, would this end of the age occur? In the words of the prophetess Maximilla: "After me there will be no more prophecy, but the End."[18]

Back We Keep Going: On to the New Testament

It appears that just about every generation from the beginning of Christianity until today has had its apocalyptic visionaries—whether honest people of integrity or power- and money-hungry scoundrels—who have predicted the imminent end of history as we know it. But how far back, really, can we push the belief that the End would come in the present generation?

Our earliest surviving Christian author is the apostle Paul, who wrote his extant letters even prior to the New Testament Gospels of Matthew, Mark, Luke, and John. Strikingly enough, like so many Christians who lived in the centuries since, Paul was convinced that the end would come in his own generation. In fact, in the very earliest writing that we have from his pen, Paul speaks about the imminent end of the age to be brought by Jesus' return. This is the first letter to the Thessalonians, written probably in 49 CE, fewer than twenty years after the death of Jesus:

> For this we declare to you by the word of the Lord, that *we who are alive, who are left* until the coming of the Lord by no means will precede those who have died. For the Lord himself, with a cry of command, with the archangel's call, and with the sound of God's trumpet, will descend from heaven, and the dead in Christ will rise first. Then *we who are alive, who are left*, will be caught up in the clouds together with them to meet the Lord in the air (1 Thess. 4:15-17).

What has long struck scholars of the New Testament is that, as seen in the words I've italicized, Paul appears to understand that he himself will be one of those living when Jesus returns. It would have been easy enough for him to talk about "those" who are alive if he did not imagine himself to be one of them.

Is it possible, then, that the Christians who through the ages have stressed the immediacy of the return of Jesus and the end of the age have done so because of Paul? That Paul started this way of thinking and that like-minded millennialists since have been affected by his words?

In fact, our survey is not yet complete. Before Paul, there was Jesus himself, a teacher and prophet of Israel, who engaged in an itinerant preaching ministry throughout the region of Galilee in what is now northern Israel. Jesus gathered disciples, gave them his message, and convinced them of his understanding of Scripture (the Hebrew Bible). He did impressive deeds that lived on long after he died. Sometime around the year 30 CE he went to Jerusalem during a Passover feast, and was arrested, tried, and crucified. What views of the end time did *he* have? Did Jesus also anticipate the end of the age?

Some Christians have refused to take the teachings of Jesus at face value, denying that his words could mean what they say. For it is within the New Testament Gospels themselves that Jesus tells his disciples: "Truly I tell you, some of you standing here will not taste death before they have seen the Kingdom of God having come in power" (Mark 9:1); "Truly I tell you, *this* generation [i.e., presumably, the one he was addressing] will not pass away before all these things take place" (Mark 13:30); "Truly I tell you, *You* will see the Son of Man...coming on the clouds of heaven" (Mark 14:62).

Is it possible that the historical Jesus himself—like so many of his followers in subsequent generations—predicted that the end of history as we know it would come *in his own generation?*

The End (at Least of This Chapter)

One of the points of the present chapter is that every single Christian who has ever claimed to know the time of the end has been dead wrong. Anyone not convinced of this point by the ongoing history of the human race will probably not have gotten this far in this book and certainly will not be interested in going farther. For my thesis in the rest of the book is that every one of these Christians could trace the lineage of their views, not just to some wide-eyed fanatics in preceding genera-tions, or to the enthusiasts who propagated the Christian religion in its earliest centuries—but to Jesus himself. Jesus, the teacher and prophet from Galilee, predicted that the God of Israel was about to perform a mighty act of destruction and salvation for his people. And he thought that some of those listening to him would be alive when it happened.

Why is it that this is not the view of Jesus taught in Christian churches and Sunday schools today? Why is it so different from what most Christians now believe about him? How can we possibly show that Jesus himself really taught such things? That he himself expected an apocalyptic climax to the history of the world within his generation?

In fact, as strange as this may seem to the general reader, this is a view of Jesus that has been maintained for most of the present century by the majority of critical scholars in both the United States and Germany—two of the bastions of biblical scholarship in the modern period. In the chapters that follow, I will try to show why.

two

who was jesus? why it's so hard to know

AS I MENTIONED AT THE END OF THE PRECEDING CHAPTER, A WIDE RANGE OF SCHOLARS WHO HAVE DEVOTED THEIR LIVES TO STUDYING THE ANCIENT SOURCES FOR THE HISTORICAL Jesus have concluded that he proclaimed the imminent end of history as we know it. I think this view is probably right (even though it is not widely held outside the scholarly community) and I'm going to try to show why. I will argue that Jesus stood within a long line of Jewish prophets who understood that God was soon going to intervene in this world, overthrow the forces of evil that ran it, and bring in a new kingdom in which there would be no more war, disease, catastrophe, despair, hatred, sin, or death. And Jesus maintained that this new kingdom was coming soon, that in fact his own generation would see it. To that extent, at least, he was not so different from the predictors of the end who have numbered themselves among his followers ever since.

I should stress, though, that not *every* modern scholar has shared this view of Jesus. Quite the contrary, in recent years, in particular, it has come under serious attack. Books about Jesus have proliferated at an alarming rate, with competent scholars (not to mention incompetent ones) setting forth their own understandings of who Jesus must have been. Many of these have tried to deny that Jesus was essentially an apocalypticist—that is, one who thought that the apocalyptic climax of history was soon to appear. And so, just within the past thirty years, we have seen books (many of which you can still find at your local book-store) arguing, instead, that Jesus was a violent revolutionary who urged his followers to take up the sword against their oppressive Roman overlords; or that he was a kind of proto-Marxist social reformer who urged his followers to adopt a new economic structure of complete equality and community of goods; or that he was an ancient precursor of the feminist movement, principally concerned with gender issues and the oppression of women; or that he was a magician—not the sleight-of-hand type but the kind that could actually perform stupen-dous feats of magic; or, most recently, that he was an ancient "Cynic" philosopher who was chiefly concerned with teaching his followers to remove themselves from the concerns and trappings of this life, to give away everything they owned, to beg for a living, and to compel every-one else to do likewise.[1] And these are only some of the more *serious* proposals!

Why is it that scholars who have devoted their entire lives to study-ing the historical Jesus have come up with such radically different answers? Isn't knowing about Jesus a straightforward matter of reading the New Testament Gospels and seeing what they say? With four such high-quality sources as Matthew, Mark, Luke, and John, why should there be any serious disagreements at all? Can't we take these ancient witnesses at face value, and thereby discount *all* of these scholarly con-structs, not to mention the more far-fetched ones (which sometimes sell much better!)?

In this chapter I'm going to begin showing why it is so difficult—not just for scholars, but for everyone interested in the question—to recon-struct what Jesus was really like, what he really said, did, and experi-enced. The problems are related directly to the nature of our sources.

The fact is that everyone today—whether a scholar, a minister, a televangelist, a simple believer, a complete agnostic—everyone who has any opinion at all about Jesus has ultimately derived that opinion from *some* kind of source—or has simply made it up, in which case there is no reason to pay it much heed, if we are interested in knowing about the *historical* Jesus. The best sources, of course, are those nearest the time of Jesus himself. That is to say, as with every person from the past, the only way to know what Jesus said and did is by seeing what his con-temporaries or near-contemporaries said about him (since he didn't leave us any writings himself)—that is, by looking at the accounts that we have about him from roughly his own time. It turns out, as I'll show later, that the oldest narrative accounts happen to be the four Gospels of the New Testament.

Why, though, is it a problem to use *these* to reconstruct the life of Jesus?

Possibly the best way for me to explain the problem is by giving a very brief history of the study of the Gospels. A full history of scholarship would be remarkably complex, as the Gospels have been and continue to be the most worked-over, discussed, and debated books in all of Western Civilization. For the sake of simplicity, though, I can speak about three major approaches to the Gospels since the beginnings of modern biblical scholarship.

What the Scholars Have Said

The Gospel Accounts as Supernatural Histories

Prior to the Enlightenment, about which I'll say a few words momentarily, virtually everyone who studied the Gospels—whether Catholic, Orthodox, or Protestant, of whatever and whichever stripe—understood them to represent "supernatural histories." That is to say, the Gospels recorded historical events, things that actually happened. If you had been there, you could have captured them on your camcorder. But, these events were by and large supernatural.

I should stress that I'm *not* saying that no one looks at the Gospels that way today. Most people still do think of the Gospels as supernatural histories. But before the Enlightenment, that's how *everyone* looked at them. Let me give just three examples of how the view worked.

In all four Gospels there is an account of the miraculous feeding of the multitudes (Matt. 14:13-21; Mark 6:30-44; Luke 9:10-17; John 6:1-13). You know the story. Jesus has been teaching some five thousand men, not counting the women and children—so let's say twelve thousand people altogether. The disciples tell Jesus to dismiss the crowds so they can go home to eat. But Jesus tells them to feed the crowds themselves. This isn't possible, though, since the disciples have only five loaves of bread and two fish. Jesus tells them to have the crowds sit down in large groups. He takes the bread and the fish, gives thanks, breaks them, and hands the pieces to the disciples. They then distribute the food to the crowds—and a miracle happens. There's enough for everyone, with basketfuls left over.

Those who see the Gospels as supernatural histories acknowledge that this was a miraculous event, and one that actually happened.

That night, when the crowds are finally dismissed, Jesus sends the disciples across the Sea of Galilee in a boat, while he stays on a hill to pray. A storm comes up, and the disciples are having trouble making any headway against the wind and waves. Jesus sees their plight and begins to walk out to them—*on* the water! They see him and are terrified, thinking that he must be a phantom. But Jesus calls out to them not to be afraid, since it is only he. In one of the Gospels, Matthew, we're told that Peter wants proof; he calls out to Jesus: "Lord, if it is you, command me to come to you on the water" (Matt. 14:28). Jesus gives the command; Peter hops out of the boat and begins to walk. But looking around he becomes frightened by the storm; he cries out and begins to sink. Jesus reaches out a hand, pulls him up, and helps him into the boat.

For those who accept the Gospels as supernatural histories, this is something you could have seen if you'd been there.

At the end of the Gospels, of course, comes the biggest miracle of all. Jesus has been condemned to death and crucified. The soldiers check and see that he is dead. He is taken from the cross, buried by a follower named Joseph of Arimathea, and mourned by his disciples. But when some women come to the tomb on the third day to complete the burial rites, they find it empty. Angelic visitors are there, who inform the women that Jesus has been raised from the dead. Jesus himself then appears to them. Later he appears to the disciples as the Lord of life who has conquered death and now sends his followers into the world to proclaim the good news to all who will hear.

Those who see the Gospels as supernatural histories maintain that this bodily resurrection of Jesus really, literally, happened.

The Gospel Accounts as Natural Histories
The Enlightenment that swept through Europe in the eighteenth century involved a whole new way of thinking and looking at the world. Such intellectuals of the Enlightenment as Descartes, Locke, Newton, and Hume had come to distrust traditional sources of authority and started to insist on the power of human reason to understand the world and the human's place in it. This was an age of science and the development of modern technology. Scholars began to assert the "logic" and importance of cause-effect relationships. They developed scientific notions of "natural law," that is, highly predictable ways that nature worked, along with the concomitant view that these "laws" could not be broken by any outside agency (e.g., a divine being). They modified the grounds of human knowledge—away, for example, from the traditional teachings and dogmas of the church to such "objective" processes as rational observation, empirical verification, and logical inference.

In terms of religious belief, scholars of the Enlightenment recognized that in earlier times, people had appealed to divine agency to explain natural phenomena that seemed mysterious and beyond the ken of normal human experience. Some ancient Greeks, for example, thought that thunderbolts were hurled to earth by Zeus and that bodily diseases were cured by the god Asclepius; Christians had analogous beliefs, that rain was sent from God or that a sick child could be made well through prayer. But during the Enlightenment all such beliefs—and others like them—were widely discounted, as scientists learned, for example, about meteorological phenomena and the body's natural defenses.

What, though, does this have to do with the Bible?

In fact, there were a number of biblical scholars who were heavily influenced by the Enlightenment, who took, therefore, a rationalistic view of the Gospels. According to these scholars, the miracles of the Bible obviously didn't happen—since modern people no longer need to appeal to the supernatural the way the ancients did. Even though the ancients thought they saw miracles (e.g., when it thundered or when a sick child was returned to health), they simply didn't understand the true nature of cause and effect. For such scholars, the Gospels do not therefore contain supernatural histories at all. They instead recount natural histories. That is to say, according to these scholars, the Gospels do record events that happened. But the ancient authors, who were decidedly not influenced by the Enlightenment, *mistook* what they saw to be miracles. Since miracles don't happen, we should look behind the accounts recorded in the Bible to see what really *did* happen. And in every case, what really happened were natural (as opposed to supernatural) events.

One of the famous rationalist interpreters of the Bible was a German theologian named Heinrich Paulus. In 1827, Paulus wrote a study of the Gospels entitled *Das Leben Jesu* (*The Life of Jesus*). In his book, Paulus subjected the Gospel accounts to serious scrutiny in order to discern what actually happened during Jesus' life. In no instance were there miracles—including the three rather stupendous examples I cited above: the feeding of the five thousand, the walking on the water, and the resurrection. In each case, Paulus tries to show that a misunderstanding occurred. The disciples ascribed a miracle to Jesus when in fact no miracle took place.

Take the feeding of the five thousand. Paulus notes that after a long period of teaching, Jesus instructed everyone to sit. He then collected five loaves and two fish from his disciples, said a blessing, and started to break the food into pieces and distribute it. What happened next, however, was not a miracle, except in the most generous meaning of the term. For according to Paulus, the crowds must have seen what Jesus and his disciples were doing—sharing their food with one another—and realized that they themselves were famished. They immediately broke out their *own* picnic baskets and started to swap all the goodies they had brought. Soon there was more than enough for everyone!

There was no supernatural intervention here. Only at a later time did someone look back on this wonderful afternoon of sharing and fellowship and decide that it was a miracle.

Well, easy enough. But what about the walking on the water? Paulus observes that it was dark when the disciples started rowing across the lake, and that a sudden storm came up, preventing them from making any headway. In fact, he claimed, they made no headway at all; they never got more than a few feet from shore. They didn't realize this, of course—it was a dark night, possibly foggy, with sheets of rain falling all around. Jesus, then, seeing their distress, came to them wading through the shallow water on the shore. They were terrified. Since they *thought* they were in the middle of the lake, they assumed the figure coming toward them must be walking on the water. They cried out. Jesus shouted to them, telling them not to be afraid, it was only he. Peter called out that that if it really were he, to allow him to come to him; Jesus ordered him to come—and why not? Peter jumped from the boat, but floundered a bit (thinking he was in over his head); Jesus steadied him with a hand, helped him back into the boat, which they managed, then, to get back onto shore.

No miracle here, just a bit of a misunderstanding.

Surely, though, Paulus cannot so simply explain the resurrection. Jesus was dead. Completely dead. He was buried. And on the third day he arose.

Or was he dead? Paulus notes that the ancient Jewish historian Josephus, whom we'll be meeting repeatedly throughout this study, mentions a time from his own life when he persuaded Roman officials to have two of his companions taken down from their crosses before they had died. One of the two actually survived to tell the tale. This historical information gives Paulus all the ammunition he needs. As he reconstructs the events of the Passion, Jesus was flogged within an inch of his life prior to being crucified. Weakened already, his life beginning to slip away, Jesus' vital signs slowed down on the cross. He practically stopped breathing. But not quite. He was at death's door, and the Roman soldiers mistook him for dead. One of them stuck a spear in his side, inadvertently performing a phlebotomy (i.e., a bloodletting, a common medical practice in Paulus's day). Then he was taken from the cross, wrapped in a clean cloth with burial spices, and laid in a sepulcher carved out of rock. Later, in the cool of the tomb, with the smell of the unguents, Jesus awakened from his death-like torpor. He arose, emerged from his tomb, and went to meet his disciples. They of course thought they had seen him—just three days earlier—dead and buried. The conclusion they drew, though completely natural, was thoroughly mistaken. They thought that Jesus had been raised from the dead. In fact, he had never died.

Paulus's explanations for the miracles of the Gospels—and he can explain them *all!*—may seem fairly outlandish to us today; but for many people of the Enlightenment, they made a lot of sense, at least, a lot *better* sense than the claim that the Gospels recorded miracles that actually happened. After all, anyone can make a mistake and we all know people who have been confused or misled or gullible. These are all among our everyday experiences. But how many of us know people who can multiply loaves, walk on water, or rise from the dead?

The Gospels as Myths

Prior to the 1830s, just about everyone understood the Gospels as either supernatural histories or natural histories. All that was to change in 1835–36 with the earthshattering publication of a two-volume book entitled *The Life of Jesus Critically Examined* (the German title was *Das Leben Jesu kritisch bearbeitet*) by the famous German theologian David Friedrich Strauss. This was an amazing book: nearly 1,500 pages of detailed and meticulous argumentation involving every story in the Gospels. It completely stood the field on its head: a remarkable feat, considering that the author was only twenty-seven years old. (Its English translation was done by none other than Mary Ann Evans—a.k.a. the novelist George Eliot—herself at a ripe young age of twenty-six. This was before she teamed up, so to say, with George Lewes and started her own writing career, which was no less brilliant than Strauss's, though markedly less germane to the subject at hand!)

Strauss disagreed with both of the prevailing ways of understanding the Gospels in his time. On the one hand, he agreed with the rationalists who said that miracles don't happen and that, as a consequence, the Gospels can't be literally true in their depictions. But on the other hand, he found the "enlightened" natural explanations of the Gospel narratives ludicrous and thought that the rationalists were completely off-base in thinking that the miracle stories represented historical events that were simply misunderstood by Jesus' pre-enlightened followers. For Strauss, the Gospels contain neither supernatural histories nor natural histories. Instead, they contain myths.

Before writing Strauss off as a crazed, dismissive skeptic, it's important to understand what he meant by the term "myth." In fact, he did not mean what most people today might think. Today, most people understand a "myth" to be something that isn't true. For Strauss it was just the opposite. A myth *was* "true." But it didn't happen. Or, more precisely (but put rather simply), for Strauss, a myth is a history-like story that is meant to convey a religious truth. That is, the story is fictional, even though it's told like a historical narrative; its intent is not to convey a history lesson, but to teach about something that is true. The Gospels are full of this kind of story.

The best way to understand how Strauss's view works is by taking an example. Consider the account of Jesus' walking on water. Strauss proceeds by summarizing the story, showing that neither the supernatural nor natural interpretation of it makes sense, and moving on to argue, then, for a mythical interpretation. Take the supernaturalist view, that the event actually happened as narrated. How, though, can it be explained? How is it, that is to say, that Jesus was able to walk on top of the water? Was it that his body did not possess (what Strauss calls) "specific gravity," that is, that it didn't weigh anything? That would mean that Jesus didn't really have a body like everyone else. But if that's the case, then Jesus himself was a phantom, a human in appearance only. Anyone who thinks this, Strauss is quick to point out, is guilty of the ancient heresy, condemned by the early church, of Docetism (from the Greek word *dokeō*, meaning "to seem" or "to appear"), which claimed that Jesus wasn't really human but only "seemed" to be. If Jesus didn't have a body, how could he shed his blood? And if he wasn't a human, how could he die? And if he didn't shed his blood and die, how could he have brought salvation?

No, for Strauss this doesn't sound right. Moreover, he points out that Jesus' body evidently had specific gravity at the *beginning* of his ministry. He was baptized by John, after all, which presupposes that he was able to get under the water *then*. So, possibly, Strauss muses, we should think that Jesus started out with a fleshly body but became more and more ethereal with the passing of time. This would explain why, at the beginning of his ministry, Jesus could be dunked under the water, in the middle he could walk on top of the water, and at the very end—when he's fully ethereal and weighs nothing—he could float right up into heaven. This option too, though, strikes Strauss as rather absurd, and it too can't deal well with the notion that Jesus suffered a real, human death.

Well, possibly then, Jesus did have a fully human body, weight and all, but had the ability to suspend his specific gravity by an act of the will, so that whenever he didn't want to, he didn't *have* to weigh anything. This too strikes Strauss as absurd. For one thing, humans can't do this, so that if Jesus really was a human—whatever else one thinks about him as divine—he too couldn't do it. And what about Peter? Was he able to suspend his specific gravity for a time? And can anyone actually do this? So that if you simply have enough faith, you can fly like a bird?

You may think so, but Strauss doesn't. And frankly, until I see you zipping through the air, I think I agree with him.

The supernatural explanation of Jesus' walking on the water, then, doesn't seem to work. But the natural explanation is scarcely any better, because it completely ignores what the text actually says. Strauss notes Paulus's explanation, but protests against it at a number of points. The text explicitly says that the boat was in the middle of the lake; it doesn't say that the disciples *thought* it was. Moreover, the text doesn't say that Jesus was wading through the water, but that he was walking on top of it. And it doesn't say that Peter floundered after getting out of the boat and then stood upright, but that he walked on water and only then began to sink. Paulus has to change the text in order to explain it, and that doesn't seem to be a very safe approach to interpretation.

As a result, the supernatural interpretation can't explain the text and the natural explanation ignores the text. So what is really going on in this story? According to Strauss, both modes of interpretation err precisely because both of them see the story as a historical account. In fact, Jesus' walking on the water is not an actual historical event but a myth—a history-like story that is trying to convey a truth.

It works like this: it was common in ancient religion, Strauss notes, and in early Christianity in particular, to liken the trials and tribulations of this life to a stormy impetuous sea that threatens life and limb. Who is able to rise above the fears, the hatreds, the enmities of this world? Who can overcome the persecutions, the sufferings, the setbacks of this life? Who can rise above the trials and tribulations of our daily existence? Who can walk upright on the stormy sea? According to this story, Jesus can. He is the one who rises above it all, who can face the wind and master the waves, who can conquer all fear, dispel all doubt, and overcome all suffering. He is the one we should follow. For if we do, we too can rise above it all and walk on the stormy sea of life, unbuffeted by the winds and unhampered by the waves. But we must take care not to be disturbed and distraught in our faith, lest we like Peter again begin to sink.

According to Strauss, the story of the walking on the water was a myth. It's not something that *happened*. It's something that *happens*.

Skipping on to Modern Times

A lot—a very lot—has happened since Strauss published his *Life of Jesus* in 1835–36. Scores of scholars have pored over every detail of the Gospels, thousands of books and articles have been churned out, countless views have been marshaled, debated, believed, and spurned. And none of that is going to end soon, unless some of our prophets from chapter 1 turn out to be right.

But one thing has remained constant since Strauss. There continue to be scholars—for most of this century, it's been the vast majority of critical scholars—who think that he was right, not in all or even most of the specific things he said, but in the general view he propounded. There are stories in the Gospels that did not happen historically as narrated, but that are meant to convey a truth. Few scholars today would follow Strauss in calling these stories "myths." The term is too loaded even still, and for most readers it conveys precisely the wrong connotations. But the notion that the Gospel accounts are not 100 percent accurate, while still important for the religious truths they try to convey, is widely shared in the scholarly guild, even though it's not nearly so widely known or believed outside of it. Just about the only scholars who disagree are those who, for theological reasons, believe that the Bible contains the literal, inspired, inerrant, no-mistakes-of-any-kind and no-historical-problems-whatsoever, absolute words directly from God. Everyone else pretty much agrees: the Gospels—whether mostly, usually, commonly, or occasionally (this is where the disputes are)—contain stories that didn't happen as told, which are nonetheless meant to teach a lesson.

Before getting into the kinds of evidence that have convinced scholars of this view, let me say something about its general credibility. Can there be such a thing as a true story that didn't happen? We certainly don't normally talk that way: if we say that something is a "true story," we mean that it's something that happened. But actually, that itself is a funny way of putting it. When my kids were younger, they learned this lesson (well, at least I meant for them to learn this lesson) just about every time we'd see a movie. Afterwards, if they'd ask me if it was a true story, I'd usually answer "yes." But since I'd say it quizzically or emphatically, depending on my mood, they'd be a bit puzzled and pursue the question: "But did it really happen?" To this I'd say "no," and then launch into an explanation (usually it didn't work) much like I'm about to give here: a story doesn't have to happen to be true.

In fact, almost all of us realize this when we think about it. Just about everyone I've ever known was told at some point during grade school the story of George Washington and the cherry tree. As a young boy,

George takes the ax to his father's tree. When his father comes home, he demands, "Who cut down my cherry tree," and young George, who is a bit inclined toward mischief but does turn out to be an honest lad, replies, "I cannot tell a lie; I did it."

As it turns out (to the chagrin of some of my students!), this story never happened. We know this for a fact, because the person who fabricated it—a fellow called Parson Weems—later fessed up to the deed. But if the story didn't happen, why do we continue to tell it? Because on some level, or possibly on a number of levels, we think it's true.

On the one hand, the story has always served, though many people possibly never realized it, as a nice piece of national propaganda. I'm reasonably sure, at least, that the story is not widely told to grade-school kids in Tehran. The reasons are obvious. This is a story about the integrity of the Father of the United States of America. Who was George Washington? He was an honest man. Really? How honest was he? Well, one time when he was a kid....The point of the story? The Father of the United States was an honest man. He could not tell a lie. The United States is founded on honesty. It cannot tell a lie.

Or so the story goes.

On the other hand—and this may be one of those cases where there are in fact several other hands—the story functions to convey an important lesson in personal morality. People shouldn't lie. Even if they mess up and do something wrong. This is a lesson I wanted my kids to learn: even if they did something that would make me mad (it would probably involve my Cuisinart or VCR rather than my cherry tree), I wanted them to come clean with me and not lie about it. People shouldn't lie. And so I myself have told the story and believed it, even though I don't think it ever happened.

The Gospels of the New Testament contain stories kind of like that, stories that may convey truths, at least in the minds of those who told them, but that are not historically accurate.

What, though, is the evidence? Or is this simply a theory cranked up by biblical scholars with too much time on their hands and not enough sense simply to let the texts of the Bible speak for themselves?

In fact there is evidence, lots of evidence, and of various kinds. Rather than go through *all* the evidence—a task that would take about twenty volumes of detailed, and possibly not altogether scintillating, demonstration—I've decided to give just a couple of examples to show what happens more widely throughout the Gospels. The evidence presupposes a certain canon of logic, namely, that two contradictory accounts of the same event cannot both be historically accurate. If you disagree with this logic, then the proof will not be persuasive. But then again, you'll also never be able to figure out what happened in the past, since you'll think that every contradictory account is true.

My examples, then, have to do with accounts about Jesus that appear to be contradictory in some of their details. Let me stress that my point is *not* that the basic events that are narrated didn't happen. Since these particular accounts deal with the birth of Jesus and his death, I think we can assume they are historically accurate in the most general terms: Jesus was born and he did die! My point, though, is that the Gospel writers have given us accounts that are contradictory in their details. These contradictions make it impossible for us to think that the stories are completely accurate. Moreover, it is precisely these contradictions that can (sometimes) point us to the "truths" that the writers wanted to convey. We'll begin with the end of Jesus' story, the accounts of his death.

"True" Stories That Didn't Happen (at Least as Narrated): Jesus' Death in John

I'll begin with an example that strikes me as particularly clear. It involves just a couple of details concerning Jesus' crucifixion. The issue relates to a very simple question: When did Jesus die? As we'll see in this example, just as something as small and seemingly insignificant as a strand of hair or a partial fingerprint can have a life-transforming importance far beyond what one might expect—for example, in the conviction of a mass murderer—so too can small and seemingly insignificant details of a story have immense implications for understanding its historical value.

All four Gospels of the New Testament agree that Jesus died sometime during the Jewish feast of the Passover. This feast was celebrated annually in Jerusalem, the capital city of Judea. According to the Jewish Scriptures, its celebration was prescribed by none other than God himself, through Moses, the giver of the Law, in commemoration of the deliverance of the nation of Israel from its four-hundred-year slavery in Egypt. According to the account still preserved in the book of Exodus, God raised up Moses to confront the Pharaoh of Egypt and to demand that he release the Israelites from their bondage. When Pharaoh refused, God sent ten plagues against the Egyptians, the tenth of which was the worst—the death of every firstborn child (and animal) of every Egyptian family. In order to protect the Israelites during this final plague, God instructed Moses to have each Israelite family sacrifice a lamb and spread its blood on the doorposts and lintels of their home.

That night, when the angel of death came, he would "pass over" the houses marked with blood. Moses was also to instruct the Israelites to eat a meal in haste that evening—there was not time even to make leavened bread. They all did as they were told, the angel of death came, the Pharaoh decided to rid his land of the people, he ordered them out, they fled to the Red Sea, with Pharaoh, who had a change of heart, in hot pursuit. God divided the sea for his people, and in the nick of time sent it rushing back in order to destroy the entire Egyptian army.

Every year thereafter, the Israelites were to commemorate the event by having a special celebratory meal in which symbolic foods were eaten: a Passover lamb, unleavened bread, bitter herbs (to recall their harsh years of slavery), several cups of wine (representing, possibly, the blood), and so on. In the days of Jesus, Jews would come from all over the world to Jerusalem to celebrate the event. Why Jerusalem? Because Jews commonly believed that the only place on earth where sacrifices could be made to God, including the sacrifice of the Passover lamb, was in the Temple of Jerusalem, which God had ordained as his special holy place and within which, in the innermost part of the sanctuary, in the holiest part of the place, called, in fact, the "Holy of Holies," God himself was believed to dwell (though no one was allowed to come in to look; the room could be entered only once a year, on the Day of Atonement, and only then by the high priest, who performed a sacrifice there in the presence of God for his people Israel).

Jews would come, then, to Jerusalem for this annual Passover event, thousands of Jews from all over the world. They would purchase a lamb once they arrived and on the afternoon before the celebratory meal was eaten, they would bring it to the Temple where a priest would sacrifice it to God, drain its blood, remove its skin, and return it to the worshiper, who would then take the carcass home to roast on a spit in preparation for the festive meal to come.

For the rest of what I have to say about the meal, it's important to remember that the ancient Jewish way of reckoning days differs from the one more commonly used today. Most people think of a new day beginning at midnight. The official Jewish day begins when it gets dark. (In the ancient sacred collection of books called the Talmud, the day begins when one can detect three stars in the sky.) That's why Sabbath—even today—begins on Friday night after sunset.

And so, in the historical scene I'm painting here, on the day of Preparation for the Passover, the Jewish celebrants would bring a lamb to the Temple in the afternoon and go home to roast it. *That night,* then—which was for them the beginning of the next day—they would eat the Passover meal. This day of Preparation was also the first day of the weeklong festival celebrated in conjunction with Passover, called the "Feast of Unleavened Bread." Passover day, then, lasted from the evening meal through the next morning and afternoon, until it got dark again, at which time it became the day *after* Passover.

So, back to the Gospels. According to all four accounts, Jesus died sometime during the feast. But when? The earliest account we have—that is, the first Gospel to have been written, as we'll see in the next chapter—is Mark's. Here the chronology of events is quite clear. In Mark 14:12 we are told that on the first day of Unleavened Bread, "when the Passover lamb is sacrificed," Jesus' disciples asked him where he wanted them "to make the preparations...to eat the Passover." In other words, this is the day of Preparation for Passover. Following his instructions, they make the arrangements, and that night eat the meal with him. This is when he takes the bread and says that it represents (or "is") his body, and the cup of wine and says that it represents (or "is") his blood, instilling new significance in these otherwise already symbolic foods. After supper, Jesus and his disciples leave to go to the Garden of Gethsemane, where Jesus prays, is betrayed by Judas Iscariot, and arrested. He appears before a Jewish council for judgment, spends the night in prison, and the next morning appears before the Roman governor Pontius Pilate, who orders his execution. Jesus is immediately taken off to be crucified. And we're told exactly when it was: "nine o'clock in the morning" (15:25)—the morning after the Passover meal was eaten.

So far so good. The problem comes when we examine closely the account of the same events in the Gospel of John, widely regarded as the *last* of our Gospels to be written. John also indicates that Jesus came to Jerusalem to celebrate the Passover (John 11:55; 12:12). Moreover, Jesus again is said to have a last meal with his disciples. But, oddly enough, we're told that this final meal took place *before* the festival of the Passover (13:1); and notably, the disciples are never said to ask Jesus where he wants them to "prepare" the Passover. Moreover, instead of talking about the symbolic significance of the bread and wine, Jesus washes the disciples' feet. There is thus no indication in John that this final meal is the Passover. Indeed, quite the contrary. After supper Jesus goes out to pray (18:1), is betrayed by Judas, and arrested. He appears before the Jewish authorities, spends the night in prison, and appears the next morning before Pontius Pilate, who condemns him to be executed. And we're told exactly when this is: "Now it was the Day of Preparation for the Passover; and it was about noon" (19:14). Jesus is immediately taken off to be crucified.

The day of *Preparation* for the Passover? How could Jesus be executed on the afternoon of the day of Preparation? According to

Mark's Gospel, he wasn't even arrested until later that night and was placed on the cross at 9:00 the next morning. How can these accounts be reconciled?

Well, they probably can't be, even though people who refuse to think that the Bible can have any mistakes of any kind have tried for years. The fact is that John claims that Jesus was executed the afternoon when the Passover lambs were sacrificed in the temple, and Mark claims that he was executed the following morning, after the lambs had been eaten.

Even though the difference can't be reconciled, it *can* be explained. Possibly the author of John, our last Gospel to be written, is actually trying to *say* something, to make a "truth-claim" about Jesus in the way he has told his story. Readers have long noted—and this can scarcely be either an accident or unrelated to our present dilemma—that John's is the only Gospel that explicitly identifies Jesus as the "Lamb of God." In fact, at the very outset of the Gospel, Jesus' forerunner, John the Baptist, sees him and says "Behold the Lamb of God who takes away the sins of the world" (1:29); and seven verses later, he says it again: "Behold the Lamb of God" (1:36). John's Gospel thus portrays Jesus as the Passover lamb, whose shed blood somehow brings salvation, just as the blood of the Passover lamb brought salvation to the children of Israel so many centuries before. What, though, does this have to do with John's chronology of Jesus' death?

To many readers it will now seem obvious: John, or someone who told him the story, made a slight change in a historical datum in order to score a theological point. For John, Jesus really *was* the Lamb of God. He died at the same time (on the afternoon on the day of Preparation), in the same place (Jerusalem), and at the hands of the same people (the Jewish leaders, especially the priests) as the Passover lambs. In other words, John has told a story that is not historically accurate, but is, in his judgment, theologically true.

The Gospels appear to be filled with this kind of story. Sometimes the historical inaccuracies relate to small and seemingly insignificant details, as here (although we should always think of these as if we were historical detectives, looking for the fingerprint or strand of hair that can blow a case open); sometimes, though, they involve entire narratives, full-length stories that don't give completely disinterested and accurate lessons in ancient history—as if any of the Gospel writers was particularly interested in regurgitating names and dates for the sake of posterity—but rather to convey theological truths about the one whom Christians considered to be the Son of God.

Eventually we'll need to see how we as modern historians—that is, those of us who want to know what actually did happen, and when, and by whom—can get behind these theologically molded accounts to uncover the actual events that lie underneath them. But for now it may be more important to provide another illustration of the problem to show how the Gospels sometimes provide entire narratives that, despite their religious or theological value, are not seen to be historically accurate by critical scholars.

"True" Stories That Didn't Happen (at Least as Narrated): Jesus' Birth in Luke

We may take an example from the familiar stories at the beginning of the Gospels of Matthew and Luke. These are the only Gospels that narrate the events of Jesus' birth (in both Mark and John, Jesus makes his first appearance as an adult). What is striking—and what most readers have never noticed—is that the two accounts are quite different from one another. Most of the events mentioned in Matthew are absent from Luke, and vice versa. In itself, this doesn't necessarily create historical problems, of course: two persons could write completely accurate accounts of World War II and never mention the same events. The problem is that some of the differences between Matthew and Luke are very difficult to reconcile with one another. At least, as we'll see, this is *one* of the problems.

Let's begin with the account in Matthew, which you may wish to read for yourself (Matt. 1:18–2:23). Here we're told that, prior to his birth, Jesus' mother Mary is engaged to Joseph, but that before they consummate the marriage, she is "found to be with child." Joseph decides to call off the marriage secretly, to avoid a scandal, but is told in a dream that Mary in fact has conceived through the Holy Spirit, in fulfilment of prophecy. Joseph takes Mary as his wife, the child is born, and they call him Jesus.

We are next told that wise men from the East come to Jerusalem, led by a star, seeking the child who was to be king. Arriving in the court of the ruler, King Herod, they learn that the future ruler of Israel was to be born in nearby Bethlehem. Herod sends them off to worship the child, and asks that they return to tell him where it is. He, unbeknownst to them, wants to destroy his opposition. The star reappears, they follow it to Bethlehem, it alights over the house of Jesus and his family, and the wise men enter to offer him worship and gifts. Warned by an angel not to return to Herod, they go back another way. Herod, though, realizing that he has been deceived, sends forth his troops to slaughter every child, two years and under, in Bethlehem. But Jesus and his family escape. Joseph is warned in a dream of Herod's wrath, and he takes his family to Egypt, where they stay until Herod's death. When he brings them home, though, he decides not to go back to Judea, since Herod's son Archelaus is now its ruler. Instead, he takes his family to a town in Galilee called Nazareth, where Jesus is then raised.

It's a coherent story, but anyone familiar with a Christmas pageant is left with questions. What about Joseph and Mary traveling to Bethlehem, only to find no room in the inn? Or what about Jesus being laid in a manger and the shepherds watching their flocks by night? In fact, these stories don't come from Matthew, but from Luke. And in his version, there is no word about any dreams to Joseph, about the wise men, the wrath of Herod, the flight to Egypt, or the fear of Archelaus. In his account (see Luke 1–2), Joseph and Mary are originally from Nazareth. As in Matthew, they are engaged, and Mary conceives through the Holy Spirit (although in Luke, she is said to be forewarned by the angel Gabriel in the Annunciation); but as the time draws near for her to give birth, Caesar Augustus, ruler of the empire, issues a decree that "all the world" should be registered. We are told that this was when Quirinius was the governor of Syria, and that everyone in the empire needs to return to their ancestral homes. Joseph, as it turns out, is from the lineage of King David, and so must return to the place of David's birth, Bethlehem. He and Mary make the fated trip together; unfortunately, there is no place for them to stay, and so when Mary gives birth, they lay the child in a manger.

News of the birth is brought by angels to shepherds who are in the fields; they come and worship the child. After eight days, Joseph and Mary have the child circumcised. Then, in obedience to the Law of Moses, as recorded in Leviticus 12, they bring him to the Temple for Mary to perform the required rites of purification. The infant Jesus is recognized in the Temple by two prophetic figures, Simeon and Anna. When all the rites of purification are completed according to the Law of Moses—which, according to Lev. 12:4, would be thirty-three days after Jesus' birth—they return home to Nazareth.

A close reading of these stories reveals not only differences—wise men in one, shepherds in the other; wrath of Herod in one, decree of Caesar in the other—but even discrepancies. Consider one simple question, for example: Where was Joseph and Mary's hometown? Most people, before reading the accounts carefully, would probably say Nazareth. And in fact that's right—for Luke. But what about Matthew? Here there's no word about Joseph and Mary coming from Nazareth. Jesus is born in Bethlehem. And he and his family appear to *live* there.

Notice that the wise men find him in a *house*, not in a stable or a cave. Moreover, the text appears to assume that these wise men have been following the star for some considerable time—months, possibly more than a year. For when Herod sends out the troops, he doesn't have just the newborns killed, but every child two years old and under. Surely soldiers would know that two-year-old kids toddling around the yard hadn't been born last week! Thus Matthew seems to assume that Joseph and Mary live in Bethlehem, that Jesus lived his first year or so there, and that when the wise men came, they had to flee to Egypt. But there's even more evidence. When Joseph is told that Herod has died, Matthew indicates explicitly that he decides *not* to return to Judea because of Archelaus. But why would he consider returning to Judea *anyway*, if his home were in Galilee? Matthew's statement makes sense only if Joseph's home was in Bethlehem, near the Judean capital of Jerusalem. Not able to return there, he goes north to relocate in a new place, in the small village of Nazareth.

There are several other points of tension that we could consider between the two accounts, but here I'll mention only one. If Luke is right that Joseph, Mary, and Jesus returned home to Nazareth after the rites of purification had been performed, that is, about a month after Jesus' birth (see Lev. 12:4), when was there time for them to flee to Egypt, as in Matthew?

It may be possible to reconcile these accounts if you work hard enough at it. I suppose you'd have to say that after Joseph and Mary returned to Nazareth, as in Luke, they decided to move into a house in Bethlehem, as in Matthew, and a year or so later the wise men arrived, leading to the flight to Egypt, and a later decision, then, to relocate again to Nazareth. But if that is the way you choose to read the two accounts, you should realize that what you've done is create your own "meta-narrative"—one not found in any of the Gospels. That is, you have decided to write a Gospel of your own!

Moreover, this approach doesn't solve other historical problems posed by the texts, problems that appear nearly insurmountable, no matter how many meta-narratives one decides to create. For purposes of illustration, I'll focus on the problems of Luke (although Matthew also has a few: How exactly, for example, does a star stop over a particular house?). Let's start with the census. We know a lot about the reign of Caesar Augustus from the writings of historians, philosophers, essayists, poets, and others living about that time. In none of these writings, including an account written by Caesar Augustus himself about his own reign, is there a solitary word about any empire-wide census. And indeed how *could* there have been one? Think about it for a second: Are we to imagine the entire Roman Empire uprooting for a weekend in order to register for a census? Joseph returns to the town of Bethlehem because he's from the lineage of David. But King David lived a *thousand* years earlier. Everyone in the empire is returning to the home of their ancestors from a thousand years earlier? How is that possible? How would people know where to go? If *you* had to go register to vote in the town your ancestors came from a thousand years ago, where would *you* go? And are we to imagine that this massive migration of millions of people, all over the empire, took place without any other author from the period so much as *mentioning* it?

There are other historical problems with the account. We know for instance—from the Jewish historian Josephus, the Roman historian Tacitus, and several inscriptions—that Quirinius was indeed the governor of Syria. Unfortunately, it wasn't until ten years after King Herod had died—even though Luke makes their rules contemporaneous.

But enough has been said to make my point. Not only do the two accounts of Jesus' birth stand at odds with one another, they are also not historically credible on their own terms.

What, then, do we do with the stories? Probably the best thing is to consider what they emphasize. They are not meant to convey precise history lessons for those of us interested in ancient times. Both Matthew and Luke—but in different ways—stress a couple of fundamental points in their accounts of Jesus' birth: his mother was a virgin and he was born in Bethlehem. What matters in these stories are these basic points. Even though he was born, his birth was not normal; and even though he came from Nazareth, he was born in Bethlehem.

The importance of the first point is fairly obvious: it shows that even though Jesus was like the rest of us, he was also different. His mother was a virgin; his father was God himself. This point is especially stressed by Luke (see Luke 1:35; Matthew emphasizes that Jesus was born of a virgin because the Scriptures *predicted* he would be; Matt. 1:23, quoting Isa. 7:14). The importance of the second point is obvious only if you are already intimately familiar with the Jewish Scriptures. For the Hebrew prophet Micah indicated that a savior of Israel would come from Bethlehem (Mic. 5:2). Both Gospel writers knew this prophecy—Matthew explicitly quotes it (Matt. 2:6). But both also knew that Jesus came from Nazareth (see also Mark 1:9; 6:1; John 1:45–46). How could he be the Savior, if he came from Nazareth? Matthew and Luke agree that Jesus was the Savior. And so, for them, even though he *came* from Nazareth, he was actually *born* in Bethlehem. But the ways they both *get* him born in Bethlehem stand at odds with one another and with the historical record that has come down to us from antiquity.

Telling It Like It Is: Story and History in the Gospels

There are dozens of other examples we could look at, but these details from the death and birth of Jesus are probably enough, for now, to make my point: there are accounts in the Gospels that are not historically accurate as narrated. This does not necessarily need to compromise our appreciation of the New Testament Gospels. These accounts were never *meant* to teach interesting facts about the first century. They are meant to teach things about Jesus. For John, he's the Lamb of God (hence the change of the day and time of his death); for Matthew and Luke, he's the Son of God (hence the virgin birth) and the Savior/Messiah (hence the birth in Bethlehem). For Christian readers who agree with these theological statements, the historical facts about Jesus' birth and death are probably far, far less important than knowing who he really is. But for historians, who for one reason or another want to know what actually happened in the past, the historical facts behind these theologically motivated accounts are themselves important.

How, though, can we get to the facts if the Gospels are filled with stories that have modified historical data in order to make theological points? It's a complicated question that requires a good deal of sustained reflection. The first step is to recognize a bit more fully how we got our Gospels in the first place—specifically, who wrote them, where these authors got their information, and how much of that information got changed.

three

how did the gospels get to be this way?

IN THE PREVIOUS CHAPTER WE SAW THAT THE GOSPELS CONTAIN STORIES THAT DIDN'T HAPPEN, OR AT LEAST THAT DIDN'T HAPPEN AS THEY ARE TOLD. BUT HOW CAN THIS BE? TO BEGIN answering the question, I should say something about the authors of these books. Who were they, and where did they get their information?

Whodunnit, Really? The Authors of Our Gospels

The titles of the Gospels in our English Bibles, of course, name their authors. These are the Gospels according to Matthew, Mark, Luke, and John. The titles represent the traditional belief that the Gospels were written by two of Jesus' own disciples—Matthew the tax collector (who is named in Matt. 9:9) and John, the "beloved disciple" (mentioned, e.g., in John 21:24)—and by two friends of the apostles—Mark, the secretary of Peter, and Luke, the traveling companion of Paul. If these traditional ascriptions are correct, then the Gospels were written by two men who would have been eyewitnesses to a lot of the stories that they narrate and two other men who knew eyewitnesses (the apostle Paul was not himself an eyewitness, but he knew several of Jesus' disciples, so that Luke, his traveling companion, would presumably have known some as well).

Scrutinizing the Tradition from the Inside

But are these traditional ascriptions correct? The first thing to observe is that the titles of the Gospels were not put there by their authors—as should be clear after just a moment's reflection. Suppose a disciple named Matthew actually did write a book about Jesus' words and deeds. Would he have called it "The Gospel According to Matthew"? Of course not. He might have called it "The Gospel of Jesus Christ" or "The Life and Death of Our Savior" or something similar. But if someone calls it the Gospel *according to Matthew*, then it's obviously someone else trying to explain, at the outset, whose version of the story this one is. And in fact we know that the original manuscripts of the Gospels did not have their authors' names attached to them.[1]

The next thing to notice is that none of the Gospels claims to be written by an eyewitness. Take Matthew, for example. Even though someone named Matthew is mentioned in Matthew 9:9, there's nothing in that verse to indicate that he's the person actually writing the account (read it and see!). Furthermore, nowhere in the entire Gospel does the author indicate that he was personally involved in the events that are described. He never says, for instance, "one time Jesus and I went up to Jerusalem, and while we were there...." Instead, he always writes in the third person—even about the disciple Matthew!—describing what *other people* were doing.

So too the other Gospels, with the possible exception of the Fourth Gospel, which ends with a passage that readers have sometimes taken to be a self-claim by the author that he was a personal observer of the events that he narrates: "this is the disciple who is testifying to these things and has written them, and we know that his testimony is true" (21:24). But even this saying, when you look at it closer, doesn't claim that the author of the Fourth Gospel *himself* was an eyewitness; it claims that the book was based on the report of a different person, whom the author believes. Note how he shifts from talking about what *that* disciple said and what "we" believe about it.

Thus the New Testament Gospels were written anonymously. The authors did not attach their names to their work. Possibly they thought their own names were relatively unimportant.

Looking at It from the Outside

It appears that the earliest readers of the Gospels agreed, that is, that *they* weren't overly concerned with who wrote these books. In fact, for half a century after the books were first put into circulation, *nobody* who quotes them, or even alludes to them, ever mentions their authors' names.

The first time we get any inkling that a Christian knew or cared about who wrote these books comes from about 120–130 CE, in the writings of an obscure author named Papias, whom the fourth-century chronicler Eusebius—the so-called Father of church history—called "a man of exceedingly small intelligence."[2] His IQ notwithstanding, Papias did make some remarks that are often taken as referring to two of our Gospels. First, he claimed that the apostle Peter, on his missionary endeavors, would speak about Jesus' words and deeds as the occasion demanded, rather than from beginning to end, and that Mark, his secretary, later wrote the stories down, but "not in order." This information came to Papias, he claimed, from an elderly Christian he knew. If so, then the tradition that our Second Gospel was written by a companion of Peter goes back to at least 110–120 CE or so. In addition, Papias claimed that the apostle Matthew wrote down the sayings of Jesus in Hebrew, and that "everyone interpreted them as they could." He says nothing about Luke or John.[3]

This tradition from Papias needs to be considered seriously. I would assume that the tradition about Mark refers to the Mark that we have in the New Testament, even though there is no way to know for sure, since Papias doesn't quote any of the materials that are found in the book he's referring to, and so we have nothing to compare it to. It is striking, though, that he emphasizes that (a) the author was not an eyewitness, (b) Peter would retell the stories at random, and (c) Mark modified the accounts he heard from Peter so as to provide an "order" for them. Moreover, the earliest we can trace this tradition is to 110–120 CE, at best—that is something like a half century after Mark itself was written. No other evidence from those years suggests that the book goes back to a companion of the apostles—and, as I've already stressed, Mark himself never claims so either!

The tradition about Matthew is even less fruitful, since the two things that Papias tells us are that (a) Matthew's book comprised only "sayings" of Jesus—whereas our Matthew contains a lot more than that—and (b) it was written in Hebrew. On this latter point, though, New Testament specialists are unified: the Gospel of Matthew that *we* have was originally written in Greek. Papias does not appear, therefore, to be referring to this book.

Apart from this tradition in Papias, we don't hear about the authors of the Gospels until near the end of the second century. By then, though, the tradition had become firmly set. Irenaeus, a Christian bishop of the church in Lyons, Gaul (ancient France), around 185 CE, maintains that there were four Gospels and only four Gospels that had been inspired by God, and that they were written by Matthew, Mark,

Luke, and John. Let me emphasize that this testimony comes nearly a hundred years after the books themselves appeared. And frankly, it looks a bit suspicious. For there were clear reasons that a writer like Irenaeus would want his readers to accept the apostolic origins of these books.

Irenaeus, along with many other Christian leaders in the second-century church, was involved in heated debates over correct doctrine. As we will see in greater detail in chapter 5, the diversity of Christian belief at the time boggles the modern mind. Irenaeus knew people who claimed to be Christian who said that there were two separate Gods—the God of the Old Testament and the God of Jesus—and that the God of Jesus, who was the God of mercy and love, had come to redeem people from the God of the Old Testament—the Creator of the world who gave his harsh and undoable Law to Moses. And Irenaeus knew yet other self-proclaimed Christians who believed that there were twelve gods; and others who said there were thirty. Some of these "Christians" insisted that the Old Testament was inspired by an evil deity, that the Creator was the enemy of Jesus, and that Jesus wasn't really a human being, but only "appeared" to be human in order to fool the Creator. These beliefs—and loads of others that may seem equally bizarre to Christians today—were held by hundreds, possibly thousands, of people in Irenaeus's day. And the striking thing is, every group that promoted these beliefs had *proof* for them: books allegedly written by the apostles of Jesus.[4]

There were lots of "apostolic" Gospels in the second and third centuries. Most of them were probably forgeries. A lot of them, though, were anonymous. But an anonymous gospel written only recently would obviously be of less value than one penned by an actual companion of Jesus or by a close follower of one of his apostles—since *these* were the people one could trust to present Jesus' teachings correctly. As a result, Christians started attaching names to the various books that were originally anonymous, and battles were fought over which ones were truly inspired by God.

It's probably no accident that the first time Christians started insisting that the Gospels they preferred were written by apostles and companions of the apostles (Matthew, Mark, Luke, and John) was after various "heresies" began to thrive, heresies in which alternative beliefs were propounded and books embracing these beliefs were distributed. It may be that earlier traditions—including the somewhat vague but tantalizing traditions about Mark and Matthew preserved by Papias—may have helped make the claims more plausible. But in the final analysis, we should return to the point from which we began: even though we might desperately want to know the identities of the authors of the earliest Gospels, we simply don't have sufficient evidence. The books were written anonymously and evidently not by eyewitnesses.

Playing the Detective: A Few Other Clues

Is this all that we can say about these books, that they were written between 65 and 95 CE by anonymous authors who weren't eyewitnesses? In fact, there are a couple of other things that can be deduced about their authors from the books themselves. First, all four Gospels are written in Greek, by authors who were reasonably well educated and literate. In comparison with most other persons in the Roman world, all four authors, in fact, evidence a high level of education. Something like 90 percent of the general population was completely illiterate—that is, unable to read and write *at all*. To be sure, the Gospels are not among the literary masterpieces of antiquity. Their style, for example, is fairly rough overall (Mark is probably the worst, Luke the best). But it's not easy to write a book, even for well-educated people today, in our highly literate and markedly literary world (although you might not know it from the number of books written about Jesus!). For someone to pull it off in antiquity required a good deal more than the average amount of literary training. And training of that kind required leisure time and money, since the vast majority of people had to work very long days (in comparison with our forty-hour weeks, where we get miffed if we have to put in a few hours on the weekend). So, these Gospel writers were relatively highly educated, Greek-speaking Christians writing between 65 and 95 CE.

The fact that we can deduce this much about the writers of the Gospels is significant because we know from the New Testament itself that Jesus' own followers, thirty-five to sixty-five years earlier, were mainly lower-class peasants—fishermen and artisans, for example—and that they spoke Aramaic rather than Greek. If they *did* have any facility in Greek, it would have been simply for rough communication at best (kind of like when I try to bungle my way through Germany, to the general consternation of native speakers). Even more strikingly, the two leaders among Jesus' followers, Peter and John, are explicitly said in the New Testament to be "illiterate" (Acts 4:13; the literal translation of the Greek word sometimes given in English as "uneducated"). In the end, it seems unlikely that the uneducated, lower-class, illiterate disciples of Jesus played the decisive role in the literary compositions that have come down through history under their names. Moreover, since the books were written in Greek, rather than Jesus' own tongue, Aramaic, they appear to have been written outside of Palestine, although some scholars would locate Mark, and even Matthew, in Galilee, where Greek was sometimes spoken.

As to where exactly they were written, we can't really say. Greek was the lingua franca of the day, spoken—and written—among the educated folk throughout the provinces of the Roman Empire. Traditionally Matthew has been located in Syria, Mark in Rome, Luke somewhere in Asia Minor, and John possibly in Ephesus, also in Asia Minor; but these proposals really amount to nothing more than guesses. As you may have inferred by now, scholars continue to call these books Matthew, Mark, Luke, and John as a matter of convenience; they have to be called *something*, and it doesn't make much sense to call them George, Jim, Fred, and Sam.

But How Did They Know? The Gospels' Sources of Information

Where, then, did these anonymous Greek-speaking authors living, probably, outside of Palestine some thirty-five to sixty-five years after the events that they narrate get their information? Here we are in somewhat better shape. Two of the sources we've already considered—Papias and the Fourth Gospel—have indicated that the Gospels were based on reports handed down, either orally or in writing, from earlier Christians, and that ultimately these reports went back to eyewitnesses.

The author of the Third Gospel makes a virtually identical claim. For Luke begins his account by explaining to his dedicatee—an otherwise unknown person named Theophilus—the purpose of his writing and the sources he had at his disposal in producing it:

> Since many have undertaken to set down an orderly account of the events that have been fulfilled among us, just as they were handed on to us by those who from the beginning were eyewitnesses and servants of the word, I too decided, after investigating everything carefully from the very first, to write an orderly account for you, most excellent Theophilus, so that you may know the truth concerning the things about which you have been instructed (Luke 1:1–4).

Several points here are of interest. First, Luke states that he had several predecessors, others before him who had written accounts of the words and deeds of Jesus. Second, he suggests that he didn't find these earlier accounts satisfactory. That's why *he*, evidently in contrast to those who came before him, is going to write an "orderly" account that will allow his reader to "know the truth." (This is a particularly telling remark if, as almost all scholars think, Luke used Mark as one of his sources!). Finally, he indicates that the stories that both he and his predecessors have told go back to oral reports, which originated, ultimately, among eyewitnesses.

But I Saw It! The Value of Eyewitness Accounts

I suppose everyone would agree that the Gospels of the New Testament in some way or another go back to the reports of eyewitnesses. That does not mean, of course, that every detail of every story found in every Gospel was originally recounted by someone who had seen it happen. As we will see momentarily, the stories were passed along from eyewitnesses to their hearers, who then retold the stories to others, who passed them on to yet others, and so on. Surely the stories were told differently on different occasions, and surely something got changed along the way. But before considering the implications of this oral process of transmission, we should think about the claim that the stories ultimately go back to eyewitnesses. For many people, who possibly haven't thought much about it, such a claim—that a story is based on an eyewitness account—provides a kind of guarantee of its accuracy. A moment's reflection, though, shows that nothing could be farther from the truth. Simply consider any two eyewitness accounts of a particular event. Are they *ever* the same? Not exactly. Sometimes they differ in what they include and exclude, often they disagree on minor details, often they are at odds on issues of major importance (did she scream at him before he threatened her with a knife or afterward?), sometimes they flat out contradict each other; *never* do they tell the story in the same words. If eyewitnesses were always completely accurate in what they say, we'd have no need for trials by jury. We could just ask someone what happened.

Now, suppose we knew of eyewitness accounts that no one had bothered to write down right away. Suppose they had waited, say, twenty or thirty years, until the ends of their lives. Or even worse, suppose that the people who had seen the episode were not the ones who wrote the story, but other people living much later did—that is, not people who had been there, but people who had heard about it from others who had heard it from, not eyewitnesses, but again, from others? What would the story be like, even if it ultimately went back to an eyewitness?

My point is that even stories based on eyewitness accounts are not necessarily reliable, and the same is true a hundredfold for accounts that—even if ultimately stemming from reports of eyewitnesses—have been in oral circulation long after the fact.

I Love to Tell the Story: The Oral Traditions about Jesus

This brings us finally to the question of the stories found in the New Testament Gospels. If the authors of the Gospels—as two of them admit—are recording events that they themselves did not see, what can we as historians say about the reliability of the accounts? Of course, the mere fact that the stories were written down for us so many years after the events does not in itself make the stories unreliable. But where did these authors get their stories in the first place?

As we have seen, the New Testament Gospels were based on oral traditions that had circulated among Christians from the time Jesus died to the moment the Gospel writers put pen to paper. How much of an interval, exactly, was this?

No one knows for certain when Jesus died, but everyone agrees that it was sometime around 30 CE. In addition, as I've already indicated, most historians think that Mark was the first of our Gospels to be written, sometime between the mid-60s to early 70s. Matthew and Luke were probably produced some ten or fifteen years later, perhaps around 80 or 85. John was written perhaps ten years after that, 90 or 95. These are necessarily rough estimates, but almost all scholars agree within a few years.

Perhaps the most striking thing about these dates for the historian is the long interval between Jesus' death and the earliest accounts of his life. Our first written narratives of Jesus appear to date from thirty-five to sixty-five years after the fact. Thirty-five to sixty-five *years*. This perhaps does not seem like a long time: after all, these books and Jesus all come from the first century. But think about it in modern terms. For the shortest interval, this would be like having the *first* written record of John F. Kennedy's presidency appear today, thirty-five years after the fact (the gap between Jesus and Mark). Imagine having no other written records—for example, no newspaper or magazine articles to go on, but simply oral traditions! For the longest interval, between Jesus and John, it would be like having stories of a famous preacher from the height of the Great Depression, say, 1935, show up in print for the first time this week. No one should think that the Gospel accounts are necessarily unreliable simply because they are late.[5] But the dates should give us pause. What was happening over these decades, these thirty, forty, fifty, and sixty years between Jesus' death and the writing of the Gospels?

Without a doubt, the most important thing that was happening for early Christianity was the spread of the religion from its inauspicious beginnings as a tiny sect of Jesus' Jewish followers in Jerusalem—the Gospels indicate that there were eleven men and several women who remained faithful to him after his crucifixion, say a total of fifteen or twenty people altogether—to its status as a "world religion," enthusiastically supported by Christian believers in major urban areas throughout the Roman Empire. Missionaries like Paul actively propagated the faith, converting Jews and Gentiles to believe in Christ as the Son of God who was crucified for the sins of the world but who then was raised by God from the dead.

We know that this tiny group of Jesus' disciples had so multiplied by the end of the first century that there were believing communities in cities of Judea and Samaria and Galilee, probably in the region east of Jordan, in Syria, Cilicia, and Asia Minor, in Macedonia and Achaia (modern-day Greece), in Italy, and probably in Spain. By this time Christian churches may also have sprung up in the southern Mediterranean, probably in Egypt and possibly in North Africa.

It is not that the Christians took the world absolutely by storm. One of the most striking facts of early Christian history is that Roman officials in the provinces appear to have taken little notice of the Christians at all until the second century. As I will point out in the next chapter, there is not a solitary reference to Jesus or his followers in pagan literature of any kind during the first century of the Common Era. Nonetheless, the Christian religion quietly and persistently spread, not converting millions of people, but almost certainly converting thousands, in numerous locations, throughout the entire Mediterranean.

What, though, did Christians tell people in order to convert them? Our evidence here is frustratingly sparse: examples of missionary sermons in the book of Acts and some intimations of Paul's preaching in his own letters (e.g., 1 Thess. 1:9–10). We cannot tell how representative these are. Moreover, there are good reasons for thinking that most of the Christian mission was conducted not through public preaching, say, on a crowded street corner, but privately, as individuals who had come to believe that Jesus was the Son of God told others about their newfound faith and tried to convince them to adopt it as well.

What would persuade people? Given what we know of that world—for example, that people were involved in religion primarily to have access to the gods, whose ongoing favor could bring health, peace, and prosperity—we are probably not too far afield to think that if faith in Jesus were known to produce beneficial, or even miraculous, results, people might be convinced. If a Christian testified, for example, that prayer to Jesus, or through Jesus to God, healed her daughter, or that one of Jesus' followers had been seen casting out an evil spirit, or that the God of Jesus had miraculously provided food for a starving family, this might spark interest in a neighbor or co-worker. But anyone interested in Jesus would want to learn more about him. Who was he? When did he live? What did he do? How did he die? The Christian, of course, would be both compelled and gratified to tell stories about Jesus to anyone who wanted to know.

Opportunities to tell stories about Jesus must have presented themselves throughout the major urban areas of the Mediterranean for decades prior to the writing of the Gospels. Otherwise there is no way to account for the spread of the religion in an age that did not enjoy the benefits of telecommunications. When people had heard enough, however much that might have been, they might themselves have decided to believe in Jesus. This would have involved, among other things, adopting aspects of Jesus' own religion, which for non-Jews meant abandoning their own gods in favor of the Jewish God, since Jews maintained that this One alone was the true and "living" God. Once the converts did so, they could join the Christian community by being baptized and receiving some rudimentary instruction. Presumably it was the leaders of the Christian congregation who performed the baptisms and taught the converts. These leaders would no doubt have been the earliest people to have adopted this new religion in the locality and/or people with special gifts for leadership—possibly the more highly educated among them, who were therefore best suited to giving instruction.

We do not know exactly what they would have told these new converts, but we might imagine that it would have included some of the essentials of the faith: information about the one true God, his creation, and his son Jesus. To some extent, this would have involved telling yet other stories about who Jesus was, about how he came into the world, about what he taught, what he did, why he suffered, and how he died. Stories about Jesus were thus being told throughout the Mediterranean for decades to convert people and to educate those who had converted, to win people to faith and to instruct those who had been brought in; stories were told in evangelism, in education, in exhortation, and probably in services of worship.

Who, then, was telling the stories? Were they always told by one of Jesus' original disciples? Impossible. The mission went on for years and years and years all over the map. Who then? Other eyewitnesses? Equally impossible. The stories must have been told, for the most part, by people who had not been there to see them happen, who had heard them from other people, who themselves had not been there to see them happen. The stories were passed on by word of mouth, from one convert to the next; they were told in different countries, in Egypt, Judea, Galilee, Syria, and Cilicia, throughout Asia Minor, Macedonia, Achaia, Italy, and Spain. They were told in different contexts, for different reasons, at different times. They were told in a language other than Jesus' own (as we have seen, he spoke Aramaic, whereas most of the converts spoke Greek), often by people who were not Jews, almost always by people who were not eyewitnesses and had never met an eyewitness.

Let me illustrate the process with a hypothetical example. Suppose I am a Greek-speaking worshiper of the goddess Artemis from Ephesus. I listen to a stranger passing through town, who tells of the wonders of Jesus, of his miracles and supernatural wisdom. I become intrigued. When I hear that this wandering stranger has performed miracles in Jesus' name—my neighbor's son was ill, but two days after the stranger prayed over him, he became well—I decide to inquire further. He explains how Jesus himself did great miracles and claims that even though he was wrongly accused by the Romans for sedition and was crucified, God raised him from the dead. Based on everything I've heard, I decide to forgo my devotion to Artemis. I put my faith in Jesus, get baptized, and join the local Christian community.

I make a trip for business in nearby Smyrna. While there, I tell friends about my new faith and the stories I've learned about my new Lord. After a time, three of them join me in becoming Christian. They begin to discuss these things with their neighbors and friends. Mostly their message is rejected; but they acquire several converts, enough to come together once a week for worship, to discuss their faith, and to tell more stories. These new converts tell their own families the stories, converting some of them, who then take the word yet farther afield. When these final converts tell the stories—where did they get them? Were they there to see these things happen? No, they heard them from family members, some of whom have probably never been outside of Smyrna! Where did the family members hear them? From the converts won by my three friends. Did these converts witness these things? No, they heard them from my friends. Were my friends eyewitnesses? No. They heard them from me. Was I an eyewitness? No, I heard them from a stranger visiting Ephesus. Was he an eyewitness? No....

And so it goes. The new converts tell the stories; and since the faith necessarily grows exponentially, most of the people telling the stories were not eyewitnesses and indeed had never laid eyes on an eyewitness or even on anyone else who had. These stories were then circulated year after year after year, primarily among people who had no independent knowledge of what really occurred. It takes little imagination to realize what happened to the stories.

You are probably familiar with the old birthday party game, "telephone." A group of kids sits in a circle, the first tells a brief story to the one sitting next to her, who tells it to the next, and to the next, and so on, until it comes back full circuit to the one who started it. Invariably, the story has changed so much in the process of retelling that everyone gets a good laugh. If it didn't work that way, who would play the game? Imagine playing "telephone" not in a solitary living room with ten kids on a sunny afternoon in July, but over the expanse of the Roman Empire (some 2,500 miles across!), with thousands of participants, from different backgrounds, with different concerns, and in different contexts, some of whom have to translate the stories into different languages all over the course of decades. What would happen to the stories?

And the situation in fact was even more complicated than that. For each of the Christian communities that sprang up around the Mediterranean encountered severe difficulties in their lives together—rejection by their families, enmity from their neighbors, and persecution by their local officials. These were difficulties for which they needed some direction from on high. The traditions about Jesus were part of the bedrock of these communities; his actions were a model they tried to emulate; his words were teachings they obeyed. Given this context, is it conceivable that Christians would ever make up a tradition that proved useful in a particular situation? Creating a story is not far removed from changing one, and presumably people would have good reasons for doing both.

Let me emphasize two points before bringing this chapter to a close. The first is that I am not engaging in mere speculation that the stories about Jesus changed in the process of retelling. We have *evidence* that the stories were changed (or invented), as seen by the two simple examples cited in the previous chapter. Second, and possibly more important, I should stress that Christians would not have to be deceitful or malicious to invent a story about Jesus, about something that he said or did. They would not even have to be conscious of having done so. There are all sorts of stories that are made up without ill intent, and we ourselves sometimes tell them.

Conclusion

And so the early Christians told and retold their stories about Jesus. These stories were not meant to be objective "history lessons" for students interested in key events of Roman imperial times. They were instead meant to convince people that Jesus was the miracle-working Son of God whose death brought salvation to the world, and to edify and instruct those who already believed. Sometimes the stories were modified to express a theological "truth," as we saw in chapter 2. That is to say, early Christians who passed along the traditions sometimes found it legitimate and necessary to change a historical fact in order to make a theological point. And these are the stories that our Gospel writers, living nearer the end of the first century, inherited.

This conclusion has some profound implications for our investigation of the Gospels. Even if the authors of our Gospels—and the Christian storytellers who preceded them—were not principally concerned with strict historical accuracy, some of us today are. (Though not all of us! Most modern readers are still far less concerned with knowing what really happened than with knowing what to believe.) But since the Gospels preserve traditions that have been modified over time in their retelling, it is impossible simply to take these stories at face value and uncritically assume that they represent historically accurate information. As a result, we will need to figure out how to use these sources to provide us with historical information. That is to say, we will need to think carefully about how to mine such theologically interested documents for historical data, how to decide which features of the Gospels represent Christianizations of the tradition and which represent the life of Jesus as it can be historically reconstructed.

This will be our task several chapters hence. Before moving there, though, we should ask a final question about the surviving sources: Are there other accounts about Jesus found *outside* the Gospels that might help us learn what he actually said, did, and experienced, other sources that might serve as external checks on the materials that we find in these canonical texts?

four

looking about a bit:
non-christian sources for the historical jesus

THE GOSPELS OF THE NEW TESTAMENT HAVE ALWAYS
BEEN CHERISHED BY CHRISTIANS WANTING TO KNOW WHAT
TO BELIEVE AND HOW TO LIVE. AS WE HAVE SEEN, THOUGH, THEY ARE
somewhat problematic for historians who want to know what really
happened during the life of Jesus. We will need to consider carefully
how to make appropriate use of these documents, if we want to reconstruct the life of the historical Jesus. That will be a task we undertake
later. Before moving there, we should look around a bit to see if there
are other sources outside of the New Testament Gospels for knowing
what Jesus said and did—other accounts of his life that might provide
us with independent information that is either less theologically motivated or, at the least, motivated by different concerns. Such sources
might provide a kind of point of comparison for us, a check on the theological tendencies of the more familiar books of Matthew, Mark, Luke,
and John. In this chapter we'll consider accounts of Jesus produced by
authors who did not believe in him.

Most people in our society probably think that Jesus must have had
an enormous effect on the people of his day—not just on his immediate followers. He was, after all, the founder of the most significant religion in the history of Western Civilization. During his time he must
have attracted masses of attention—not only among the crowds that
he taught and healed, but throughout society at large. Anyone who

could deliver such brilliant teachings and produce such incredible miracles must have turned the world on its ear. Even those who had never seen him must have been abuzz with his spectacular deeds. Reports about this son of God come to earth must even have filtered into the highest reaches of government. Possibly the order for his execution came from on high—from the emperor himself, fearful that his own claims to divinity might be compromised by the appearance of one who was truly divine. Better to have the threat crushed than to confront him oneself.

In this "commonsensical" view, Jesus' impact on the society of his day must have been immense, like a comet striking the earth. In that case, we could expect to find scores of accounts of his words and deeds written by contemporaries outside the group of his closest disciples. Surely people had a lot to say about him, whether his friends or enemies. If so, we would be well advised to see what they said.

Unfortunately, the commonsensical view is not even close to being right—biblical epics on the wide screen (the source of many people's knowledge about the Bible!) notwithstanding. If we look at the historical record itself—and, I should emphasize, for historians there is nothing *else* to look at—it appears that whatever his influence on subsequent generations, Jesus' impact on society in the first century was practically nil, less like a comet striking the planet than a stone tossed into the ocean.

This becomes especially clear when we consider what his own contemporaries had to say about him. Strangely enough, they said almost nothing.

Non-Christian Sources for the Life of Jesus

Early "Pagan" Sources

When historians use the term "pagan," it does not have a derogatory connotation (i.e., it's not what *you* mean when you say that the guy down the street is a "complete pagan"). Instead, it refers to anyone who followed any of the polytheistic religions of the ancient world—that is, anyone who wasn't either a Jew or a Christian. The vast majority of people in the Roman Empire, therefore, were pagans. What sorts of things do pagan authors from the time of Jesus have to say about him?

Nothing. As odd as it may seem, there is no mention of Jesus at all by any of his pagan contemporaries. There are no birth records, no trial transcripts, no death certificates; there are no expressions of interest, no heated slanders, no passing references—nothing. In fact, if we broaden our field of concern to the years after his death—even if we include the entire first century of the Common Era—there is not so much as a solitary reference to Jesus in any non-Christian, non-Jewish source of any kind. I should stress that we do have a large number of documents from the time—the writings of poets, philosophers, historians, scientists, and government officials, for example, not to mention the large collection of surviving inscriptions on stone and private letters and legal documents on papyrus. In none of this vast array of surviving writings is Jesus' name ever so much as mentioned.

PLINY THE YOUNGER. The first reference to Jesus in any surviving pagan account does not come until the year 112 CE. It appears in a letter written by a governor of the Roman province of Bithynia-Pontus (northwestern part of modern-day Turkey), a Roman official named Pliny. Historians usually refer to him as Pliny the Younger, to distinguish him from his equally famous uncle—called, as you might imagine, Pliny the Elder, a widely read and prolific scientist (whose scientific curiosity led to his demise, as it turns out; when Mount Vesuvius erupted in 79 CE he decided to investigate at close range and, well, that was the end of Pliny the Elder). During his tenure as governor of his province, Pliny the Younger was in close contact with the Roman emperor, Trajan. Copies of the letters that they sent back and forth at the time still survive.

Difficulties had arisen in Bithynia-Pontus because of a Roman policy that disallowed groups of people to come together socially—a policy meant to discourage social uprisings: if you couldn't meet together, you couldn't plan a revolution. It also led to less desirable results, however, since among other things, it made it impossible to form fire brigades, leading to enormous problems in some of the communities in Pliny's province. In the context of addressing some of these difficulties to the emperor, Pliny mentioned, in what is now his Epistle 10, another group that had been meeting together illegally. It was a group of Christians.

The letter tells us some interesting things about these followers of Jesus. We learn, for example, that they comprised a range of ages and socioeconomic classes, that they met in the early morning before it was light, that they partook of food together, and—the chief point for our present investigation—that they worshiped "Christ as a god." The name "Jesus" itself is not given here, but it's pretty clear whom Pliny had in mind. Unfortunately, he doesn't give us any information about Jesus—for example, who he was, where he lived, what he said or did, or how he died—only that he was worshiped as divine by his followers. Thus, while the letter has proved important for historians interested in knowing about early Christianity from an outsider's perspective—it shows us, for example, where Christianity had spread and how Christians worshiped in the early second century—it is of practically no use for helping us learn more about the historical Jesus.

SUETONIUS.   A few years later, the Roman historian Suetonius made a casual comment that some scholars have taken to be a reference to Jesus. Suetonius wrote a set of biographies on the twelve Roman Caesars who had ruled up to his own time, starting with Julius Caesar. There is a lot of valuable historical information in these books, along with a lot of juicy gossip—a gold mine for historians interested in major events of the early Roman Empire. In his *Life of Claudius*, emperor from 41 to 54 CE, Suetonius mentions riots that had occurred among the Jews in the city of Rome and says that the riots had been instigated by a person named "Chrestus." Some historians have maintained that this is a misspelling of the name "Christ." If so, then Suetonius is indicating that some of Jesus' followers had created havoc in the capital, a view possibly confirmed in the New Testament (see Acts 18:2). Unfortunately again, though, Suetonius tells us nothing about the man "Chrestus." If he does have Jesus in mind—and it's only a possibility, since he may be referring, actually, to someone called Chrestus!—he must be referring only to Jesus' followers, since Jesus himself had been executed some twenty years before these riots occurred.

TACITUS.   At about the same time (115 CE), another Roman historian, Tacitus, also mentions the early Christians. But in this case, we actually learn something about the founder of their religion. Tacitus is probably best known for the *Annals*, a sixteen-volume history of the Roman Empire covering 14–68 CE.   Probably the most famous passage in the *Annals* (book 15) reports the megalomania of the emperor Nero, who had Rome torched in order to implement some of his own architectural designs for the city. When he was suspected for the fire, Nero sought to place the blame elsewhere and found in the Christians a ready scapegoat. He rounded up members of this despised sect (Tacitus himself says that the Christians were widely held in contempt for their "hatred of the human race") and made a public display of them, having some rolled in pitch and set aflame to light his public gardens, and others wrapped in animal skins to be torn to shreds by savage dogs. Nero was not known for his timid tactics.

In any event, in the context of his discussion of Nero's excesses against the Christians, Tacitus does manage to say something about where they had acquired their (to him) strange beliefs and so provides us with the first bit of historical information to be found about Jesus in a pagan author: "Christus, from whom their [i.e., the Christians'] name is derived, was executed at the hands of the procurator Pontius Pilate in the reign of Tiberius" (*Annals* 15.44). Tacitus goes on to indicate that the "superstition" that emerged in Jesus' wake first appeared in Judea before spreading to Rome itself.

It is a pity that Tacitus does not tell us more. I suppose we should assume either that he didn't think additional information about Jesus was of much historical importance or that this was all he knew. Some scholars have noted that even this bit of knowledge is not altogether reliable: Pilate was in fact not a "procurator" but a "prefect"; that is, he not only oversaw revenue collection, but also had some military forces at his command. In any event, Tacitus's report confirms what we know from other sources, that Jesus was executed by order of the Roman governor of Judea, Pontius Pilate, sometime during Tiberius's reign. We learn nothing, however, about why Pilate ordered the execution, let alone about Jesus' life and teachings.

These are the only references to Jesus in pagan sources from the hundred years after his death. As you can see, they provide scarcely any information—nothing at all, for example, about what he said and did. For this kind of information, we will need to turn elsewhere.

Early Jewish Sources

In contrast to pagan sources, we have very few Jewish texts of any kind that can be reliably dated to the first century of the Common Era. And here again, even among the ones that do survive—for example, the Dead Sea Scrolls, about which I'll say some words later, and the extensive writings of Philo, the great Jewish philosopher of Alexandria, Egypt (20 BCE–50 CE)—Jesus is never mentioned. With one important exception. This is the Jewish historian Josephus (37–100 CE), probably our most important source for understanding Jewish life and history during the first century.

In the many volumes of writings that have come down to us from his pen, Josephus does not say much about Jesus. But he does mention him briefly on two occasions, and we will do well to consider what he says. First some background.

JOSEPHUS. Josephus was born to an aristocratic family just six or seven years after Jesus' death. He himself became an important figure in the political scene in Palestine. When the Jewish War against Rome broke out in 66 CE (a war that would lead, in 70 CE, to the catastrophic fall of Jerusalem and the destruction of the Temple), he was given charge of the Jewish forces in Galilee in the north. His troops were no match for the Roman legions, however, who marched through the region with relative ease. When Josephus's army was surrounded, as he himself later reported, his men made a suicide pact to prevent the Romans from taking any prisoners. Each soldier was to draw a numbered lot; the one who drew the second lot was to kill the one who drew the first, the third was to kill the second, and so on, until the one remaining soldier was to kill himself. As it turns out (one wonders if this was by chance), one of the final two lots fell to Josephus himself. After the rest of his troops were dead, he convinced his one remaining companion to turn themselves in.

When he was brought before the conquering Roman general, Vespasian, Josephus continued to demonstrate his political savvy and good sense. He told Vespasian that he had a revelation from God that he, Vespasian, would soon be the emperor of Rome. As things turned out, Josephus was right. After a much beleaguered Nero committed suicide, the imperial government was thrown into serious turmoil. Three different emperors had three very short reigns, with imperial assassinations and suicides the order of the day. Vespasian's troops eventually proclaimed him emperor; he marched to Rome, restored order, and settled in for a relatively long haul.

And he never forgot that Josephus had predicted it. As a reward, he gave Josephus an annual stipend and appointed him as a kind of court historian. From the perspective of posterity, Josephus used his situation and time well, producing several important books that have survived until today. One of the best known is his insider's account of the Jewish War of 66–73 CE, in which he not only played a key role early on, but was also used later by Vespasian's son and eventual successor to the emperorship, Titus, as an interpreter to try to convince the Jewish forces besieged in Jerusalem to surrender. Another is his twenty-volume history of the Jewish people extending from Adam and Eve up to near his own time, entitled *The Antiquities of the Jews*.

There are scores of important and less important Jews discussed in these historical works, especially Jews close to Josephus's own time. Jesus does not play a significant role in these books. He is not mentioned at all in Josephus's treatment of the Jewish War—no surprise, really, since Jesus' crucifixion took place some three decades before the war began. But he does make two tantalizingly brief appearances in the *Antiquities*.

I'll take the references in reverse order, since the second is of less historical interest. It occurs in a story about the Jewish high priest Ananus, who abused his power in the year 62 CE by unlawfully putting to death a man named James, whom Josephus identifies as "the brother of Jesus who is called the messiah" (*Ant.* 20.9.1). From this reference we can learn that there was indeed a man named Jesus (Josephus actually discusses lots of different people with that name—many of them at far greater length than the Jesus *we* are concerned about), that he had a brother named James (which we already knew from the New Testament; see Mark 6:3 and Gal. 1:19), and that he was thought by some people to be the Jewish messiah. The information is not much, but at least it's *something*. I should point out that Josephus himself does not happen to agree with those who called Jesus the messiah. We don't know how much he knew about the Christians, but it is clear that he remained a non-Christian Jew until his dying day.

Indeed, Josephus's own religious commitment has made the other reference to Jesus a source of considerable puzzlement over the years. For in it Josephus not only mentions Jesus as a historical figure, but also, in this case, appears to profess faith in him as the messiah—somewhat peculiar for a person who never converted to Christianity! The passage reads as follows:

> At this time there appeared Jesus, a wise man, if indeed one should call him a man. For he was a doer of startling deeds, a teacher of people who receive the truth with pleasure. And he gained a following both among many Jews and among many of Greek origin. He was the messiah. And when Pilate, because of an accusation made by the leading men among us, condemned him to the cross, those who had loved him previously did not cease to do so. For he appeared to them on the third day, living again, just as the divine prophets had spoken of these and countless other wondrous things about him. And up until this very day the tribe of Christians, named after him, has not died out (*Ant.* 18. 3. 3).

This "testimony" to Jesus has long perplexed scholars. Why would Josephus, a devout Jew who never became a Christian, profess faith in Jesus, suggesting that he was something more than a man, calling him the Messiah, rather than merely saying that others thought he was, and claiming that he was raised from the dead in fulfilment of prophecy?

Many scholars have recognized that the problem can be solved by understanding how, and by whom, Josephus's writings were transmitted over the centuries. For they were not preserved among Jews, many of whom considered him to be a traitor because of his conduct during and after the war with Rome. It was Christians who copied Josephus's writings through the Middle Ages, including of course this peculiar passage.

Is it possible that this reference to Jesus has been "beefed up" a bit by a Christian scribe who wanted to make Josephus appear more appreciative of the "true faith"?

If we take out the "Christianized" portions of the passage, we are left with something like the following:

> At this time there appeared Jesus, a wise man. He was a doer of startling deeds, a teacher of people who receive the truth with pleasure. And he gained a following both among many Jews and among many of Greek origin. And when Pilate, because of an accusation made by the leading men among us, condemned him to the cross, those who had loved him previously did not cease to do so. And up until this very day the tribe of Christians, named after him, has not died out.[1]

It is useful to know that Josephus had this much information about Jesus. Unfortunately, there is not much here to help us understand specifically what Jesus said and did. We might conclude that he was considered important enough for Josephus to mention, though not as important, say, as John the Baptist or many other Palestinian Jews who were considered to be prophets at the time, about whom Josephus says a good deal more. We will never know if Josephus had additional information about Jesus at his disposal, or if he told us all that he knew.

No other non-Christian Jewish source written before 130 CE, that is, within a hundred years of Jesus' death, so much as mentions him.

There *are* some references in later documents, however, and even though these are not of much use for us as historians, I should perhaps say at least a brief word about them. They come in the collections of Jewish lore and learning that are preserved under the names of the ancient Jewish rabbis, principally in the Jewish Talmud.

Rabbinic Sources

The Talmud represents a compilation of Jewish legal disputes, anecdotes, folklore, customs, and sayings. Even though some of these rabbinic materials—that is, materials relating to the teachings of the Jewish rabbis—may have originated all the way back in the period of our concern, scholars have increasingly realized that it is difficult to establish accurate dates for them. The collection itself was made long after the period of Jesus' life. The core of the Talmud is the Mishnah, a collection of rabbinic opinions about the Jewish Law that was not put into writing until the early third century CE, nearly two centuries after Jesus' death. The bulk of the Talmud consists of commentaries, called the Gemara, on the Mishnah. One set of commentaries was produced by Jewish scholars in Palestine in the fourth century CE. Another, usually seen to be more authoritative, came from Babylonia in the fifth century CE. In view of the dates of these writings, and the complications of establishing the origins of their traditions, scholars by and large realize that they can no longer (as they once did) simply quote a passage from the Talmud and assume that it reflects conditions in the first century of the Common Era, any more than one can quote a modern newspaper editorial and assume that it reflects conditions of colonial America.

Jesus is never mentioned in the Mishnah itself—the oldest portion of the Talmud—but only in the commentaries on the Mishnah that were produced much later.[2] Even though scholars generally recognize that these references are of little use for reconstructing the life of the historical Jesus, they are interesting in their own right. One of the problems with the references, though, is knowing whether they actually refer to Jesus, since he is not called by name. There are some texts, for example, that refer to a person named "Ben [i.e., son of] Panthera." Panthera was allegedly a Roman soldier who seduced a Jewish hairdresser named Miriam (= Mary). She gave birth, then, out of wedlock. This tradition, as scholars have long recognized, may represent a subtle attack on the Christian view of Jesus' origins—namely, that he was the "son of a virgin." In Greek, the term for virgin is *parthenon*, close in spelling to Panthera.

In other references in the Talmud, we learn that Jesus was a sorcerer, who acquired his black magic in Egypt. Recall the Gospel accounts of Jesus as a miracle worker, who as a youth had fled with his family to Egypt. He is said to have gathered five disciples around him (as opposed to twelve), and to have been hanged on the eve of the Passover, after a herald went about for forty days proclaiming the charges of sorcery against him. This account may be a response to the Gospels, which indicate that the trial of Jesus took place with injudicious speed, his execution occurring just twelve hours or so after his arrest.[3]

These references, as I've said, come hundreds of years after Jesus' life and appear to represent Jewish responses to the Christian claims about Jesus. They do not, that is, appear to provide historically reliable information about what Jesus said, did, and experienced.

A Sobering Subtotal: Jewish and Pagan Sources for Jesus

What, then, do we learn about Jesus from non-Christian sources of his day? Not much. I have given here every single reference to Jesus that survives in pagan or Jewish sources written within an entire century of his death. As a result, if we want to know what Jesus said and did during his life, we have no choice but to turn to sources produced by his followers. Fortunately, there are some such sources that exist outside of the New Testament Gospels. Before returning to the Gospels themselves, we may do well to consider the character of these other sources, to see what they can tell us about Jesus' life and death.

looking about a bit more:
other christian sources for the historical jesus

WE HAVE ALREADY BEGUN TO CONSIDER THE RELIABIL-
ITY OF THE CANONICAL GOSPELS FOR RECONSTRUCTING THE
LIFE OF JESUS. DESPITE A GOOD DEAL OF MEDIA HYPE IN RECENT YEARS, A
lot of people still don't realize that we have other Gospels that did not
make it into the New Testament. Lots of other Gospels, in fact—over a
couple of dozen of them. Many of these Gospels make for fascinating
reading and can be of real significance for a scholar interested in knowing about how Jesus came to be understood in later times. But most of
them are latecomers—the bulk of them date from the third to the
eighth centuries, hundreds of years after Jesus himself. And nearly all of
them are based on the New Testament Gospels themselves. For these
reasons, they are not, as a rule, useful for the historian seeking independent verification of the things Jesus said and did.

Rather than belabor the point by discussing all of these other books,
I'll mention just three of the earliest ones and say something about
their character and historical value. In fact, two of these, as it turns out,
have made a real impact on the historical investigation into the life of
Jesus, as scholars, especially over the past twenty years or so, have
argued that they contain historically authentic tradition not found in
Matthew, Mark, Luke, and John. I personally find these claims to be a
bit extravagant, and want to explain why in the discussion that follows.
But before doing so, I'd like to mention an ancient Gospel that *no one*

thinks is historically accurate, despite its early date (possibly the first half of the second century) and interesting content. This will show the kind of legendary accounts of Jesus that eventually turn up with some regularity. It is a Gospel that narrates Jesus' life as a boy—a period almost entirely overlooked by the Gospels of the New Testament (with the exception of the brief account in Luke 2:41–52).

Christian Sources Outside the Canon

The Infancy Gospel of Thomas

The motivating question behind this "infancy Gospel," a term used to designate these later accounts of Jesus' birth and early life, has continued to intrigue readers of the New Testament ever since: If Jesus was a miracle-working Son of God as an adult, what was he like as a kid?

It turns out that he was a bit mischievous. And the alleged author is one who would be expected to know. The book is attributed to a person named "Thomas," a word that means "twin." In some parts of early Christianity, it was believed that Jesus had a twin brother, Thomas (fathered, possibly, by Joseph rather than God).[1] If this author is claiming to be Jesus' twin brother—what better source for knowing the miraculous doings of the divine *Wunderkind*?

The Gospel begins with Jesus as a five-year-old, making clay sparrows by a stream on the Sabbath. A Jewish man passing by sees what the boy has done and reproaches Joseph for allowing his son to break the Law of Moses by not keeping the Sabbath day holy. But when Joseph comes to reprimand the boy, Jesus claps his hands and commands the sparrows to be gone. They come to life and fly off—thereby destroying any evidence of malfeasance!

One might have expected that with his supernatural powers, Jesus would be a useful and entertaining playmate for the other kids in town. It turns out, though, that the boy has a temper and is not to be crossed. When a child muddies a pool of water that Jesus has dammed up near a stream, he curses the boy—who, to the anguish of his parents, withers on the spot. When another child inadvertently runs into him on the street, Jesus turns in anger and declares, "You shall go no farther on your way." The child falls down dead. (Jesus later raises him from the dead, along with others that he has cursed on one occasion or another.) And Jesus' wrath is not reserved only for other children. Joseph sends him to school to learn to read, but Jesus refuses to recite the alphabet. His teacher pleads with him to cooperate, until Jesus replies with a scornful challenge, "If you really are a teacher and know the letters well, tell me the power of Alpha and I'll tell you the power of Beta." More than a little perturbed, the teacher cuffs the boy on the head, the single largest mistake of an illustrious teaching career. Jesus zaps him on the spot. Joseph is stricken with grief and gives an urgent order to his mother: "Do not let him go outside: anyone who makes him angry dies."

As time goes on, however, Jesus begins to use his powers for good—saving his friends from deadly snake bites, healing the sick, and proving remarkably handy around the house: when Joseph miscuts a board, he has Jesus there to provide a miraculous solution. The account concludes with Jesus as a twelve-year-old in the Temple, surrounded by scribes and Pharisees who hear him teach and who bless Mary for the wonderful child she has brought into the world.

Clearly a book such as this is based on legend and pious, or not so pious, Christian imagination. It is not, however, of much use to anyone wanting to know what Jesus himself said and did.

Two other early Gospels, though, may provide us greater assistance. One of them was allegedly written by Jesus' closest disciple, Peter.

The Gospel of Peter

We have known about the Gospel of Peter for centuries, since it is mentioned in the writings of the fourth-century church father Eusebius.[2] But we have actually had it in our possession—or rather, we have had a *fragment* of it in our possession—little more than a century, since its final pages were discovered in 1886 in the grave of a Christian monk in Egypt.

Eusebius indicates that the Gospel was popular in parts of Syria during the second half of the second century. According to his account, Serapion, the bishop of Antioch, approved the Gospel of Peter for use in the church of Rhossus, even though he had not taken the trouble to read it himself. When Serapion was told, though, that the book contained heretical teachings about Christ, he perused a copy and quickly dashed off a letter forbidding its use and detailing the offensive passages. Eusebius quotes from this letter but does not cite the passages Serapion had in mind. This is a bit of a shame, since without them we can't be sure that the fragmentary pages discovered at the end of the nineteenth century come from the same "Gospel of Peter" that Serapion had read. In any event, the manuscript we have—a Gospel written in the first person, allegedly by Peter himself—is of considerable interest in its own right.

From the few pages that survive, it's impossible to know how long the entire account was—whether, for example, it included stories of Jesus' entire ministry or only of his trial, execution, and resurrection.

The text begins in the middle of a passage with the statement that "None of the Jews washed his hands, neither did Herod nor any of his judges. As they did not wish to wash, Pilate got up." Evidently the preceding passage narrated the story, otherwise known only from Matthew, of Pilate's washing his hands at Jesus' trial (Matt. 27:24). In Peter's account, however, the emphasis is not on Pilate, who is throughout portrayed as innocent of Jesus' death, but on Herod, the king of the Jews, and on the Jewish leaders who collaborated with him. They do *not* wash their hands—that is, they are seen as guilty for Jesus' blood. In the next verse, it is Herod who orders Jesus to be taken out and crucified.

The narrative continues with the request of Joseph (of Arimathea) for Jesus' body, the mockery of Jesus, and his crucifixion. These accounts are both like and unlike what we read in the canonical Gospels. For example, in verse 10, Jesus is said to be crucified between two criminals, as in the other Gospels. But then we find the unusual statement that "he was silent as if he had no pain." This last statement could well be taken to imply the early Christian heresy known as "Docetism" (i.e., it may imply that Jesus only "appeared" to be human; see chapter 2)—perhaps Jesus appeared to have no pain because he in fact did not have any. Some scholars have seen this as supporting evidence that this is the "heretical" Gospel known to Serapion. Further confirmation may come several verses later. When Jesus is about to die, he utters his "cry of dereliction" in words similar to, but not identical with, those found in Mark's account: "My power, O power, you have left me" (v. 19). He is then said to be "taken up," even though his body remains on the cross. We know of some second-century "heretics" ("Gnostics," whom I'll discuss more fully in a minute) who believed that the divine element was not actually part of Jesus, but had entered into him at his baptism, empowered him for his ministry, and then departed from him before his death. This idea guaranteed that the divine element—which by definition should not be able to experience the limitations, pain, and finitude of our mortal existence—never actually suffered. Does this Gospel itself portray Jesus as bemoaning the departure of the divine Christ from him prior to his death?

The account continues by describing Jesus' burial and then, in the first person, the distress of the disciples: "we fasted and sat mourning and crying night and day until the Sabbath" (v. 27). As in Matthew's Gospel, the Jewish leaders ask Pilate for soldiers to guard the tomb. This Gospel, however, provides more elaborate detail. The centurion in charge is named Petronius, who along with a number of soldiers rolls a huge stone in front of the tomb and seals it with seven seals. They then pitch their tent and stand guard.

Then comes perhaps the most striking passage of the narrative, an actual account of Jesus' resurrection and emergence from the tomb, an account found in none of our other early Gospels. A crowd has come from Jerusalem and its surrounding neighborhoods to see the tomb. During the night hours, they hear a great noise and observe the heavens open up; two men descend in great splendor. The stone before the tomb rolls away of its own accord, and the two men enter. The soldiers standing guard awaken the centurion, who comes out to see the incredible spectacle.

From the tomb there emerge three men; the heads of two of them reach into heaven. They are supporting the third, whose head reaches up beyond the heavens. Behind them emerges a cross. A voice then speaks from heaven, "Have you preached to those who are sleeping?" The cross replies, "Yes" (vv. 41–42).

The soldiers run to Pilate and tell him all that has happened. The Jewish leaders beg him to keep the story quiet, for fear that they will be stoned once the Jewish people realize what they have done in putting Jesus to death. Pilate commands the soldiers to silence, but only after reminding the Jewish leaders that Jesus' crucifixion was indeed their fault, not his.

The next day at dawn, not knowing what has happened, Mary Magdalene goes with several women companions to the tomb to provide a more adequate burial for Jesus' body. But the tomb is empty, save for a heavenly visitor who tells her that the Lord has risen and gone. The manuscript then ends in the middle of a story that apparently described Jesus' appearance to some of his disciples (perhaps similar to that found in John 21): "But I, Simon Peter, and Andrew, my brother, took our nets and went to the sea; and with us was Levi, the son of Alphaeus, whom the Lord..." (v. 60). Here the manuscript breaks off.

Scholars continue to debate certain aspects of this fascinating account. Did this Gospel contain a narrative of Jesus' ministry or only of his Passion? Was it written by a heretical Christian? When was it written? Did its author use any of the canonical Gospels as sources? If not, where did he get his information? Are some of the traditions preserved here earlier (and more reliable) than those found in Matthew, Mark, Luke, and John?

Rather than go into all of the details of these debates, let me simply indicate the view that strikes me as the most reasonable and explain why. This Gospel appears to have been written later than the canonical Gospels, but it does not appear to have relied on them. Instead it was based on popular traditions about Jesus' Passion, stories in circulation in a number of Christian circles. Its author may have had "heretical" leanings and certainly felt considerable antipathy toward non-Christian Jews.

That the Gospel of Peter represents a later stage of development in the traditions about Jesus than what we find in the first-century Gospels is suggested first of all by the heightened legendary accretions: especially, the heightened Jesus (!) and the cross that walks behind him and speaks to the heavens. The treatment of "the Jews" in this account is also significant for dating its traditions, for here they are made even more culpable for Jesus' death than in the canonical Gospels. Indeed, Pilate, representing the Roman authorities, is altogether blameless. Rather, the king of the Jews, Herod, and the other Jewish leaders are at fault for Jesus' unjust condemnation.

This portrayal coincides with views that were developing in Christian circles in the second century, a period in which, as we know from other historical sources, Christian anti-Judaism began to assert itself with particular vigor. One by-product of this heightened animosity is that Christians began to exonerate Pilate for Jesus' death and to blame Jews (indeed, all Jews) more and more. In the Gospel of Peter, it is Jews who actually do the dirty work of crucifying Jesus. Later they regret it, and explicitly express their fears that Jerusalem will now be destroyed as a result of their actions. The interpretation of the destruction of Jerusalem as God's vengeance upon the Jewish people for the execution of Jesus became a common theme in Christian writers of the second century. It appears therefore that the account as we now have it was written after the Gospels that eventually became part of the New Testament. Is it based on any of these earlier narratives?

The Gospel of Peter does have a number of close parallels to the canonical Gospels—particularly to Matthew, where one also reads of Pilate washing his hands and of a guard being posted at the tomb. At the same time, we would be hard-pressed to explain why this author left out so many canonical passages that would have suited his purposes so admirably, had he known them, including the cry from the Jewish crowds in which they assume full responsibility for Jesus' death after Pilate washes his hands ("His blood be upon us and our children," Matt. 27:25), or the account of Jesus' carrying his cross, or the mocking of Jesus during his crucifixion. Moreover, I should stress a methodological point that we will come back to later: scholars have long recognized that the best grounds for thinking that one document was the source for another is when they have extensive verbal agreements with one another. If they agree word for word, it's hard to deny that one of them copied the other. But there are no full sentences that the Gospel of Peter shares with the other Gospels; indeed, there are virtually no verbatim agreements of any kind that extend for more than two or three words at a stretch.

Perhaps it is best, then, to see the accounts of this narrative as having been drawn from stories about Jesus' Passion and resurrection that were in wide circulation among Christians. An author living perhaps at the beginning of the second century did what others had done before him and yet others would do afterward, collecting the stories he had heard, or possibly read, and creating out of them a narrative of the words, deeds, and experiences of Jesus. The result is that this Gospel may provide some independent verification of some of the accounts found in our earlier Christian sources, the New Testament Gospels. But we should always recognize that it was written at a later date, removed some ninety or a hundred years from the events that it narrates.

The Coptic Gospel of Thomas

The Coptic Gospel of Thomas (not to be confused with the Infancy Gospel of Thomas) is without question the most significant Christian book discovered in modern times. It was accidently uncovered by a bedouin farmer near the village of Nag Hammadi, Egypt, in 1945, just a year or so before the discovery of the Dead Sea Scrolls. Digging for fertilizer out in the wilderness, the bedouin (whose name, memorably enough, was Mohammed Ali) uncovered a jar beneath a boulder at the face of a cliff. Inside were thirteen leather-bound books which—as scholars later discovered once they got their hands on them—contained a collection of fifty-two texts, most of them in some way or another "Gnostic" in character, as I'll explain momentarily.

The cliff was near an ancient Christian monastery. Some scholars have speculated that the jar was hidden by monks in the late fourth century, when ecclesiastical higher-ups began to assert pressure on Christians to restrict their reading to "approved" literature. It is clear, in any event, that whenever the jar was actually hidden, the books that it contained were manufactured in the fourth century. The bindings of the covers were strengthened by scraps of paper, some of which are dated. The writings in the books, of course, were much older: some of them are mentioned by name by authors of the second century (just as the New Testament sitting on my desk was published in 1979, even though the books it contains were written nineteen centuries earlier). Among these fifty-two writings, the Gospel of Thomas has caused by far the greatest stir. Some scholars think of it as—and call it!—the Fifth Gospel.

Unlike the Gospel of Peter, discovered sixty years earlier, this particular Gospel is completely preserved. And yet it has no narrative at all, no stories about anything that Jesus did, no references to his death and resurrection. The Gospel of Thomas is a collection of 114 sayings of Jesus.

The sayings are not arranged in any recognizable order. Nor are they set within any context, except in a few instances in which Jesus is said to reply to a direct question of his disciples. Most of the sayings begin simply with the words "Jesus said." In terms of genre, the book looks less like the New Testament Gospels and more like the book of Proverbs in the Hebrew Bible. Like Proverbs, it is a collection of sayings that are meant to bring wisdom to the one who can understand. In fact, the opening statement indicates that the correct understanding of these sayings will provide more than wisdom; it will bring eternal life: "These are the secret words which the living Jesus spoke, and Didymus Judas Thomas wrote them down. And he said, 'The one who finds the meaning of these words will not taste death'" (G. Thom. 1).

Who is this Didymus Judas Thomas, the one who allegedly penned these words? Whereas there may be some doubt concerning the alleged author of the Infancy Gospel of Thomas that I discussed earlier, in this case the author's claim is unambiguous. Both "Didymus" and "Thomas" are words that mean "twin" (the first is Greek, the second Semitic); Judas is his proper name. According to the ancient Syrian writing called the Acts of Thomas, he was a blood relation of Jesus, the one mentioned also in the New Testament (Mark 6:3). In other words, Didymus Judas Thomas was Jesus' twin brother.

Many of the sayings in this book will be familiar to those who have read the Gospels of the New Testament: "Jesus said, 'If a blind man leads a blind man, the two of them fall into a pit'" (G. Thom. 34); "Jesus said, 'Blessed are the poor, for yours is the Kingdom of Heaven'" (G. Thom. 54); "Jesus said, 'The harvest is great, but the workers are few; but beseech the Lord to send workers to the harvest'" (G. Thom. 73). Other sayings sound vaguely familiar, yet somewhat peculiar: "Jesus said, 'Let the one who seeks not cease seeking until he finds, and when he finds, he will be troubled, and when he is troubled, he will marvel, and he will rule over the All'" (G. Thom. 2).

And still other sayings in the Gospel of Thomas sound quite unlike anything known from the New Testament: "Jesus said '...On the day when you were one, you became two. But when you have become two, what will you do?'" (G. Thom. 11); "Jesus said, 'If the flesh exists because of spirit, it is a miracle, but if spirit exists because of the body, it is a miracle of miracles. But I marvel at how this great wealth established itself in this poverty'" (G. Thom. 29); "Jesus said, 'I stood in the midst of the world, and I appeared to them in the flesh. I found all of them drunk; I did not find any of them thirsting. And my soul was pained for the sons of men because they are blind in their hearts, and they do not see that they came empty into the world.... When they have shaken off their wine, then they shall repent'" (G. Thom. 28); "His disciples said, 'On what day will you be revealed to us and on what day shall we see you?' Jesus said, 'When you undress without being ashamed, and you take your clothes and put them under your feet as little children and tramp on them, then you shall see the Son of the Living One, and you shall not fear'" (G. Thom. 37).

The meanings of these sayings are in no way obvious. If they were, they would not be called "secret"! They seem far less obscure, however, when understood in light of the basic myth that was shared by various groups of Christians commonly called "Gnostics." Here I should take a brief detour to explain what that myth was.

A Brief Detour into the Gnostic Myth

Gnosticism is a blanket term used by modern scholars to cover a wide range of religions that emerged in the world of the Mediterranean at about the same time as Christianity, or slightly later. Until the mid-twentieth century—prior, in fact, to the discovery of the Gospel of Thomas and the other writings of the Nag Hammadi Library—we were ill-informed about these religions, since virtually all of our information came from attacks leveled against them by their opponents. This of course was a problem: an enemy can scarcely be trusted to provide a fair or accurate portrayal of one's views.

Unfortunately, the discovery of the Nag Hammadi texts did not completely remedy the situation. For one thing, these texts themselves don't present a unified view of Gnosticism, but represent a remarkable range of opinion and belief. Even more problematic, these documents do not purport to lay out what the Gnostics believed and practiced, but presuppose such matters as the backdrop for what they do want to discuss. That is to say, these books were written by Gnostics for Gnostics, and so do not go to any great lengths to explain what the authors and readers together assume to be true, any more than an article on the sports page about the first game of the World Series explains the history and rules of baseball. Modern readers who want to know what Gnosticism was about, then, have to read between the lines a bit to reconstruct their underlying assumptions about such fundamental matters as the divine realm, the world, and the place of humanity in it, as well as to see what kinds of ritual practices and ethical systems were found among such groups.

As a result, scholars continue to dispute rather basic issues, such as where Gnosticism came from, whether it was originally connected with Christianity, and what its various permutations were. It is generally agreed, however, (a) that the term "Gnosticism" can be applied to a wide range of religious groups, many of them Christian, that thrived in the second century of the Common Era, and (b) that most of these groups stressed "knowledge" (=gnosis, hence the term "Gnostic") as a way of salvation from this evil world, which was not created by the one true God.

More specifically, based on a careful reading of the Gnostics' texts themselves and the reports of their enemies—the church fathers who opposed them—it appears that the overarching views of most Gnostics may be summarized under the following, rather simplified, rubrics.

1 *The World.* Most Gnostics differentiated between "matter," which was evil, and "spirit," which was good. This world, as a material realm, was evil.

2 *The Divine Realm.* The true God did not, therefore, create this world. He was completely spirit. According to the myths that Gnostics told, in eternity past the true God generated other divine offspring (often called "aeons") who themselves, often in pairs, produced offspring. A catastrophe occurred in the divine realm, as one of these divine beings (sometimes named "Sophia," Greek for "Wisdom") fell or became separated from the rest, and spontaneously generated another divine being. The latter, born outside the divine realm, was evil. With his minions that also then came into being, he created the material world as a place of imprisonment for the one who had fallen. He is therefore known as the "Demiurge," that is, the "Maker."

3 *Humans.* The aeon (Sophia) that had fallen from the divine realm was captured and imprisoned in this material world in the bodies of humans. Many humans have this spark of the divine within them. People with the spark have a longing to escape this world; those who do not are simply animals like other animals, destined to die and then cease to exist.

4 *Salvation.* The divine spark within humans can escape only by learning where it came from, how it got here, and how it can return. Deliverance from this material world, in other words, can come only by liberating knowledge (*gnosis*).

5 *The Divine Redeemer.* This knowledge, though, cannot be gained from within this world since the world is evil; it must, therefore, be brought from the outside. In Christian forms of Gnosticism (there are other forms that show no clear ties to Christianity), the

one who brings this knowledge is Christ, who comes from above to convey the *gnosis* necessary for salvation. Since he cannot really belong to this world, though, he was not actually born here. Some Gnostics maintained that Jesus only seemed to be a human, that is, that his body was a phantasm, physical in appearance only. This is the docetic view we've seen already. Others claimed that Christ was a divine aeon who temporarily inhabited the real body of the man Jesus, starting with his baptism, and who then left him at the end of his life, prior to his crucifixion. Afterward, he raised him from the dead and repossessed him, so as to convey his secret teachings after his resurrection.

6 *The Church*. Many Gnostics maintained that Christians who have faith in Christ and do good works can have some modicum of salvation after they die. But the real and glorious afterlife will come only to the Gnostics themselves, those who have the divine spark within and who have come to acquire the full knowledge of the secrets of salvation. These are the "elect."

7 *Ethics*. As a rule, Gnostics appear to have believed that since the human body was evil, it was to be treated harshly to facilitate the spirit's escape from it. These Gnostics, then, urged a rigorously ascetic style of life.

Several of the texts from Nag Hammadi represent explications of the myths that convey these views; these are probably to be allowed poetic license rather than taken as propositional truths or historical sketches of what "really" happened in the mythic past. Many of these are interpretations of the Jewish Scriptures, especially the opening chapters of Genesis, which provided fuel for the mythological imagination. Other texts are poetical reflections on the divine realm, the need for liberating knowledge, and the nature of the world or of the human place in it. Yet others contain attacks on literal-minded Christians who failed to recognize the truth. The few Gnostic texts that have survived in other places, that is, outside of the Nag Hammadi collection, also seem to share many of these basic perspectives.

Back on Track: Thomas as a Gnostic Gospel

Scholars continue to debate whether the Gospel of Thomas is best seen as a Gnostic Gospel. The book clearly does not spell out the Gnostic myth of creation and redemption. But then again, neither do a lot of other Gnostic texts. Moreover, as we've seen already, there are a number of sayings attributed to Jesus here that occur also in non-Gnostic sources. At the same time, a large number of the sayings that may strike a first-time reader as altogether puzzling *do* make good sense when read in light of the basic Gnostic myth that I've just laid out. For example, many of these sayings reflect the notion that within the hearer is a spark of the divine that had a heavenly origin. This spark has tragically fallen into the material world, where it has become entrapped in a body (sunk into poverty); and in that condition it has become forgetful of its origin (or "drunken"). It needs to be reawakened (or "sobered up") by learning the truth about this material world and the impoverished physical body that it inhabits. Jesus is the one who conveys this truth. Once the spirit learns the meaning of his words, it will be able to strip off this body of death, symbolized sometimes as garments of clothing, and escape this material world. It will then have salvation, life eternal; it will rejoin the divine realm and rule over all. These sayings do indeed look Gnostic.

Moreover, as I've indicated, there is not a word in this Gospel about Jesus' crucifixion and resurrection. Indeed, for this author none of Jesus' earthly activities appears to matter: there is no word here of his miracles or encounters or experiences. What matters are Jesus' secret teachings. He brings salvation not through his Passion but by conveying the message necessary for deliverance from this impoverished material existence.

Not only are Jesus' bodily experiences of no importance for the Gospel of Thomas, but the physical existence of believers is irrelevant as well. For this reason, neither human events on the personal level nor history itself are of any consequence. The Kingdom of God is not something to be expected in the future. Consider, for instance, saying 113:

> His disciples said to him, "On what day will the Kingdom come?" [He said,] "It will not come by expectation. They will not say, 'Look here,' or, 'Look there,' but the Kingdom of the Father is spread out on the earth and people do not see it."

The Kingdom is here, now, for those who know who they are and whence they have come; it is not a physical place outside the person, but a salvation of "oneness," of unity with the divine realm whence the Gnostic has come:

> "Jesus said, 'If the ones who lead you say, "There is the kingdom, in heaven," then the birds of heaven shall go before you. If they say to you, "It is in the sea," then the fish shall go before you. Rather the kingdom is within you and outside you. If you know yourselves, then you will be known, and you will know that you are sons of the living Father. But if you do not know yourselves, then you are in poverty and you are poverty" (G. Thom. 3).

Thus this material world and the body that we inhabit are poor excuses for existence. Only through knowledge (= Gnosis)—knowledge of one's true identity, as revealed by the living Jesus—can one escape and enjoy the riches of the Kingdom of the Father. This is a powerful message, and one that stands in stark contrast to the views proclaimed by other early Christians, who maintained, for example, that the material world was good because it was created by God, that the Kingdom of God would be a physical presence on earth to come in the near future, and that salvation came not by understanding the secret message of Jesus but by believing in his death and resurrection.

It seems unlikely that the historical Jesus taught *both* things, which raises a number of interesting and important historical questions. When the sayings of Thomas represent slight, or even large, variations from those of the Synoptic Gospels—that is, when they are basically similar, but with a few twists here and there—is it possible that Thomas preserves Jesus' words more accurately than the Synoptics? Others of Thomas's sayings cannot be found in the New Testament. Could some of these be authentic? Is the entire collection early, from the first century itself? Or was it compiled only later?

Scholars have fought tooth and nail over these questions ever since the book was discovered. And even now, more than fifty years later, the heat of the debate has not subsided. Instead of going through all the ins and outs, let me explain the position that strikes me as the most plausible.

On the one hand, it does not appear to me that the Gospel of Thomas actually used the Synoptic Gospels to formulate its sayings of Jesus. The burden of proof in such matters, as I've already mentioned, is on the one who claims that an author used another document as a source. The surest indicators of reliance on a source are detailed and extensive verbal parallels. But this is precisely what we don't find between Thomas and the Synoptics. There are many similar sayings but few extensive verbal correspondences, even after taking into account the fact that the Synoptics are in Greek but Thomas is in a Coptic translation. Moreover, I should point out that if Thomas did use the Synoptics, we would be hard-pressed to explain why he left out most of their sayings of Jesus, many of them relevant to his agenda.

It is probably better, therefore, to assume that the author who calls himself Thomas knew a number of the sayings of Jesus, and that he understood these sayings in a particular way, based on his knowledge of what I have called the Gnostic myth. He collected these sayings, some of them old, some of them new, and put them into a Gospel designed for his community, a community that held to the importance not of

Jesus' death and resurrection, but of his secret message. His collection—judging from the Gnostic underpinnings of some of the sayings—was probably made sometime in the early second century. Nonetheless, some of the sayings he preserved may represent actual teachings of Jesus. As we will see in the next chapter, each of these sayings—as well as all the sayings allegedly from Jesus in every other surviving source—must be considered on a case-by-case basis.

Outside the Canon: Conclusion

In sum, there does not appear to be much information about the historical Jesus outside the canon of the New Testament. I should stress that this conclusion is not based on a theological judgment about the supreme importance of the New Testament. It is a judgment that *anyone* who looks carefully at the historical record would have to draw, whether Christian, Jewish, Muslim, Buddhist, Hindu, agnostic, or atheist! Even though there are lots of other Gospels out there, they are almost entirely late and legendary. To be sure, the Gospel of Peter may theoretically provide some corroborating information about Jesus' last hours, and the Coptic Gospel of Thomas may preserve some independently attested sayings of Jesus. But even on a generous estimate, these books will not provide any *significant* help in our quest to learn what Jesus actually said, did, and experienced. No matter how you slice it, you have to rely on the New Testament if you want to know about the life of the historical Jesus.

Christian Sources Within the Canon

But we are not necessarily limited in our investigation to the four Gospels. For there are twenty-three other books in the New Testament. Surely, one might think, *they* can provide us with additional information. They were, after all, written by some of Jesus' earliest followers. What do these other New Testament books tell us about the historical Jesus?

Unfortunately, again, not much. You can see this for yourself: simply read through the entire New Testament after the Gospels, from Acts to Revelation, and make a list of everything said about Jesus' life. You may be surprised. You won't need a full sheet of paper. These books say a lot, of course, about Christ's work of salvation, his resurrection, and his present doings. But they say scarcely anything at all about what he said, did, and experienced between the time he was born and the time he died—which is, after all, the time period we're interested in if we want to know about the "historical" Jesus.

Just to illustrate the problem, consider the author outside of the Gospels who tells us the most about Jesus' life, the apostle Paul. If we were to peruse his writings, what would we find? In the following list, I've tried to be exhaustive. Paul tells us that Jesus was born of a woman (Gal. 4:4; this, of course, is not a particularly useful datum—one wonders what the alternative may have been!), and that he was born a Jew (Gal. 4:4), reputedly from the line of King David (Rom. 1:3). He had brothers (1 Cor. 9:5), one of whom was named James (Gal. 1:19). He had twelve disciples (1 Cor. 15:5; at least, I assume this is what he means when he refers to "the twelve" here) and conducted his ministry among Jews (Rom. 15:8). He had a last meal with his disciples on the night in which he was betrayed (1 Cor. 11:23).3 Paul knows what Jesus said at this last meal (1 Cor. 11:23–25). Finally, he knows that Jesus died by being crucified (1 Cor. 2:2). He also knows of Jesus' resurrection, of course, but here I am interested only in what he tells us about Jesus' life prior to his death.

In addition to the words spoken at the Last Supper, Paul refers to two of the sayings of Jesus, to the effect that Christians shouldn't get divorced (1 Cor. 7:11; cf. Mark 10:11–12) and that they should pay their preacher (1 Cor. 9:14; cf. Luke 10:7). Still other teachings of Paul sound similar to sayings of Jesus recorded in the Gospels—for instance, that Christians should pay their taxes (Rom. 13:7; cf. Mark 12:17) and that they should fulfill the Law of Moses by loving their neighbors as themselves (Gal. 5:14; cf. Matt. 22:39–40). But Paul gives no indication that he knows that Jesus himself spoke these words.

Paul does say a lot about the *importance* of Jesus, especially the importance of his death, resurrection, and imminent return from heaven. But in terms of historical information, what I've just listed is about all there is. Imagine what we wouldn't know about Jesus if these letters were our only sources of information. We hear nothing here of the details of Jesus' birth or parents or early life, nothing of his baptism or temptation in the wilderness, nothing of his teaching about the coming Kingdom of God. We have no indication that he ever told a parable, that he ever healed anyone, cast out a demon, or raised the dead. We learn nothing of his transfiguration or triumphal entry, nothing of his cleansing of the Temple, nothing of his interrogation by the Sanhedrin or trial before Pilate, nothing of his being rejected in favor of Barabbas, of his being mocked, of his being flogged, and so on. The historian who wants to know about the traditions concerning Jesus—or indeed, about the historical Jesus himself—will not be much helped by the surviving letters of Paul. Or indeed, by the other authors of the New Testament.

As strange as it may seem, though, this conclusion does not completely exhaust the possibilities of canonical sources outside of our surviving Gospels. You might think that if we aren't helped by any other New Testament author, that there would be no place to turn except the Gospels. But as it turns out, this is not quite true!

The Q Source

One of the most controversial and talked-about sources that scholars have used for studying the life of the historical Jesus is, oddly enough, a document that does not exist. Most scholars are reasonably sure, though, that at one time it did exist, and that it can, at least theoretically, be reconstructed. The document is called "Q."

To understand what Q is (or was), we need to consider a couple of important aspects of the New Testament Gospels. As I've already mentioned, the first three are called the "Synoptic Gospels." This is because, unlike the Gospel of John, they tell so many of the same stories, sometimes word for word the same, that they can actually be laid out on a page next to each other in parallel columns for the sake of comparison. That is to say, they can be "seen together," the literal meaning of the Greek term "synoptic." How does one account for the fact that three ancient documents include so many of the same episodes, often in the same sequence, and often even in the same wording? This question is sometimes called ".the Synoptic Problem." For almost everyone who has worked on the problem at any length, the answer is pretty obvious. All three of these Gospels must have had one or more sources in common. That is, they, or at least two of them, copied. Either they all copied the same source, or two of them copied the third, or one copied another and served, then, as a copy for the third, or...actually the possibilities are nearly endless (as anyone with the hankering to investigate the history of the scholarship on this one will quickly see!).

In the mid-nineteenth century, scholars developed a view that can be called the "four-source hypothesis." The hypothesis is ultimately founded on the premise that the Gospel of Mark was the first to be written, and that Matthew and Luke both—independently of one another—used it as a source for their Gospels. This is by far the most commonly held view among scholars in the field today; you can easily read up on the evidence for it if you're so inclined.[4]

Among other things, the view readily explains why all three Gospels sometimes have exactly (or almost exactly) the same story (Matthew and Luke copied it from Mark), why sometimes Matthew and Mark have a story not found in Luke (Matthew copied it from Mark, but Luke decided not to), and why Mark and Luke have some stories not found in Matthew (Luke copied it but Matthew didn't). It can also explain those very few cases where Mark has a story, or part of a story, not found in either Matthew or Luke. They both, possibly for reasons of their own, decided not to include it. But there remains a fairly obvious problem (and lots of not-so-obvious ones): What about the sayings and stories found in Matthew and Luke—which again are sometimes given in exactly the same words—that are not found in Mark? There are in fact lots of these—entire stories like the devil's three temptations of Jesus in the wilderness (Matt. 4:1–11; Luke 4:1–13), parables like the great wedding feast (Matt. 22:1–14; Luke 14:15–24), groups of sayings like the Beatitudes (Matt. 5:3–12; Luke 6:17, 20–23), and lots of individual sayings. Nearly all this non-Markan material found in both Matthew and Luke consists of Jesus' sayings (the temptation narrative is one of the major exceptions). Since they couldn't have gotten this material from Mark, what was their source?

There are reasons for thinking that neither Matthew nor Luke copied these stories from the other.[5] That leaves only one plausible explanation for their agreements in these non-Markan traditions (well, one explanation with lots of variable ways of imagining how it happened): they both had access to another source, one that no longer survives on its own.

This is the source that scholars call Q. Its existence was first hypothesized by German scholars, who, somewhat lacking in ingenuity, decided to call it "Source" (German *Quelle*—hence the one-letter abbreviation "Q" that you'll see scattered throughout New Testament scholarship and the rest of this book). By strict definition, Q consists of material that is common to Matthew and Luke but not found in Mark. As I've indicated, this material consists almost entirely of sayings—but not completely so: in addition to the temptation narrative, Q also contained a story of Jesus healing a centurion's son (Matt. 8:5–13; Luke 7:1–10).

What else did it contain? It certainly had some of the most familiar sayings of Jesus. It contained, for example, the Beatitudes (Luke 6:20–23) and the Lord's Prayer (Luke 11:2–4); it included the commands to love your enemies, not to judge others, and not to worry about what to eat and wear (Luke 6:27–42; 12:22–32); and it provided a number of familiar parables (e.g., Luke 12:39–48; 14:15–24). The reality, though, is that we don't have a full picture of what Q contained, since our only access to it is through the agreements of Matthew and Luke in passages not found in Mark. So, while we can say what probably *was* in it, we're hard-pressed to say what was *not*. I stress this point because a number of scholars have built massive arguments—castles in the air, actually—on the fact that Matthew and Luke do not share stories of Jesus' Passion that are not found in Mark, and have concluded from this that Q must not have had a Passion narrative. In fact, we don't *know* whether it contained a Passion narrative. We don't *have* it!

Many scholars have been particularly impressed by the similarities evident between Q, insofar as we can reconstruct it, and the Gospel of Thomas. Interestingly enough, prior to the discovery of Thomas one of the principal arguments sometimes used against the hypothetical existence of Q was that early Christians could not *possibly* have created a collection of Jesus' sayings without much interest at all (*if* at all!) in his death and resurrection. And then Thomas turned up—a Gospel comprised exclusively of Jesus' sayings without an account of his death and resurrection!

The similarities between Thomas and Q should probably not be pressed too far, though, for reasons I've already alluded to. Q did have some narratives; that is, it wasn't exclusively sayings. It may have had a Passion narrative; we simply can't know. And it was produced much earlier than Thomas. Since it was used independently by both Matthew and Luke, presumably sometime in the early 80s, it must have been in circulation before then. Most scholars think it was written well before then, probably before Mark (whose author, evidently, did not use it himself), possibly in the 50s or 60s CE.

If so, it represents our earliest—though nonsurviving!—source for the historical Jesus. In this connection, and in anticipation of some of the issues I'll be raising later, I should point out that Q is chock-full of apocalyptic sayings on the lips of Jesus, sayings in which he predicts the imminent end of the age in a catastrophic act of judgment sent by God.

Other Early Sources

Let me conclude this discussion by pointing out, very briefly, the reason for calling the most common explanation of the relationship of the Synoptic Gospels the *four*-source hypothesis. We have already seen two of the sources lying behind the Gospels of Matthew and Luke, namely, Mark and Q. There are some stories, though, that are found only in Matthew (e.g., the visit of the wise men, Jesus' instructions on almsgiving, and the parable of the pearl of great price; Matt. 2:1–12; 6:1–8; 13:45–46), and others found only in Luke (e.g., Jesus as a twelve-year-old; Zacchaeus in the sycamore tree; and the parables of the good Samaritan and of the prodigal son; Luke 2:1–52; 10:29–37; 19:1–10; 15:11–32). It is generally assumed that the Gospel writers didn't make up these stories whole-cloth (they certainly *may* have; but given their use of other sources for their accounts, it seems somewhat unlikely). If not, then they must have gotten them from someplace—either written documents that no longer survive or oral traditions that they had heard. For the sake of convenience, scholars designate the special source(s) available to Matthew as "M" and the one(s) available to Luke as "L." Since these are sources that provide material found in either Matthew or Luke alone, there is nothing to compare them with in order to decide their basic character. We do not know, for instance, whether M (or L) was only one source or a group of sources, whether it was written or oral. It could represent a single document available to the author of Matthew (or Luke), or several documents, or a number of stories that were transmitted orally, or a combination of all of these things.

Since these sources also predated the Gospels into which they were incorporated, they, too, could provide early access to the sayings and deeds of Jesus.

Sources within the Canon: Conclusion

We could talk further about the sources lying behind the Gospels of the New Testament, but I've said enough to allow us to proceed with our investigation. The basic points to recall at this stage are these: (1) There is very little mention of Jesus by early and reliable sources outside of the New Testament—whether pagan, Jewish, or Christian—with the notable exceptions of the Gospels of Peter and Thomas. (2) Within the New Testament, apart from the four Gospels, there is very little information about Jesus' life. (3) The Gospels themselves are therefore our best sources for trying to establish what Jesus himself actually said and did. (4) These Gospels were based on earlier sources—such as Q—that can be reconstructed, at least to some extent.

At the same time, I should stress that the *sources* of the Gospels are riddled with just the same problems that we found in the Gospels themselves: they, too, represent traditions that were passed down by word of mouth, year after year, among Christians who sometimes changed the stories—indeed, sometimes invented the stories—as they retold them. It's now time to figure out what to do with these problems. Given the fact that the sources at our disposal are not always historically accurate, how can we best use them to determine what actually happened in the life of the historical Jesus?

six

moving on to the past:
how can we reconstruct the life of jesus?

WE HAVE SPENT A GOOD DEAL OF TIME LOOKING AT THE HISTORICAL SOURCES THAT CAN INFORM US ABOUT JESUS OF NAZARETH. THE HISTORIAN'S SOURCES ARE LIKE THE AUTO MECHANIC'S tools: it's one thing to have them, but another thing to know how to use them. At this stage we need to consider what to do with the sources we have in order to help us determine what Jesus said, did, and experienced. I'll begin by considering what a historian might hope for in a set of sources and then reflect on how our available sources stack up against this historian's wish list.

A Historian's Wish List

Historians obviously have to devise criteria for determining which sources can be trusted and which cannot—much as a jury in a murder trial has to decide which of the witnesses called to the stand can be believed. In reconstructing any past event—whether an air disaster in 1930, a heresy trial in 1030, or a crucifixion in 30—an ideal situation would be to have sources that (a) are numerous, so that they can be compared to one another (the more the better!); (b) derive from a time near the event itself, so that they were less likely to have been based on hearsay or legend; (c) were produced independently of one another, so that their authors were not in collusion; (d) do not contradict one another, so that one or more of them is not necessarily in error; (e) are internally consistent, so that they show a basic concern for reliability; and (f) are not biased toward the subject matter, so that they have not skewed their accounts to serve their own purposes.

Are the New Testament Gospels—our principal sources for reconstructing the life of Jesus—these kinds of sources? Before pursuing the question, let me emphasize once again that I am not passing judgment on the worth of these books, trying to undermine their authority for those who believe in them, or asking whether they are important as religious or theological documents. I am instead asking the question of the historian: Are these books reliable for reconstructing what Jesus actually said and did? How do they stack up against our wish list?

On the up side, we are obviously fortunate that Jesus' life is presented in multiple ancient sources. We aren't *as* well informed about him, in some ways, as we are about his follower Paul or some other ancient figures like Cicero, who left us numerous writings from their own hands (we have nothing, of course, written by Jesus himself). But for a person living two thousand years ago, we have an uncommon number of sources for Jesus, more than for all but a handful of his contemporaries. And it is particularly useful to have so many *independent* accounts of his words and deeds—that is to say, the author of Mark didn't know Q; John probably hadn't read the Synoptics; Paul, who was writing before any of the Gospels had been written, obviously didn't know what they were going to say, just as they show no evidence of having read Paul, and so on. We thus have relatively numerous and independent reports about Jesus from the ancient world, and this is all clearly to the good.

On the down side, these reports are not, as we have seen, disinterested accounts by impartial observers, written near the time of the events they narrate. They are all—with minor exceptions like the accounts of Josephus and Tacitus—provided by Jesus' own followers, who had a vested interest in what they had to say about him, and who were writing a long time after the fact (thirty-five to sixty-five years). Moreover, these authors were not themselves eyewitnesses. They were Christians who, so far as we can tell, did not even *know* any eyewitnesses. They spoke a different language from the eyewitnesses, lived in different countries, and addressed different audiences with different needs and concerns. And even if they were eyewitnesses, we would still have to examine their testimony carefully. For the beliefs of these authors, and the needs of their audiences, affected the ways they told their stories about Jesus.

Each of these authors—as two of them actually tell us—inherited his stories from earlier written sources. Each of these sources had its own perspective as well. And before anyone bothered to *write* stories about Jesus, they had circulated by word of mouth for years and years, among Christians who recounted them for a variety of reasons: to magnify the importance of Jesus, to convince others to believe in him, to instruct them concerning his relationship with God, to show how he understood the Hebrew Scriptures, to encourage his followers with the hope that his words could bring, and so forth. As the stories circulated orally, they were changed to suit the purposes at hand. And they were modified yet further when they were written down in such lost documents as Q and further still when rewritten by the authors of our Gospels.

It is important to recall that this view is not based simply on scholarly imagination. We have evidence for it, some of which I have laid out in earlier chapters.

Precisely because these documents were of such importance to people who believed in Jesus as the Son of God, their concerns, to put it somewhat simplistically, were less historical than religious. They were not interested in providing the brute facts of history for impartial observers, but in proclaiming their faith in Jesus as the Son of God. This was "Good News" for the believer. But it is not necessarily good news for historians, who are invested in getting behind the perspectives of the authors of the Gospels, and those of their sources, to reconstruct what Jesus really said, did, and experienced. How can "faith documents" such as the Gospels—writings produced by believers for believers to promote belief—be used as historical sources?

Using Our Sources: Some of the Basic Rules of Thumb

Before elaborating on some specific criteria that scholars have devised, let me say something about a few very basic methodological principles that most historians would agree should be applied to our sources.

The Earlier the Better

In general, historical sources closest to an event have a greater likelihood of being accurate than those at a further remove. This isn't a hard and fast rule, of course—sometimes later sources can recount events more accurately than earlier ones. But not usually, and especially not in antiquity, when later authors did not have the research techniques and data retrieval systems available to us today. The rule of thumb, particularly in the ancient world, is that earlier is better.

The logic of the principle, especially when dealing with ancient sources, is that as an event gets discussed and reports about it circulate, there are greater and greater opportunities for it to be changed—until just about everyone gets it wrong. The less time that has elapsed in the transmission process, the less time there is for alteration and exaggeration. Thus if you want to know about the Montanists who lived near the end of the second century, it's better to consult sources from about their time than sources produced two centuries later.

In terms of our own study, this means that the earliest sources should be especially valued. Of our four New Testament Gospels, John is the latest, written, probably, about sixty or seventy years after the events it narrates. On the whole, it is less likely to be accurate than Mark, written some thirty years earlier. (Recall what John did with the date and time of Jesus' death!) So, too, the Gospels of Peter and Thomas, which, while relying on earlier materials, were themselves evidently produced in the early second century. Following this principle, our best source of all would be Paul (who regrettably doesn't tell us very much), and then Q (i.e., the common source shared by Matthew and Luke for stories not found in Mark) and Mark, followed by M (Matthew's special source[s]) and L (Luke's), and so on.

Theological Merits / Historical Demerits

Over the course of Christian history, probably the most religiously significant and theologically powerful account of Jesus' life has been the Gospel of John. John says things about Jesus found nowhere else in Scripture: only here, for example, is Jesus identified as the "Word" that was from the beginning of all time, who was with God and who was God, the Word that became flesh and dwelt among us (1:1–14); only here does Jesus claim to be equal with God (10:30); only here does Jesus say that anyone who has seen him has seen the Father, that anyone who rejects him has rejected the Father, and that anyone who believes in him will have eternal life with the Father (5:22–24; 6:40; 14:9). These are powerful theological statements. But if they were actually said by Jesus, the historian might ask, why do they never occur in sources that were written earlier than John? Nothing like them can be found in Mark, Q, M, or L—let alone Paul or Josephus. As true as these statements about Jesus may be to the believer, it is difficult to think that they represent things he really said to his disciples.

And thus a second rule of thumb that historians follow: accounts of Jesus that are clearly imbued with a highly developed theology are less likely to be historically accurate. The reason relates to our first rule of thumb: later sources tend to be more theologically oriented than earlier ones, since the greater passage of time has allowed greater sustained theological reflection. And so, books like John and Thomas—which may indeed preserve important historical information on occasion— are not as valuable to the historian as sources that do not promote as distinctive a theological agenda.

Beware the Bias

The final rule of thumb is closely related to the preceding two. It is sometimes possible to detect a clear bias in an author—for example, when just about every story in his or her account drives home, either subtly or obviously, the same point. We've seen a bit of this, for example, in the Gospel of Peter, whose vendetta against the Jewish people colors just about every episode.

Whenever you can isolate an author's biases, you can take them into account when considering his report. That is to say, statements supporting his bias should then be taken with a pound of salt (not necessarily discarded, but scrutinized carefully). An example is the report in the Gospel of Peter that it was the Jewish king Herod and his court that had Jesus crucified. In all of our other early sources, the Roman governor Pilate is said to be responsible. Peter's established bias against the Jews should therefore give one pause when evaluating his account.

Having said all this by way of general evaluation of our sources, what *specific* criteria can we apply to the traditions about Jesus preserved in them?

Specific Criteria and Their Rationale

Over the course of the past fifty years, historians have worked hard on precisely this question, developing methods for uncovering historically reliable information about the life of Jesus. I need to say up front that this is a hotly debated area of research, with some very smart and competent historians (and quite a few less than competent ones) expressing divergent views both about what criteria to use and about what conclusions to draw, once they agree on the criteria.

Here I'd like to sketch several of the methodological principles that have emerged from these debates. As you will see, there is a real logic behind each of them, and the logic needs to be understood for the criterion itself not to seem hopelessly arbitrary. In particular, it might help to use an analogy: in many respects, the historian is like a prosecuting attorney. He or she is trying to make a case and is expected to bear the burden of proof. As in a court of law, certain kinds of evidence are acknowledged as admissible, and witnesses must be carefully scrutinized. How, then, can we go about it?

Piling on the Testimony:
The Criterion of Independent Attestation

In any court trial, it is better to have a number of witnesses who can provide consistent testimony than to have only one, especially if the witnesses can be shown not to have conferred with one another in order to get their story straight. A strong case will be supported by several witnesses who independently agree on a point at issue. So, too, with history. An event mentioned in several independent documents is more likely to be historical than an event mentioned in only one. This is not to deny that individual documents can provide reliable historical information. But without corroborating evidence, it is often impossible to know whether an individual source has made up an account, or perhaps provided a skewed version of it.

As we've seen, we do in fact have a number of independent sources for the life of Jesus. It is probably safe to say, for example, that Mark, the apostle Paul, and the authors of Q, M, L, and John all wrote independently of one another. Moreover, we have seen that the Gospel of Thomas, possibly the Gospel of Peter, and certainly Josephus were all produced independently of our other surviving accounts. This means that if there is a tradition about Jesus that is preserved in more than one of these documents, no one of them could have made it up, since the others knew of it as well, independently. And if a tradition is found in several of these sources, then the likelihood of its going back to the very beginning of the tradition from which they all ultimately derive, that is, back to the historical Jesus himself, is significantly improved.

I should emphasize that this criterion does not work for sources that are not independent. For example, the story of Jesus and the so-called rich young ruler is found in three of our Gospels (Matt. 19:16–22; Mark 10:17–22; Luke 18:18–23). But since Matthew and Luke took the story over from Mark—assuming the four-source hypothesis that we discussed in chapter 5—it is not independently attested. For this reason, the criterion of independent attestation does not work for stories found among all three Synoptic Gospels, since the source for such stories is Mark, or among any two of them, since these are either from Mark or Q.

In what circumstances, then, could the criterion work? Some examples can help to clarify the matter: (a) Stories in which John the Baptist encounters Jesus at the beginning of his ministry can be found in Mark, in Q (where John's preaching is expounded), and in John. Why did all three sources, independently of one another, begin Jesus' ministry with his association with John the Baptist? Possibly because it really did start this way. (b) Jesus is said to have brothers in Mark (6:3), John (7:3), and Paul's first letter to the Corinthians (9:5); moreover, Mark, Paul (Gal. 1:19), and Josephus all identify one of his brothers as James. Conclusion? Jesus probably did have brothers and one of them was probably named James. (c) Jesus tells parables in which he likens the Kingdom of God to seeds in Mark, Q, and the Gospel of Thomas. Conclusion?

Obviously there are limitations to this criterion. It is important to emphasize that merely because a tradition is found in only one source— for example, the parable of the Good Samaritan occurs only in Luke—it is not automatically discounted as historically inaccurate. That is to say, the criterion shows which traditions are more likely to be authentic, but does not show which ones are necessarily inauthentic, a critical difference!

At the same time, multiply attested traditions are not necessarily authentic either. Instead, they are simply more *likely* to be authentic. That is to say, if a tradition is attested independently by two or more sources, then at the very least it must be older than all of the sources that record it. But this is not the same thing as saying that it must go all the way back to Jesus. It could well be, for example, that a multiply attested tradition derives from the years immediately after Jesus' death, with different forms of the story being told in a variety of communities thereafter. For this reason, our first criterion has to be supplemented with others.

What an Odd Thing to Say! The Criterion of Dissimilarity

The most controversial criterion that historians use, and often misuse, to establish authentic tradition from the life of Jesus is sometimes called the "criterion of dissimilarity." The criterion is not so difficult to explain, given what we have already seen about the Gospels.

Any witness in a court of law will naturally tell things the way he or she sees them. Thus, the perspective of the witness has to be taken into account when trying to evaluate the merits of a case. Moreover, sometimes a witness has a vested interest in the outcome of the trial. A question that perennially comes up, then, involves the testimony of interested parties: Are they distorting, or even fabricating, testimony for reasons of their own? The analogy does not completely work, of course, for ancient literary sources (or for modern ones either). Authors from the ancient world were not under oath to tell the historical facts, and nothing but the facts. But when examining ancient sources, the historian must always be alert to the perspective of the witness.

We know that early Christians modified and invented stories about Jesus. There is no one who disputes this: otherwise we would have to think that Jesus really did make clay sparrows come to life when he was a five-year-old, and zap his young playmates when they irritated him, and come forth from his tomb at his resurrection with his head reaching above the clouds, supported by angels as tall as skyscrapers, and reveal the secret Gnostic doctrines to his disciples long after his resurrection. No one believes that all of these stories actually happened (at least no one I've ever met). How, then, did they come to be written down? Somebody made them up, and told them to other people, and eventually they came into the hands of an author—unless he himself made them up.

How can we know which stories were made up, and which ones are historically accurate? The first thing to do is to determine the sorts of things the early Christians were saying about Jesus, for example, from other surviving documents, and to ascertain whether the traditions told about his own sayings and deeds clearly support these Christian views. What if they do? Then there is at least a theoretical possibility that these sayings and deeds were made up precisely in order to advance the views that some Christians held dear.

What if a saying or deed attributed to Jesus, on the other hand, does not obviously support a Christian cause, or even goes against it? A tradition of this kind would evidently not have been made up by a Christian. Why, then, would it be preserved in the tradition? Perhaps because it really happened that way. "Dissimilar" traditions, that is, those that do not support a clear Christian agenda, or that appear to work against it, are difficult to explain unless they are authentic. They are therefore more likely to be historical.

I want to be perfectly clear about the limitations of this criterion. Just because a saying or deed of Jesus happens to conform to what Christians were saying about him does not mean that it cannot be accurate. Obviously, the earliest disciples followed Jesus precisely because they appreciated the things that he said and did. They certainly would have told stories about him that included such things. Thus, on the one hand, the criterion may do no more than cast a shadow of doubt on certain traditions. For example, when in the Infancy Gospel of Thomas the young Jesus raises kids from the dead or miraculously solves his father's mistakes in the carpenter's shop, these look like things drawn from later Christian imagination. And when in the Coptic Gospel of Thomas Jesus is said to reveal the secret doctrines of *gnosis* to a handful of followers, this is too closely aligned with Gnostic theology to be above suspicion. But the criterion of dissimilarity is best used not in the negative way of establishing what Jesus did not say or do, but in the positive way of showing what he likely did.

Perhaps the criterion can be clarified by providing a couple of brief examples of where it might work. As we have seen, Jesus' association with John the Baptist at the beginning of his ministry is multiply attested. In some traditions, Jesus is actually said to have been baptized by John. Is this a tradition that a Christian would have "made up"? Well, probably not. For it appears that most early Christians understood that a person who was baptized was spiritually inferior to the one who was doing the baptizing. This view is suggested already in the Gospel of Matthew, where we find John protesting that he is the one who should be baptized by Jesus, not the other way around (Matt. 3:14). What conclusion could be drawn? If it is hard to imagine a Christian inventing the story of Jesus' baptism, since this could be taken to mean that he was John's subordinate, then it is more likely that the event actually happened. The story that John initially refused to baptize Jesus, on the other hand, is not multiply attested (it is found only in Matthew) and appears to serve a clear Christian agenda. On these grounds, even though John's reluctance cannot be proven to be a Christianized form of the account, it might appear to be suspect.

Another example. According to all four canonical Gospels, and perhaps Paul, at the end of Jesus' life he was betrayed by one of his own followers. Is this a story that a Christian believer would invent? Would Christians want to admit that Jesus was turned in by one of his closest friends and allies? It seems unlikely: surely Jesus would have had a commanding presence over those closest to him. Why, then, do we have the tradition, which is, as I've pointed out, independently attested? Perhaps it's something that really happened.

A final, fairly obvious example. The earliest Christians put a good deal of effort into convincing non-Christian Jews that the Messiah had to suffer and die, that in fact Jesus' crucifixion was according to the divine plan. Why was it so difficult for them to persuade others? Because prior to the Christian proclamation of Jesus, there were no Jews, at least so far as we know, who believed that the Messiah was going to be crucified. On the contrary, the Messiah was to be the great and powerful leader who delivered Israel from its oppressive overlords. Christians who wanted to proclaim Jesus as Messiah would not have invented the notion that he was crucified, because his crucifixion created such a scandal. Indeed, the apostle Paul calls it the chief "stumbling block" for Jews (1 Cor. 1:23). Where, then, did the tradition come from? It must have actually happened.

Other sayings and deeds of Jesus do not pass this criterion. In Mark's Gospel, for example, when Jesus predicts that he is to go to Jerusalem, and that he will be rejected by the scribes and elders and be crucified, and then in three days be raised from the dead, he is proclaiming precisely what the early Christian preachers were saying about him. The Passion predictions cannot pass the criterion of dissimilarity. Does that mean that Jesus did not predict his own death? Not necessarily. It means that if he did, we can't establish it through this criterion. Again, in John's Gospel Jesus claims to be equal with God, a claim that coincides perfectly with what some Christians were saying about him near the end of the first century, when John's Gospel was written. Does this mean that Jesus did not really make this claim? Not necessarily. It means that the tradition cannot pass this criterion.

The point is that historians have to evaluate all of the traditions about Jesus so as to determine whether they coincide with the beliefs and practices of the early Christians who were proclaiming them, so as to make some kind of judgment concerning their historical reliability. One of the problems inherent in the criterion, as you might have guessed, is that we do not know as much about what the early Christians believed and practiced as we would like. Moreover, what we do know indicates that they believed and practiced a whole range of things. For these reasons, it is easier to make a judgment concerning a particular tradition when it passes both of the criteria we have discussed (independent attestation and dissimilarity). And the judgment can be made yet more easily when a tradition passes the third criterion as well.

If the Shoe Fits.... The Criterion of Contextual Credibility
You're probably not going to believe a witness in a court of law if his or her testimony doesn't conform with what you otherwise know to be the facts of the case. The same applies to historical documents. If a recently "discovered" diary purports to be from the hand of "Joshua Harrison, explorer of the Western territories of the United States," and is dated AD 1728, you know that you have a problem.

For ancient documents, reliable traditions must conform to the historical and social contexts to which they relate. For the traditions of the Gospels, this means that the sayings, deeds, and experiences of Jesus have to be plausibly situated in the historical context of first-century Palestine in order to be trusted as reliable. Any saying or deed of Jesus that does not "make sense" in this context is automatically suspect.

As an obvious example of the sort of thing I have in mind, I might cite the Gnostic sayings of the Gospel of Thomas. For instance, in saying 37, when Jesus replies to the disciples' question about when they will see him again, he says, "When you undress without being ashamed, and you take your clothes and put them under your feet as little children and tramp on them, then you shall see the Son of the Living One, and you shall not fear." It is much easier to situate the saying in the context of the second century, when the Gnostic myth that makes sense of the saying was having an influence, than in the days of Jesus.

Some of the traditions of the New Testament Gospels do not fare well by this criterion either. For example, in Jesus' conversation with Nicodemus in John 3, there is a play on words that creates a certain confusion in Nicodemus's mind. Jesus says, "You must be born from above," but Nicodemus misunderstands him to mean "You must be born again." The misunderstanding is understandable, so to say, since the Greek word for "from above" also means "again." Nicodemus has to ask for clarification, which leads Jesus to enter into an extended discourse about experiencing a heavenly birth. From a historical point of view, the problem with this passage (one of the favorite passages of many Christians today!) is that the confusion created by the word Jesus uses makes sense in Greek, the language of the Fourth Gospel, but it cannot be replicated in Aramaic, the language spoken by Jesus himself. In Aramaic, the word for "from above" does not also mean "again." The result? If this conversation did take place (it passes neither of our other criteria), it would not have occurred exactly in the way described by John's account.

A somewhat different problem of contextual credibility occurs in John 9:22, where we are told that some people were afraid to admit publicly that they believed in Jesus, because "the Jews" had already agreed that anyone who professed belief in Jesus as the Messiah was to be "put out of the synagogue." We have good reason for thinking that something of this sort did happen later in the first century—but not during the days of Jesus, when Jewish leaders had not in fact passed legislation concerning Jesus or his followers. It is likely, then, that the story as narrated in the Fourth Gospel is not historically accurate.

Unlike the other two criteria, this one serves a strictly negative function. The others are used to argue *for* a tradition, on the grounds that it is attested by two or more independent sources or that it is a story that Christians would not have invented. This third criterion is used to argue *against* a tradition, on the grounds that it does not conform to what we know about the historical and social context of Jesus' life.

Conclusion

To sum up. We know that Christians were modifying and inventing stories about Jesus, and that our written sources preserve both historically reliable information and theologically motivated accounts. In light of this situation, the traditions that we can most rely on as historically accurate are those that are independently attested in a number of sources, that do not appear to have been created in order to fulfill a need in the early Christian community, and that make sense in light of a first-century Palestinian context.

Finally, I should emphasize that with respect to the historical Jesus, or indeed, with respect to any historical person, the historian can do no more than establish historical probabilities. In no case can we reconstruct the past with absolute certitude. All that we can do is take the evidence that happens to survive and determine to the best of our abilities what probably happened. Scholars will always disagree on the end results of their labors. But nothing can be done about this. The past can never be empirically proved, it can only be reconstructed.

Illustration of the Criteria: Jesus' Early Life

I would like to conclude this chapter by showing how the criteria I've just laid out can be used by considering the early traditions of Jesus' birth and early life. I've arranged the traditions under two major rubrics: what we can't know (or have serious reason to doubt), and what, evidently, we can.

What We Can't Know (or What We Might Doubt)

THE VIRGIN BIRTH.   The tradition that Jesus' mother was a virgin is given by both Matthew and Luke, and to that extent, it's independently attested.[1] But it has always struck scholars as odd that the tradition—which surely would be an important thing to know!—isn't attested anywhere else in our earliest sources, even among writers who would have had a real interest in publicizing the fact that God himself was actually Jesus' father. Mark, for example, understands Jesus to be the Son of God in some sense (Mark 1:11), but when it mentions his family, including his mother, it says nothing about the unusual circumstances of his birth (e.g., Mark 3:31). John actually mentions Joseph and calls him Jesus' father (John 1:45), seeming to assume, therefore, that Jesus was born in a normal way. And Paul, who also thinks of Jesus as the Son of God, says that Jesus was born of a woman (Gal. 4:4), but says nothing about the woman being a virgin.

Moreover, the two sources that mention the virgin birth both have a vested interest in the doctrine. For Matthew the virgin birth fulfills prophecy (Matt. 1:23) and for Luke it shows that he really was God's son (Luke 1:35). That is to say, in view of the criterion of dissimilarity, there are ample reasons for an early Christian to have made up the idea of a virgin birth, leading most historians to question it as a historical datum.

At the end of the day, of course, there's simply no way to know anything about the sex lives of Jesus' parents before he was born.

BETHLEHEM.   All four of our Gospels assume that Jesus came from Nazareth. But two of them—Matthew and Luke again—independently claim that he was born in Bethlehem. We examined these traditions in chapter 2, and saw that (a) the sources are inconsistent with one another at key points (if Matthew's account is right, it's hard to see how Luke's can be also, and vice versa); (b) both present serious historical problems when taken on their own terms (e.g., the worldwide census under Caesar Augustus in Luke); and (c) both had a clear reason for wanting to affirm that Jesus came from Bethlehem, since a Hebrew prophet had predicted that a ruler would come from there (Mic. 5:2; quoted in Matt. 2:6). As a result, most critical historians consider the tradition of Jesus' birth in Bethlehem to be highly problematic.

OTHER UNIQUE TRADITIONS.   The birth stories that are unique to either Matthew or Luke have even less claim to historical authenticity, since, obviously, they aren't multiply attested (they're unique!). Moreover, none of them passes the criterion of dissimilarity. For example, Matthew's account of the visit of the wise men who followed a star functions, among other things, to show that heaven itself proclaimed this child's birth to all who had eyes to see (in fullfilment, probably, of Num. 24:17). Furthermore, the story shows that the Jewish leaders rejected Jesus (they didn't join the wise men in worshiping the child who would be king, even though they knew where he was to be born) and that they—with Herod as their ultimate leader—actually sought the boy's life. These themes anticipate the end of Matthew's Gospel story, where Jewish animosity leads to Jesus' execution. In other words, these are all theologically driven traditions (i.e., they don't pass the criterion of dissimilarity), that appear in only one source (no independent attestation), which is not particularly early (M). Similar points could be made of the even more problematic accounts we've already discussed of Luke—the census when Quirinius was governor of Syria, the adoration in the Temple by Simeon and Anna, and the rest.

What We Probably Can Know
Other traditions relating to Jesus' early life, on the other hand, probably can be accepted as historically reliable, when tested by our various criteria.

RAISED IN NAZARETH.   Jesus is said to have come from Nazareth in all four Gospels (Matt. 4:13; Mark 1:9; Luke 4:16; John 1:45), and is sometimes actually *called* "Jesus of Nazareth" in other ancient sources (e.g., Acts 3:6). That is to say, the tradition passes the criterion of independent attestation with flying colors. Moreover, as we've just seen again, Matthew and Luke had to go out of their way to explain how it was that Jesus was born in Bethlehem, since everyone knew he came from Nazareth. To this extent, the tradition passes the criterion of dissimilarity (i.e., neither Matthew nor Luke was comfortable with it).

Even more significantly, with respect to dissimilarity, it is difficult to imagine why Christians would have wanted to make the tradition up. Nazareth was a little, unknown, and completely insignificant village. Modern archaeologists estimate its size at around 1,500 to 2,000 persons in Jesus' day. It's not mentioned in the Hebrew Bible, or even in the writings of Josephus, who, as you may recall, was in charge of the Jewish military operations in Galilee and had a lot to say about the region in his many volumes of writings. What would be gained by claiming that Jesus came from a small, one-horse town like Nazareth (cf. John 1:45)? If you wanted to speak about the powerful Messiah of Israel, surely you'd have him come from the center of power, Jerusalem, or possibly Bethlehem. There is little doubt that the tradition of Jesus coming from Nazareth is so firmly entrenched in the tradition precisely because it's historically accurate. Jesus grew up in an out-of-the-way rural village.

BORN AND RAISED A JEW.   There's probably no reason to belabor the point that all of our sources portray Jesus as Jewish—he came from a Jewish home, he was circumcised as a Jew, he worshiped the Jewish God, he kept Jewish customs, followed the Jewish Law, interpreted the Jewish Scriptures, and so on. Despite some wild claims by modern ideologues, for example, some Nazis who would have preferred that Jesus was a blond, blue-eyed Aryan, the tradition of Jesus' Jewish origin and upbringing is firmly entrenched in all of our traditions at every level.

HIS PARENTS.   Jesus' parents are everywhere assumed to be Jewish. They, as we've seen, came from Nazareth, a small rural village in Galilee, the northern part of what we today think of as Israel. They are consistently named Joseph and Mary in our sources (e.g., independently, Matt. 1:16–18; Mark 6:3; Luke 2:5, 16; 3:23; John 1:45; even rabbinic sources call his mother "Miriam"). In none of our traditions are there stories about Joseph after Jesus begins his public ministry. It is usually assumed that he had died by then. The idea that he was already an old man when he became betrothed to Mary is not found until the second century, when it is is sometimes used to explain why they never had sex. But it has absolutely no basis in the earliest Gospel accounts.

About the only thing said about Joseph in the Gospels, outside the birth narratives, is that he was a common laborer (Matt. 13:55, also found, possibly independently of Matthew, in the Infancy Gospel of Thomas, 13). The Greek word used to describe his profession is *tekton*, usually translated as "carpenter." But the word could refer to a number of occupations that involved working with the hands—stone mason or metal worker, for example. In any event, a *tekton* was a lower-class, blue-collar worker. If Joseph worked with wood, it would have been to make things like plows, yokes, and gates, not fine cabinetry (so Infancy Gospel of Thomas). For a rough analogy from the modern period, we might think of Joseph as a construction worker. It is hard to imagine why Christians would have wanted to make up this tradition.

Mary is reported in several of our earliest sources to have outlived her son. We don't have any reliable information concerning what she actually thought of him, since the traditions that she knew that he was the Son of God even before he was born are not multiply attested— they occur only in Luke—and obviously don't pass the criterion of dissimilarity.

HIS BROTHERS AND SISTERS. Jesus evidently had siblings. As I've pointed out, his brothers are mentioned in Mark, John, Josephus, and Paul. His sisters show up in Mark (3:32; 6:3). It has sometimes been maintained that these were not in fact his actual brothers and sisters. The famous translator of the Latin Vulgate, Jerome, for example, claimed that they were his cousins—even though there is a Greek word for "cousin" that is not used of these people in our sources. Jerome was persuasive, in large part, because very few people in his context could read Greek! Others have claimed they were his half siblings, from Joseph's previous marriage. These claims relate to the Roman Catholic doctrine that Mary was a virgin not only when Jesus was born, but for the rest of her life, when, since she was not tainted by sin, she ascended into heaven. There is nothing about this in the Gospels, however, and so the natural assumption is that Joseph and Mary engaged in sexual relations and had a large family. Jesus was presumably the oldest child.

HIS LANGUAGE AND EDUCATION. There are multiply attested traditions that Jesus spoke Aramaic. Sometimes, for example, the Gospels quote his words directly without translating them into Greek (see Mark 5:41; 7:34; John 1:42). This would make sense contextually, since Aramaic was the normal spoken language of Jews in Palestine in the first century. Moreover, there would be no reason for anyone to make up the tradition. Thus it passes all three of our criteria. It is also indicated in the Gospels that Jesus could read the Scriptures in Hebrew (e.g., Luke 4:16–20; see also Mark 12:10, 26), and that he eventually became known as an interpreter of them. He is sometimes, for example, called "rabbi," that is, "teacher" (see Mark 9:5; John 3:2). At the same time, there are independently attested traditions that those who knew about Jesus' background were surprised by his learning (Mark 6:2; John 7:15). Together, these data suggest that he did learn to read as a child—that is, that he had some modicum of education—but that he was not considered an intellectual superstar by the people who knew him as he was growing up.

There are no traditions that specifically indicate that Jesus spoke Greek, although some historians have surmised that living in Galilee, where Greek was widely known, he may have learned some. Moreover, some have suspected that he communicated with Pontius Pilate in Greek at his trial—although we will see later that it is very difficult to know exactly what happened then. At best we can say that it is at least possible that Jesus was trilingual—that he normally spoke Aramaic, that he could at least read the Hebrew Scriptures, and that he may have been able to communicate a bit in Greek. The final point is, in my judgment, the least assured.

HIS EARLY LIFE. We are completely in the dark about Jesus' early life otherwise. The one tradition about him between his infancy and adulthood, discounting what we find in the later infancy Gospels, occurs only in Luke. That is, it is not independently attested. Moreover, it serves a clear theological agenda of portraying Jesus as a *Wunderkind* already at the age of twelve (Luke 2:41–52). We might assume that he had a normal childhood—but unfortunately we aren't even sure what a "normal" childhood would have been like in rural Galilee. He probably would have been apprenticed to his father's line of work—whether as a carpenter making yokes and gates or something along a similar line. He himself is called a *tekton* in Mark 6:3.

The first we learn anything historically certain about Jesus after his early life is when he comes to be baptized by John as an adult. His baptism, as I'll emphasize in chapter 9, is as historically certain as anything in the Gospels, apart from his crucifixion. Most readers of the Gospels, however, have failed to see its significance. For us not to make the same mistake, we will need to learn a lot more about the context in which Jesus emerged as a public figure in Galilee and Judea, sometime in the late 20s of the Common Era.

seven

finding a fit: jesus in context

AS I INTIMATED AT THE END OF THE PREVIOUS CHAPTER,
WE CAN'T SIMPLY JUMP INTO A CONSIDERATION OF JESUS'
WORDS AND DEEDS, EVEN BASED ON A CAREFUL APPLICATION OF THE CRI-
teria I've spelled out, without first considering something about their
historical context. For if we don't situate Jesus in his own context, we
take him out of context, and almost certainly, then, we'll misunder-
stand him. Before moving forward, let me emphasize this point.

Introduction to the Problem

The reality is that anytime you change the context of something (a
word, a statement, a gesture, an action) you change what it means.
Indeed, nothing that we experience through any of our senses makes
any sense without a context, which is another way of saying that context is determinative of meaning. I could demonstrate this in a number
of different ways, but since the following chapters will be considering
words—the words of Jesus and the words that describe both his words
and deeds—I've decided to show that if you change a word's context,
you change what it means.

I could illustrate the point, I think, with any word that any of us has ever heard or read. To move about as far afield as we can, though, let's consider the word "dude."

"Dude" is the kind of word (actually, every word is this kind of word) that always means something that is pretty obvious to its hearers, depending on their context—that is, who they are, where they are living, and when. At one time and place the word "dude" typically referred to a dandy—an urbane and sophisticated fellow who dressed to the nines and liked to appear cultured. Eventually, the word came to refer to anyone who was a modern city-person, as opposed to someone who lived in the country. And so, dude ranches were, and are, places that city-folk could go in order to learn how to ride horses, lasso cattle, chew straw, and do whatever else suited their rural fancies.

When I was in high school back in the 1970s, the word "dude" had taken on a completely different meaning. It was a term that a guy would use to greet another guy: "Hey dude." In that context, you would never say this to someone you didn't know and never, ever to someone you didn't like. It was a kind of insider term that denoted a bond of friendship—usually among guys who would cringe to hear such words called "terms of affection" (and so far as I can recall, the term was a completely male thing).

In different contexts, the word has meant different things (see, e.g., the Jack Nicholson jail scene in Dennis Hopper's film classic *Easy Rider*). But recent developments have become even more interesting. About six years ago my fifth-grade son came home from school. When he walked in the door I said, "Hey dude." His reaction shocked me: "Dad, don't *call* me that!"

"Why not?"

"Don't you know what a dude is?"

"Uh, well, I *thought* I did. What's a dude?"

"A dude is a camel's gonads."

Personally, I thought this was terrific. I told a good friend about it, and he thought so too. Now when he answers the phone, I say, "Hey camel's gonads."

And if you've hung out with high-school or college kids in the mid- to late 1990s, you'll know that dude has grown to mean something else altogether. In fact, now it doesn't mean *anything*. It's an interjection completely devoid of content that begins a sentence and is intended to convey a sense of enthusiasm: "*Dude*, you should have been at the mall yesterday" (contrary to what you might suspect, dude is not used in this sentence as a vocative—that is, to address a person whom you're calling a dude; it's a null term expressing interest or excitement).

And so it goes. New contexts, new meanings; change the context, change the meaning. The same is true of every word in every language ever spoken. And of every combination of words: Does the sentence "this is so bad" always mean the same thing? And every gesture: What does it mean to stand with your arm raised over your head and your first finger pointed up? And every action: What does it mean to kiss someone on the cheek? And in fact everything in our human experience.

My immediate point: if you want to understand words and deeds—including the words and deeds of Jesus—you have to understand their context.

To give a full account of Jesus' context would take a huge multivolume study of its own. But I can give enough here at least to get us started and to help us make sense of the things Jesus said and did. To begin with, Jesus was a Jewish man living in the first century of the Common Era, in the Roman territory of Galilee. What was that like?

Political Crises in Palestine and Their Consequences

The ancient history of Palestine was long and complex, and here I'll deal with only a minute aspect of it, namely, that which had a direct bearing on the context of Jesus' adult life in the 20s of the Common Era.[1] In a nutshell, the political history of the land had not been happy for some eight hundred years; these had been eight centuries of periodic wars and virtually permanent foreign domination. The northern part of the land, the kingdom of "Israel," was overthrown by the Assyrians in 721 BCE; then, about a century and a half later, in 587–86 BCE, the southern kingdom of "Judah" was conquered by the Babylonians. Jerusalem was leveled, the Temple destroyed, and the leaders of the people taken into exile. Some fifty years later, the Babylonian Empire was overrun by the Persians, who brought an end to the forced exile and allowed the Judean leaders to return home. The Temple was rebuilt, and the priest in charge of the Temple, the "high priest," was given jurisdiction as a local ruler of the people. This was a man from an ancient family that traced its line back hundreds of years to a priest named "Zadok." Ultimately, of course, the Persian king was the final authority over the land and its people.

This state of affairs continued for nearly two centuries, until the conquests of Alexander the Great, ruler of Macedonia. Alexander overthrew the Persian Empire, conquering most of the lands around the eastern Mediterranean as far as modern-day India. He brought Greek culture with him into the various regions he conquered, building Greek cities and schools and gymnasia (centers of Greek culture), encouraging the acceptance of Greek culture and religion, and promoting the use of the Greek language. Alexander died a young man in 323 BCE. The generals of his army divided up his realm, and Palestine fell under the rule of Ptolemy, the general in charge of Egypt. During all of this time, the Jewish high priest remained the local ruler of the land of Judea. And that did not change when the ruler of Syria wrested control of Palestine from the Ptolemeans in 198 BCE.

It is hard to know how widespread or intense the antagonism toward foreign rule was throughout most of this period, given our sparse sources. No doubt many Jews resented the idea that their own rulers were answerable to a foreign power. They were, after all, the chosen people of the one true God of Israel, the God who had agreed to protect and defend them in exchange for their devotion. This was the land that he had promised them, and for many of them it must have been more than a little distressing, both politically and religiously, to know that ultimately someone else was in charge. In any event, there is no doubt that the situation became greatly exacerbated under the Syrian monarchs. Over the century and a half or so since Alexander's death, Greek culture had become more and more prominent throughout the entire Mediterranean region. One Syrian ruler in particular, Antiochus Epiphanes, decided to bring greater cultural unity to his empire by requiring his subjects to adopt aspects of Greek civilization. Some of the Jews living in Palestine welcomed these innovations. Indeed, some men were enthused enough to undergo surgery to remove the marks of their circumcision, allowing them to exercise in the Jerusalem gymnasium without being recognized as Jewish. By all accounts, the operation was not pleasant. Others, however, found this process of "Hellenization," this imposition of Greek culture, absolutely offensive to their religion. In response to their protests, Antiochus tightened the screws even further, making it illegal for Jews to circumcise their baby boys and to maintain their Jewish identity, converting the Jewish Temple into a pagan sanctuary, and requiring Jews to sacrifice to the pagan gods.

A revolt broke out, started by a family of Jewish priests known to history both as the "Maccabeans," based on the name given to one of its powerful leaders, Judas "Maccabeus" ("the Hammerer"), and also as the "Hasmoneans," based on the name of a distant ancestor. The Maccabean revolt began as a small guerrilla skirmish and ended with much of the country in armed rebellion against its Syrian overlords. It started in 167 BCE; in less than twenty-five years, the Maccabeans had successfully driven the Syrian army out of the land and assumed full and total control of its governance, creating the first sovereign Jewish state for over four centuries. They rededicated the Temple (one of their first acts, in 164 BCE, commemorated still by Hanukkah) and appointed a high priest as supreme ruler of the land. To the dismay of many Jews in Palestine, however, the high priest was not from the traditional and ancient line of Zadok, but from the common stock of priests of the Hasmonean family itself.

The Hasmoneans ruled the land as an autonomous state for some eighty years, until 63 BCE, when the Roman general Pompey came in conquest. The Romans allowed the high priest to remain in office, using him as an administrative liaison with the local Jewish leadership. But there was no doubt who controlled the land. Eventually, in 40 BCE, Rome appointed a king to rule the Jews of Palestine; this was Herod the Great, renowned both for his ruthless exercise of power and for his magnificent building projects, which served not only to beautify the cities but also to elevate the status of Judea and to employ massive numbers of workers. Many Jews, however, castigated Herod as an opportunistic collaborator with the Romans, a traitorous half-Jew at best. The latter charge was based in part on his lineage: his parents were from the neighboring country of Idumea and had been forced to convert to Judaism before his birth.

During the days of Jesus, after Herod's death, Galilee, the northern region of the land, was ruled by Herod's son Antipas; and starting when Jesus was a boy, Judea, the southern region, was governed by Roman administrators known as prefects. Pontius Pilate was prefect during the whole of Jesus' ministry and for some years after his death. His headquarters were in Caesarea, but he came to the capital city Jerusalem, with troops, whenever the need arose.

The point of this brief sketch is not to indicate what Jewish children learned in their fifth-grade history classes; indeed, there is no way for us to know whether a boy like Jesus would ever have even heard of such important figures from the remote past as Alexander the Great or Ptolemy. But the historical events leading up to his time are significant for understanding his life because of their social and intellectual consequences, which affected the lives of all Palestinian Jews. For it was in response to the social, political, and religious crises of the Maccabean period that the Jewish "sects" of Jesus' day (e.g., the Pharisees, Sadducees, and Essenes) were formed; and it was the Roman occupation that led to numerous nonviolent and violent uprisings during Jesus' time, uprisings of Jews for whom any foreign domination of the Promised Land was both politically and religiously unacceptable. Moreover, it was the overall sense of inequity and the experience of suffering during these times that inspired the ideology of resistance known as "apocalypticism," a worldview that was shared by a number of Jews in first-century Palestine.

One Consequence: The Formation of Jewish "Sects"

It was during the rule of the Hasmoneans, and largely in reaction to it, that various Jewish sects emerged. The Jewish historian Josephus mentions four of these groups; the New Testament makes explicit reference to three. In one way or another, all of them play a significant role for our understanding of the life of the historical Jesus.

The first thing to note, though, is that most Jews did not belong to any of these groups. We know this much from Josephus, who indicates that the largest sect, the Pharisees, claimed six thousand members and that the Essenes claimed four thousand. The Sadducees probably had far fewer. These numbers should be considered in light of the overall Jewish population in the world at the time; the best estimates put the number at something like three and a half million.

What matters for our purposes here, however, is not the size of these groups—for they were influential, despite their small numbers—but the ways in which they understood what it meant to be Jewish, especially in light of the political crises that they had to face. Members of all of the sects, of course, would have subscribed to the basic principles of the ancient Jewish religion: each believed, for example, in the one true God, the Creator of all things, who was revealed in the Scriptures, who had chosen his people Israel, and who had promised to protect and defend them in exchange for their committed devotion to him through following his laws. The groups differed in significant ways, however, when it came to knowing what obedience to God's laws required and to knowing how to react both to the rule of a foreign power and to the presence of a high priest from a line other than Zadok's.

PHARISEES. The Pharisees represent probably the best known and least understood Jewish sect. Because of the way they are attacked in parts of the New Testament, especially in Matthew, Christians through the ages have considered the Pharisees' chief attribute to be hypocrisy; indeed, *Webster's Dictionary* gives "hypocrite" as a definition of "Pharisee." This would be somewhat like a dictionary from the year 3040 CE defining a Methodist as a "liar" or a Baptist as an "adulterer" or an Episcopalian as a "drunkard." To be sure, there probably are liars and adulterers and drunkards in these denominations, just as there were hypocrites among the Pharisees. But to define them as such really misses the point. Pharisees were not required to take a "hypocritic" oath upon joining.

It appears that this sect began during the Maccabean period as a group of devout Jews intent above all else on following the entire will of God. Rather than accepting the culture and religion of the Greeks, these Jews insisted on knowing and obeying the Law of their own God to the fullest extent possible. One of the difficulties with the Law of Moses, though, is that in many places it is ambiguous. For example, Jews are told in the Ten Commandments to keep the Sabbath day holy. But nowhere does the Law indicate precisely how this is to be done. Pharisees devised rules and regulations to assist them in keeping this and all the other laws of Moses. These rules eventually formed a body of tradition, which, to stay with our example, indicated what a person could and could not do on the Sabbath day in order to keep it holy, that is, set apart from all other days. Thus, for example, when it was eventually determined that a faithful Jew should not go on a long journey on the Sabbath, it had to be decided what a "long" journey was and consequently what distance a Jew could travel on this day without violating its holiness. So, too, a worker who believed that he or she should not labor on the Sabbath had to know what constituted "work" and what therefore could and could not be done.

Or a second example. The Law of Moses commands Jewish farmers to give one-tenth of their crops, that is, a tithe, to the priests and Levites (e.g., Num. 18:20–21). Priests performed sacrifices in the Temple, and Levites were their assistants; a person became a priest or Levite by birth, not by choice. Since they themselves were not allowed to farm, the tithes were their means of support for their service to God. What should a person do, though, who purchased food from a farmer, not knowing whether the food had been properly tithed? To be on the safe side, some Pharisees maintained that they should tithe the food they *purchased*, as well as the food they grew. This way they could be certain that God's Law was being followed. And if it got followed twice in this case, so much the better—especially for God's priests and Levites!

The rules and regulations that developed among the Pharisees came to take on a status of their own and were known in some circles as the "oral" Law, which was set alongside the "written" Law of Moses (and was sometimes believed to have come, like the written Law, directly from Moses). It appears that Pharisees generally believed that anyone who kept the oral law would be almost certain to keep the written law as a consequence. The intent was not to be legalistic but to be obedient to what God had commanded.

The Pharisees may have been a relatively closed society in Jesus' day, to the extent that they stayed together as a group, eating meals and having fellowship only with one another, that is, with those who were like-minded, who similarly saw the need to maintain a high level of obedience before God. Those who did not do so were thought to be unclean.

It is important to recognize that the Pharisees were not the "power players" in Palestine in Jesus' day. That is to say, they appear to have had some popular appeal but no real political clout. In some ways they are best seen as a kind of separatist group, one that wanted to maintain its own purity and did so in isolation from other Jews. Many scholars think that the term "Pharisee" itself originally came from a Persian word that means "separated ones." Eventually, however, some decades after Jesus' execution, the Pharisees did become powerful in the political sense. This was after the Jewish War, described more fully below, which culminated in the destruction of Jerusalem and the Temple in the year 70 CE. With this calamity, the other groups passed off the scene for a variety of reasons, and the Pharisees were given greater authority by the Roman overlords. The oral tradition continued to grow and eventually took on the status of divinely revealed law. This law was eventually written down around the year 200 CE and is known as the Mishnah, the heart of the Jewish sacred collection of texts, the Talmud.

Why are the Pharisees important for understanding the historical Jesus? In part because, as we will see, he set his message over against theirs: he did not think that scrupulous and detailed adherence to the laws of Torah were the most important aspect of a Jew's relationship with God, especially as these laws were interpreted by the Pharisees.

SADDUCEES. It is difficult to reconstruct exactly what the Sadducees stood for because not a single literary work survives from the pen of a Sadducee, in contrast to the Pharisees, who are represented to some extent by the later traditions of the Talmud, by Josephus, who was a Pharisee, and, interestingly enough, by the one Pharisee who left us writings before the destruction of the Temple—after he had converted to Christianity!—the apostle Paul (see Phil. 3:5). For the Sadducees, on the other hand, we are restricted to what we read in other sources, such as the works of Josephus and the New Testament.

During Jesus' own day, the Sadducees were evidently the real power players in Palestine. They appear to have been by and large members of the Jewish aristocracy in Jerusalem and to have been closely connected with the Jewish priesthood in charge of the Temple cult. Most of the Sadducees were themselves priests, though not all priests were Sadducees. As members of the aristocracy, granted some limited power by their Roman overlords, Sadducees appear to have been conciliatory toward the civil authorities, that is, cooperative with the Roman governor. The local Jewish "council" that was occasionally called together to decide local affairs, commonly called the "Sanhedrin," was evidently made up principally of Sadducees. Given their connection with the Temple, Sadducees emphasized the need for Jews to be properly involved in the cultic worship of God as prescribed in the Torah. In fact, it appears that the Torah itself—that is, the five books of Moses— was the only authoritative text that the Sadducees accepted. In any event, we know that they did not accept the oral traditions formulated by the Pharisees. Less concerned with personal purity and regulations of such daily affairs as food laws, travel on the Sabbath, and definitions of "work," the Sadducees focused their religious attention on the sacrifices in the Temple, and expended their political energy on working out their relations with the Romans so that these sacrifices could continue.

It may have been their rejection of all written authority outside of the five books of Moses that led the Sadducees to reject several doctrines that later became characteristic of other groups of Jews: they denied, for example, the existence of angels and disavowed the notion of the future resurrection of the dead, doctrines held by the Pharisees and the Essenes. Their views of the afterlife may well have conformed, essentially, with those of most non-Jews throughout the empire: either the "soul" perishes with the body, or it continues on in a kind of shadowy netherworld, regardless of the quality of its life here on earth.

Why are the Sadducees of importance for understanding the historical Jesus? In part because he roused their anger by predicting that God would soon destroy the locus of their social and religious authority, their beloved Temple. In response, some of their prominent members urged Pontius Pilate to have him executed.

ESSENES. The Essenes are the one Jewish sect not explicitly mentioned in the New Testament. Ironically, they are also the group about which we are best informed. This is because the famous Dead Sea Scrolls were evidently produced by a group of Essenes, who lived in a community east of Jerusalem in the wilderness area near the western shore of the Dead Sea, in a place that is today called Qumran. I say that they "evidently" produced the Scrolls because the term "Essene" never occurs in them. But we know from other ancient authors such as Josephus that a community of Essenes was located in this area; moreover, the social arrangements and theological views described in the Dead Sea Scrolls correspond to what we know about the Essenes from these other accounts. Most scholars are reasonably certain, therefore, that the Scrolls represent a library used by this sect, or at least by the part of it living near Qumran.

As was the case with the Gnostic documents uncovered near Nag Hammadi, Egypt, the discovery of the Dead Sea Scrolls was completely serendipitous. In 1947, a shepherd boy searching for a lost goat in the barren wilderness near the northwest shore of the Dead Sea happened to toss a stone into a cave and heard it strike something. Going in he discovered an ancient earthenware jar that contained a number of old scrolls. The books were recovered by bedouin shepherds, news of the discovery reached antiquities dealers, biblical scholars learned of the find, and a search was conducted both to find more scrolls in the surrounding caves and to retrieve those that had already been found by the bedouin.

Some of the caves in the region yielded entire scrolls; others contained thousands of tiny scraps that are virtually impossible to piece back together. The problem is that so many of the pieces are missing: imagine trying to do an immense jigsaw puzzle under these conditions—or rather dozens of immense jigsaw puzzles, not knowing what the end product of any of them is to look like, when most of the pieces are lost, and those that remain are all mixed together! All in all there are hundreds of documents that are represented, many of them only by fragments the size of postage stamps, others, a couple dozen or so, in scrolls of sufficient length to give us a full idea of their contents.

Most of the Scrolls are written in Hebrew, others in Aramaic, a few in Greek. Different kinds of literature are represented here. There are at least partial copies of every book of the Jewish Bible, with the exception of the book of Esther. Some of them are fairly complete. These are extremely valuable because of their age; they are nearly a thousand years older than the oldest copies of the Hebrew Scriptures that we previously had. We can therefore check to see whether Jewish scribes over the intervening centuries reliably copied their texts; the short answer is that, for the most part, they did. There are also commentaries on some of the biblical books, written principally to show that the predictions of the ancient prophets had come to be fulfilled in the experiences of the Essene believers and in the history of their community. In addition there are books that contain psalms and hymns composed by members of the community, prophecies that indicate the future course of events that were believed to be about to transpire in the authors' own day, and rules for the members of the community to follow in their lives together.

Sifting through all of these books, scholars have been able to reconstruct the life and beliefs of the Essenes in considerable detail. It appears that their community at Qumran was started during the early Maccabean period, perhaps around 150 BCE, by pious Jews who were convinced that the Hasmoneans had usurped their authority by appointing a non-Zadokite as high priest. Believing that the Jews of Jerusalem had gone astray, these Essenes chose to start their own community, in which they could keep the Mosaic Law rigorously and maintain their own ritual purity in the wilderness. They did so fully expecting the apocalypse of the end of time to be imminent. When it came, there would be a final battle between the forces of good and evil, the children of light and the children of darkness. The battle would climax with the triumph of God and the entry of his children into the blessed Kingdom.

Some of the Scrolls indicate that this Kingdom would be ruled by two Messiahs, one a king and the other a priest. The priestly Messiah would lead the faithful in their worship of God in a purified Temple, where sacrifices could again be made in accordance with God's will. In the meantime, the true people of God needed to be removed from the impurities of this world, including the impurities prevalent in the Jewish Temple and among the rest of the Jewish people. These Essenes therefore started their own monastic-like community, with strict rules for admission and membership. A two-year initiation was required, after which, if approved, a member was to donate all of his possessions to the community fund and share the common meal with all the other members. Rigorous guidelines dictated the life of the community: members had fixed hours for work and rest and for their meals; there were required times of fasting; and strict penalties were imposed for unseemly behavior such as interrupting one another, talking at meals, and laughing at inappropriate times.

It appears that when the Jewish War of 66–73 CE began, the Essenes at Qumran hid some of their sacred writings before joining in the struggle. It may well be that they saw this as the final battle, preliminary to the end of time when God would establish his Kingdom and send its Messiahs.

Why are the Essenes important for understanding the historical Jesus? In part because Jesus appears to have shared many of the Essenes' apocalyptic views, even though he did not belong to their sect; he too believed that the end of time was near, and that people had to prepare for the coming onslaught.

THE "FOURTH PHILOSOPHY." When Josephus writes about Judaism for a Roman audience, he describes each of the sects that we have discussed as a "philosophy," by which he means a group with a distinctive and rational outlook on the world. He never gives a name to the fourth sect that he discusses, but simply calls it the "fourth philosophy." The tenets of this "philosophy," however, are clear, and were manifested in several different groups that we know about from various ancient sources. Each of these groups in its own way supported active resistance to Israel's foreign domination.

The view that characterized these sundry groups was that Israel had a right to its own land, a right that had been granted by God himself. Anyone who usurped that right, and anyone who backed the usurper, was to be opposed, by violent means if necessary. Among those who took this line in the mid-first century were the "Sicarii," a group whose name comes from the Latin word for "dagger." These "daggermen" planned and carried out assassinations and kidnappings of high-ranking Jewish officials who were thought to be in league with the Roman authorities. Another group that subscribed to this philosophy, somewhat later in the century, were the "Zealots." These were Jews who were "zealous" for the Law and who urged armed rebellion to take back the land God had promised his people. More specifically, based on what we find in Josephus, Zealots were Galilean Jews who fled to Jerusalem during the Jewish revolt, around the year 67 CE, who overthrew the priestly aristocracy in the city in a bloody coup, and who urged the violent opposition to the Roman legions that ultimately led to the destruction of Jerusalem and the burning of the Temple in 70 CE.

Why are such groups important for understanding the historical Jesus? In part because he too thought that the Romans were to be overthrown. But it was not to be by armed resistance.

A Related Consequence:
Popular Modes of Resistance to Oppression

As we have seen, Jews in Palestine had been under direct foreign domination for most of the eight centuries prior to the birth of Jesus. In particular, the struggles of the Hasmoneans against the Hellenizing policies of their Syrian overlords led to the formation of sects that were active in Jesus' day. But there was much more to his world than this. As I have indicated, most Jews did not belong to any of these parties. All Jews, however, were directly affected by the policies of domination enforced by Rome.[2]

As a conquered people, Jews in Palestine were required to pay taxes to the empire. Since the Roman economy was agrarian, taxation involved payment of crops and of monies to fund the armies and infrastructure provided by Rome, including roads, bridges, and public buildings. In monetary terms, the oppression of Jews appears to have been no worse than that of other native populations of the Roman provinces. We have no reliable numbers from ancient sources themselves, but the best estimates among modern scholars suggest that a typical Jewish farmer was taxed on average something like 12 or 13 percent of his income to support the Roman presence in the land, on top of taxes to support the Temple and local Jewish administration, which might run an additional 20 percent or so. His total taxes, then, were perhaps a third of his overall income.

This may not appear exorbitant by the standards of today's highly industrialized nations; we must recall, however, that in ancient agrarian societies, without modern means of irrigation, labor-saving machinery, and sophisticated technology, most farmers did well to eke out an existence in the best of circumstances. When one is living close to the edge, having to provide financial support for a foreign oppressor is not a cheery prospect. Or to put it less euphemistically, paying for Rome's excesses was seen by many Jews, as well as by many others in the empire, to be both unmanageable and perverse.

At the same time, it must be conceded that the treatment of the Jews was better in some respects than that of other inhabitants of the empire. Since the days of Julius Caesar, Jews were not required to supply Rome with soldiers from their ranks. This was an exemption that was in Rome's best interest as well, since devout Jews refused to soldier every seventh day. Nor did they have to provide direct support for Roman legions stationed nearby or marching through to the frontiers. In another respect, though, the Jewish situation could be seen as far worse than average, in that many Jews considered it blasphemous to pay taxes to support the Roman administration of the land that God had given them. How, then, did Jews react to their domination by Rome?

The short answer is that different Jews reacted in different ways. For many Jews, especially members of the aristocratic upper class, the Roman occupation was no doubt tolerable and had its advantages, for example, protection from hostile nations to the east; but for others, it was beyond toleration, a political and religious nightmare. Resistance to the Roman occupation appears to have been widespread, but rarely was it active or violent. Throughout the first century, Jews of Palestine locked horns with their Roman overlords on a number of occasions. It will be useful for our understanding of the historical Jesus to examine the nature of these conflicts.

SILENT PROTESTS. In chapter 2, I discussed the annual Passover celebration in Jerusalem. The population of Jerusalem would swell many times over during the weeklong festival, and there is little doubt that those who came to the celebration did not do so for purely antiquarian reasons. That is to say, Jews celebrating the Passover were not simply remembering the past, when God acted on their behalf to save them from their subjugation to the Egyptians; they were also looking to the future, when God would save them yet again, this time from their present overlords, the Romans.

Roman officials appear to have understood full well the potentially subversive nature of the celebration. They typically brought armed troops in just for the occasion, stationing them in the Temple, the locus of all activity. No need to allow a religious festival to turn into a fanatical uprising. Most Jews, for their part, did not much appreciate the Roman presence on such sacred occasions.

At no time did the tension become more evident than during a Passover celebration in the 50s of the Common Era, when a Roman governor named Cumanus was procurator of Judea. During the feast, one of the soldiers stationed on the wall of the Temple decided to show his disdain for the Jews and their religion. In the words of Josephus, he "stooped in an indecent attitude, so as to turn his backside to the Jews, and made a noise in keeping with his posture" (*Jewish War* 2.224–27). The worshipers present were not amused. Some picked up stones and began to pelt the soldiers; a report was sped off to Cumanus, nearby. He sent in reinforcements and a riot broke out. According to Josephus, who probably exaggerated the numbers, some twenty thousand Jews were killed in the mayhem that ensued.

Thus, the Passover feast represented an implicit protest against the Roman presence in the Promised Land; but on occasion, things could get out of hand, leading to violent resistance and death. As a rule, the Romans worked hard at keeping the situation under control, resolving problems before they led to massive uprisings or public riots. You may recall that Jesus was arrested and removed from the public eye during Passover.

NONVIOLENT UPRISINGS. Roman administrators would occasionally do or threaten to do something that offended Jews in Palestine, who would in turn rise up in protest. It appears that for most of the first century, these protests were nonviolent. In the year 26 CE, for example, when Pilate assumed the prefectorship of Judea, he had Roman standards brought into Jerusalem at night and set up around the city. These standards bore the image of Caesar. Jews in the city erupted in protest and demanded their removal. Pilate refused. According to Josephus, hundreds of the leading citizens staged a kind of "sit-in" at his residence in Caesarea (*Jewish War* 2.169–74; *Antiquities* 18.55–59). After five days, Pilate had the protesters surrounded by soldiers three deep and threatened to have them all put to the sword. The Jews responded by flinging themselves to the ground and stretching out their necks, claiming to prefer death to such a flagrant transgression of their Law. Pilate relented, and had the standards removed.

Something similar happened fourteen years or so later, when the megalomaniac emperor Caligula required the inhabitants of the empire to worship him as a god (the first Roman emperor to have done so). Jews from around the world erupted in protest; some from outside of Palestine came in delegations to Rome to explain why the act would be offensive and blasphemous for them. Caligula responded with intransigence, ordering that a statue of himself, with the body of Zeus (!), be set up in the Jerusalem Temple. According to Josephus, tens of thousands of Jews in Palestine appeared in protest before the Roman legate of Syria, Petronius, who had arrived with two full legions to enforce the policy (*Antiquities* 18.261–72, 305–09). They vowed not to plant their crops if he carried out his orders and offered themselves as martyrs rather than live to see the desecration of their Temple. Petronius was himself powerless to revoke the emperor's order, although he was impressed both by the strength of the opposition and by the danger to the crops, knowing that Rome could collect no tribute if the land lay fallow. Fortunately for him, he was saved from the consequences of failing to follow the emperor's order. For reasons unrelated to the protest, Caligula was assassinated.

PROPHETIC PROCLAMATIONS. One particularly noteworthy form of Jewish protest against foreign domination involved the occasional appearance of self-styled prophets predicting the imminent intervention of God on behalf of his people, an intervention to be modeled on earlier acts of salvation as recorded in the Hebrew Scriptures. Some of these prophets gathered a large following among the Jewish masses. For obvious reasons, they were not well received by the Romans.

Less than fifteen years after Jesus' execution, a prophet named Theudas led a large crowd of Jews to the Jordan River, where he publicly proclaimed that he would make the waters part, allowing his people to cross on dry land (see Josephus, *Jewish War* 20.97–99). Word of his activities reached the Roman authorities, who evidently knew enough Jewish tradition to recognize the allusion to the Exodus event under Moses, when the children of Israel were delivered from their slavery in Egypt and the Egyptian army was routed during the crossing of the Red Sea. Rather than risk an uprising, the governor sent out the troops. They slaughtered Theudas's followers and brought his head back to Jerusalem for display.

About a decade later another prophet arose, who was called simply the "Egyptian" by Josephus and the New Testament book of Acts, the two sources that refer to him (*Jewish War* 2.261–63; Acts 21:38). This prophet acquired a large following among the masses—according to Josephus, thirty thousand people—which he led to the Mount of Olives. There he proclaimed the imminent destruction of the walls of Jerusalem, another transparent reference, this time to the conquest of Jericho, when the children of Israel came into the Promised Land and "the walls came tumbling down." Again, the Roman troops were sent forth to hunt down and slaughter the group.

Other prophets arose and experienced similar fates. Roman administrators of Judea appear to have had no qualms about destroying those whose proclamation of God's intervention on behalf of his people could win them a following and, potentially, lead to riots. Especially in Jerusalem.

VIOLENT INSURRECTIONS. There were also violent insurrections in Palestine during the first century, incidents in which Jews with forethought and intent engaged in armed revolt against the Romans. It should not be thought, however, that these were everyday occurrences. On the contrary, incidents of this sort appear to have been isolated.

One of them occurred around 6 CE during Jesus' childhood, when Archelaus, son of Herod the Great, was deposed as ruler of Judea and replaced by a Roman prefect. A local census was imposed for tax purposes and a group of Jews led by a freedom fighter named Judas the son of Hezekiah resisted with the sword. The revolt was crushed, effectively and brutally (*Jewish War* 2.117–18; *Antiquities* 18.1–10).

The second, and more disastrous, uprising came sixty years later, when such Roman atrocities as the governor's plundering of the Temple treasury led to a widespread revolt. The Romans sent in the legions from the north, and within a year subjugated Galilee (this was when Josephus had been the commander of the Jewish troops there, prior to surrendering). A group of Galilean Jews who fled from the Roman army arrived in Jerusalem and eventually provoked a bloody civil war against the priestly aristocracy who had been in charge of the Temple and the rest of the city. Once they acquired control, these "Zealots" pressed the fight against the Romans to the end. This led to a horrifying three-year siege of Jerusalem, in which, among other things, reports of starvation and cannibalism were rampant. The war ended in a bloodbath in which tens of thousands of Jews were slaughtered or enslaved, rebel leaders crucified, much of the city leveled, and the Temple burned to the ground.

CONCLUSION. In sum, Palestine was under Roman domination in the first century and Jews in the land reacted to the situation in a variety of ways. Some, especially members of the upper classes, cooperated with and even supported the Romans; others protested in silence, anticipating a deliverance to be wrought by God; others engaged, when necessary, in acts of nonviolent resistance; others became caught up in spontaneous rioting, provoked by their insensitive treatment at the hands of the Roman rulers and soldiers; others publicly proclaimed the imminent end of their suffering through the supernatural intervention of God; yet others sought to take matters into their own hands, taking up the sword to engage in violent resistance. The nonviolent protesters had some success in getting the Romans to back down on particular issues. The violent protesters—whether rioting masses, prophetic figures, or guerrilla warriors—had none whatsoever. In the cases we know of, the Romans effectively and ruthlessly destroyed those who preached or practiced violence against them.

A Third Consequence: An Ideology of Resistance

We must consider one final aspect of Jesus' historical context before seeing where he himself stood within it. This involves one of the "worldviews" evident in a number of Jewish writings from around his time. Modern scholars have called this worldview "apocalypticism," based on the Greek term *apocalypsis*, which means an "unveiling" or a "revealing." Jews who subscribed to this worldview maintained that God had revealed to them the future course of events, in which he was soon to overthrow the forces of evil and establish his Kingdom on earth.

We know about Jewish apocalyptic thought from a number of ancient sources. It is first attested in some of the latest writings of the Hebrew Bible, especially the book of Daniel, which scholars date to the time of the Maccabean revolt. It is also prominent in the Dead Sea Scrolls, the writings of the Essene community at Qumran from around the time of Jesus. In addition, it is found in a range of other Jewish writings that did not make it into the Bible, books called "apocalypses" because their authors claim that the actual course of future events had been "revealed" to them.

Before describing what apocalypticists believed about this world and their place in it, I should say something about the origin of their worldview itself. Most ancient Jews, as I have intimated, believed that God had made a covenant with his people to be their divine protector in exchange for their devotion to him through keeping his Law. This point of view naturally came to be challenged by the political history of Palestine. For if God had promised to protect and defend Israel against its enemies, why was it constantly being dominated by foreigners? Why was it conquered, in succession, by the Assyrians, the Babylonians, the Persians, the Greeks, the Syrians, and the Romans? How could Jews claim that God was on their side, to protect and defend them, if they were constantly being overthrown?

One of the popular answers was given by ancient Jewish prophets, including those whose writings were later canonized in the Hebrew Bible, prophets like Isaiah, Jeremiah, Amos, and Hosea. According to these authors, Israel continued to suffer military and political setbacks because it had disobeyed God. He was still their God and he remained the all-powerful ruler of the world, able to dictate the course of human events. But the people of Israel had sinned against him, and their military defeats and economic disasters represented God's punishment for their sins. According to the prophets, if the people would only return to the ways of God, and again become devoted to keeping his Law, he would relent and establish them once more as a sovereign power in their own land.

This basic point of view has always been popular, not only among Jews but also among Christians: people suffer because they have sinned, and this is their punishment. Some Jewish thinkers eventually became dissatisfied with this answer, however, because it could not adequately explain historical realities. For in fact it was not only the sinners who suffered, but people who were righteous as well. And matters never improved even when people did repent and return to God and commit themselves to keeping his Law. Why would Israel continue to suffer after it returned to God, while other nations that made no effort to please him prospered?

Around the time of the Maccabean revolt, when the oppressive policies of Antiochus Epiphanes became too much for many Jews in Palestine to bear, when they were forbidden on pain of death from keeping the Law of Moses, some of them came up with another solution. In their view, the suffering of God's people could not be explained as a penalty for their sin. God surely would not punish his people for doing what was right, for keeping his laws, for example. Why, then, did the people suffer? There must have been some other supernatural agency, some other superhuman power that was responsible. God was not making his people suffer; his enemy, Satan, was.

According to this new way of thinking, God was still in control of this world in some ultimate sense. But for unknown and mysterious reasons he had temporarily relinquished his control to the forces of evil that opposed him. This state of affairs, however, was not to last forever. Quite soon, God would reassert himself and bring this world back to himself, destroying the forces of evil and establishing his people as rulers over the earth. When this new Kingdom came, God would fulfill his promises to his people.

This point of view, as I have said, is commonly called apocalypticism. It was an ideology that tried to make sense of the oppression of the people of God. As you have probably inferred, and as I will lay out more fully in chapter 8, I think it was a view embraced by Jesus.

COSMIC DUALISM. Jewish apocalypticists were dualists. That is to say, they maintained that there were two fundamental components to all of reality: the forces of good and the forces of evil. The forces of good were headed by God himself, the forces of evil by his superhuman enemy, sometimes called Satan, or Beelzebub, or the Devil. On the side of God were the good angels; on the side of the Devil were the demons. On the side of God were righteousness and life; on the side of the Devil were sin and death. These were actual forces, cosmic powers to which human beings could be subject and with which they had to be aligned. No one was in neutral territory. People stood either with God or with Satan, they were in the light or in darkness, they were in the truth or in error.

This apocalyptic dualism had clear historical implications. All of history could be divided into two ages, the present age and the age to come. The present age was the age of sin and evil, when the powers of darkness were in the ascendency, when those who sided with God were made to suffer by those in control of this world, when sin, disease, famine, violence, and death were running rampant. For some unknown reason, God had relinquished control of this age to the powers of evil. And things were getting worse.

At the end of this age, however, God would reassert himself, intervening in history and destroying the forces of evil. There would come a cataclysmic break in which all that was opposed to God would be annihilated, and God would bring in a new age. In this new age, there would be no more suffering or pain; there would be no more hatred, despair, war, disease, or death. God would be the ruler of all, in a kingdom that would never end.

HISTORICAL PESSIMISM. Even though, in the long run, everything would work out for those who sided with God, in the short term things did not look good. Jewish apocalypticists maintained that those who sided with God were going to suffer in this age, and there was nothing they could do to stop it. The forces of evil would grow in power as they attempted to wrest sovereignty over this world away from God. There was no chance of improving the human condition through mass education or advanced technologies. The righteous could not make their lives better, because the forces of evil were in control, and those who sided with God were opposed by those who were much stronger than they. Things would get worse and worse until the very end, when quite literally, all hell would break loose.

ULTIMATE VINDICATION.   But at the end, when the suffering of God's people was at its height, God would finally intervene on their behalf and vindicate his name. For in this perspective God was not only the Creator of this world, he was also its Redeemer. And his act of vindication would be universal: it would affect the entire world, not simply the Jewish nation. Jewish apocalypticists maintained that the entire creation had become corrupt because of the presence of sin and the power of Satan. This universal corruption required a universal redemption; God would destroy all that is evil and create a new heaven and a new earth, one in which the forces of evil would have no place whatsoever.

Different apocalypticists had different views concerning how God would bring about this new creation, even though they all claimed to have received the details by a revelation from God. In some apocalyptic scenarios, God was to send a human Messiah to lead the troops of the children of light into battle against the forces of evil. In others, God was to send a kind of cosmic judge of the earth, sometimes also called the Messiah or the "Son of Man" to bring about a cataclysmic overthrow of the demonic powers that oppressed the children of light.

This final vindication would involve a day of judgment for all people. Those who had aligned themselves with the powers of evil would face the Almighty Judge and render an account of what they had done; those who had remained faithful to God would be rewarded and brought into his eternal Kingdom. Moreover, this judgment applied not only to people who happened to be living at the time of the end. No one should think, that is, that he or she could side with the powers of evil, oppress the people of God, die prosperous and contented, and so get away with it. God would allow no one to escape. He was going to raise all people bodily from the dead, and they would have to face judgment, eternal bliss for those who had taken his side, eternal torment for everyone else. And there was not a sweet thing that anyone could do to stop him.

IMMINENCE. According to Jewish apocalypticists, this vindication by God was going to happen very soon. Standing in the tradition of the prophets of the Hebrew Bible, apocalypticists maintained that God had revealed to them the course of history, and that the end was almost here. Those who were evil had to repent, before it was too late. Those who were good, who were suffering as a result, were to hold on. For it would not be long before God would intervene, sending a savior—possibly on the clouds of heaven in judgment on the earth—bringing with him the good Kingdom for those who remained faithful to his Law. Indeed, the end was right around the corner. In the words of one first-century Jewish apocalypticist: "Truly I tell you, there are some standing here who will not taste death until they see that that Kingdom of God has come with power." These in fact are the words of Jesus (Mark 9:1). Or as he says elsewhere, "Truly I tell you, this generation will not pass away before all these things have taken place" (Mark 13:30).

On to Jesus

Some of the earliest traditions about Jesus portray him as a Jewish apocalypticist who responded to the political and social crises of his day, including the domination of his nation by a foreign power, by proclaiming that his generation was living at the end of the age, that God would soon intervene on behalf of his people, sending a cosmic judge from heaven, the Son of Man who would destroy the forces of evil and set up God's Kingdom. In preparation for his coming, the people of Israel needed to turn to God, trusting him as a kindly parent and loving one another as his special children. Those who refused to accept this message would be liable to the judgment of God, soon to arrive with the coming of the Son of Man.

Is this ancient portrayal of Jesus, which is embodied in a number of our oldest traditions, historically accurate? Was Jesus a Jewish apocalypticist?

eight

jesus the apocalyptic prophet

FEW AUTHORS IN MODERN TIMES CAN BE SAID TO HAVE REDIRECTED THE COURSE OF AN ENTIRE FIELD OF STUDY. IN 1906, ALBERT SCHWEITZER DID, WITH HIS BRILLIANT MONOGRAPH, *The Quest of the Historical Jesus* (original German title: *Von Reimarus zu Wrede*). Although not the first scholar to take the view of Jesus that was to become prevalent in the academy, Schweitzer was certainly the most forceful. Like a handful of historians before him and a myriad since, Schweitzer was convinced that Jesus was an apocalypticist.

Schweitzer is best known, of course, for his humanitarian endeavors. After giving up an extraordinarily promising academic career as a philosopher-theologian in Strasbourg to establish a medical mission in French Equatorial Africa, he spent his life curing the sick in his jungle clinic, far removed from the ivy towers of the European intellectual scene. But a major portion of his writings, some done even while keeping his clinic, were devoted to the New Testament. And none of his books had a more far-reaching effect than *The Quest*. It was published when Schweitzer was only thirty-one years old, written while he was working toward his medical degree. He was also producing his French biography of J. S. Bach at the time, lecturing at the university in Strasbourg, serving as director of the theological seminary there, and performing regularly as a concert organist in Paris. Schweitzer was no couch potato.[1]

The bulk of his book recounts the attempts since the Enlightenment to produce a life of Jesus. With scathing wit, penetrating analysis, and inimitable turns of phrase, Schweitzer shows that every generation of scholars that attempted to write a life of Jesus in fact portrayed Jesus in its own image. So, too, the individual scholar: "Thus each successive epoch of theology found its own thoughts in Jesus; that was, indeed, the only way in which it could make Him live. But it was not only each epoch that found its reflection in Jesus; each individual created Him in accordance with his own character. There is no historical task which so reveals a man's true self as the writing of a Life of Jesus" (*Quest of the Historical Jesus*, 4).

Schweitzer demonstrates this thesis through an exhaustive analysis of the entire history of scholarship on Jesus—from its beginnings in 1776 with a posthumously published account of a German scholar named H. Reimarus, who argued that Jesus was a political revolutionary whose violent activities were covered up by the Gospel writers, to the rationalist views of Heinrich Paulus and the myth-oriented response of D. F. Strauss, which we discussed in chapter 5, on down to his own day. Throughout his account, Schweitzer sympathizes with scholars who sought to free Jesus from the dogma of the church (as if the historical Jesus himself would have recited the Nicene Creed). At the same time he scorns every attempt to make Jesus into a modern man, who promoted, in substance, the religious, political, cultural, or social agenda of modern European intellectuals. For Schweitzer, Jesus was a man of the past. To understand what he was really like, we must situate him in his own context, not pretend that he fits perfectly well into our own.

> The historical Jesus will be to our time a stranger and an enigma. The study of the Life of Jesus has had a curious history. It set out in quest of the historical Jesus, believing that when it had found Him it could bring Him straight into our time as a Teacher and Savior. It loosed the bands by which He had been riveted for centuries to the stony rocks of ecclesiastical doctrine, and rejoiced to see life and movement coming into the figure once more, and the historical Jesus advancing, as it seemed to meet it. But He does not stay; He passes by our time and returns to His own.... He returned to his own time, not owing to the application of any historical ingenuity, but by the same inevitable necessity by which the liberated pendulum returns to its original position (*Quest of the Historical Jesus*, 399).

More people should read this book. And more people who read this book should pay attention to it. Schweitzer himself might be a bit bemused—if not a shade befuddled—by New Testament scholars who cite his warnings against portraying a Jesus who fits comfortably into our own time, before themselves going on to do so yet again. Schweitzer did not think that the historical Jesus shared the problems or perspectives of the twentieth century. Instead, Jesus was a first-century apocalypticist, who never expected that there would *be* a twentieth century. He thought that the end of the world was coming within his own lifetime. In fact, he expected it to come before the year was out. When it didn't come, Schweitzer argued, Jesus decided that he himself needed to suffer in order for God to bring the heavenly Kingdom here to earth. And so he went to his cross fully expecting God to intervene in history in a climactic act of judgment. When at his last meal he told his disciples that he would not drink wine again until he drank it anew with them in the Kingdom, he was not thinking that this would be two thousand years hence, but in the next day or two. It turns out that Jesus was wrong. He died on the cross mistaken about his own identity and the plan of God.

No one any longer agrees with Schweitzer's particular reconstruction of Jesus' message and mission (at least no one I've ever met). But his basic emphases—that Jesus is to be situated in the context of first-century Palestinian Judaism and that he was himself an apocalypticist—have carried the day for much of the twentieth century, at least among critical scholars devoted to examining the evidence. In recent years, however, the apocalyptic view of Jesus has come under increasing attack in academic circles. For anyone conversant with the ebb and flow of historical study, this should come as no surprise.[2]

For one thing, very few people who devote their lives to studying the historical Jesus actually *want* to find a Jesus who is completely removed from our own time. What people want—especially when dealing with such potentially dry matters as history and such potentially inflammatory matters as religion—is *relevance*. If Jesus was completely a man of his own time, with a worldview and a message totally out of sync with our own materialist, postcolonialist, secular-humanist, or whatever-ist society, then he may be an interesting historical figure, but he is scarcely relevant (or so it's commonly thought) to the issues and concerns people need to confront today. And so it's no wonder that some scholars—who are human after all—want to make Jesus into something else—a proto-feminist, for example, or a Neo-Marxist, or a countercultural Cynic.

But, as I've insisted, historians who try to reconstruct the past are obliged to follow their own self-imposed rules. And these rules include things like looking at what they call evidence. And the evidence is rooted in the ancient sources. And there are certain ways these sources are to be used. So whatever the real reasons scholars may have for debunking the idea that Jesus was an apocalypticist, one can always look at the sources and see whether what the scholars say is probably right.

In what follows I am not by any stretch of the imagination binding myself to Schweitzer's particular reconstruction of what Jesus was up to. I think Schweitzer was dead wrong on a number of critical points, which I won't need to go into, since this is a book about Jesus, not Schweitzer. But I do think that he was essentially right that Jesus was an apocalypticist. And this, I think, can be shown by considering the ancient sources in view of the methodological principles and criteria sketched out in chapter 6 above. I'll begin by considering our general rules of thumb, which so far as I know, are agreed upon by all historians. From there I'll consider the specific criteria that can be used with these materials. I'll end with an argument that in my mind clinches the view that Jesus was almost certainly an apocalypticist. In the chapters that follow, then, we'll have a more detailed look at Jesus' words, deeds, and death in light of this basic apocalyptic framework.

Considering the Rules of Thumb

Scholars of antiquity agree that, as a rule, we should give preference to sources that are closest to the time of the events they narrate and that are insofar as possible not tendentious. What do we have in the case of Jesus? There is in fact a very clear and consistent trend when it comes to the apocalyptic materials. The earliest sources at our disposal—Q, Mark, M, and L, for example—all portray Jesus apocalyptically. Our later sources—for example, John and Thomas—do *not*. Is this an accident?

I'll not provide all of the relevant data in this chapter, since we will be considering more of it at length in chapters 9–11. But I do want to say enough to make my point. Throughout the earliest accounts of Jesus' words are found predictions of a Kingdom of God that is soon to appear, in which God will rule. This will be an actual kingdom here on earth. When it comes, the forces of evil will be overthrown, along with everyone who has sided with them, and only those who repent and follow Jesus' teachings will be allowed to enter. Judgment on all others will be brought by the Son of Man, a cosmic figure who may arrive from heaven at any time. Being a member of Israel will not be enough to escape the coming judgment. People need to heed Jesus' words, return to God, and follow his commandments before it's too late.

Jesus is said to have proclaimed this message in Q, Mark, M, and L. Consider the following examples:

1 Mark

> "Whoever is ashamed of me and of my words in this adulterous and sinful generation, of that one will the Son of Man be ashamed when he comes in the glory of his Father with the holy angels.... Truly I tell you, there are some standing here who will not taste death until they see that the Kingdom of God has come in power" (Mark 8:38–9:1).

> "And in those days, after that affliction, the sun will grow dark and the moon will not give its light, and the stars will be falling from heaven, and the powers in the sky will be shaken; and then they will see the Son of Man coming on the clouds with great power and glory. And then he will send forth his angels and he will gather his elect from the four winds, from the end of earth to the end of heaven.... Truly I tell you, this generation will not pass away before all these things take place" (13:24–27, 30).

2 Q

> "For just as the flashing lightning lights up the earth from one part of the sky to the other, so will the Son of Man be in his day.... And just as it was in the days of Noah, so will it be in the days of the Son of Man. They were eating, drinking, marrying, and giving away in marriage, until the day that Noah went into the ark and the flood came and destroyed them all. So too will it be on the day when the Son of Man is revealed" (Luke 17:24; 26–27, 30; cf. Matt. 24:27, 37–39).

> "And you, be prepared, because you do not know the hour when the Son of Man is coming" (Luke 12:39; Matt. 24:44).

3 M

> "Just as the weeds are gathered and burned with fire, so will it be at the culmination of the age. The Son of Man will send forth his angels, and they will gather from his Kingdom every cause of sin and all who do evil, and they will cast them into the furnace of fire. In that place there will be weeping and gnashing of teeth. Then the righteous will shine forth as the sun, in the Kingdom of their Father" (Matt. 13:40–43).

4 L

"But take care for yourselves so that your hearts are not overcome with wild living and drunkenness and the cares of this
life, and that day come upon you unexpectedly, like a sprung
trap. For it will come to all those sitting on the face of the
earth. Be alert at all times, praying to have strength to flee from
all these things that are about to take place and to stand in the
presence of the Son of Man" (Luke 21:34–36).

At this stage my point is quite simple. The earliest sources record
Jesus as propounding an apocalyptic message. But, interestingly
enough, some of the most clearly apocalyptic traditions come to be
"toned down" as we move further away from Jesus' life in the 20s to
Gospel materials produced near the end of the first century. Let me give
one example. I've already pointed out that Mark was our earliest
Gospel and was used as a source for the Gospel of Luke (along with Q
and L). It's a relatively simple business, then, to see how the earlier traditions of Mark fared later in the hands of Luke. Interestingly, some of
the earlier apocalyptic emphases begin to be muted.

In Mark 9:1, for example, Jesus says, "Truly I tell you, there are some
who are standing here who will not taste death until they see that the
Kingdom of God has come in power." Luke takes over this verse—but it
is worth noting what he does with it. He leaves out the last few words,
so that now Jesus simply says: "Truly I tell you, there are some who are
standing here who will not taste death until they see the Kingdom of
God" (Luke 9:27). The difference might seem slight, but in fact it's
huge: for now Jesus does not predict the imminent arrival of the Kingdom *in power*, but simply says that the disciples (in some sense) will see
the Kingdom. And strikingly, in Luke (but not in our earlier source,
Mark), the disciples *do* see the Kingdom—but not its coming in power.
For according to Luke, the Kingdom has already "come to you" in Jesus
own ministry (Luke 11:20, not in Mark), and it is said to "be among
you" in the person of Jesus himself (Luke 17:21, also not in Mark).

Let me stress that Luke continues to think that the end of the age is
going to come in his own lifetime. But he does *not* seem to think that it
was supposed to come in the lifetime of Jesus' companions. Why not?
Evidently because he was writing after they had died, and he knew that
in fact the end had not come. To deal with the "delay of the end," he
made the appropriate changes in Jesus' predictions.

This is evident as well near the end of the Gospel. At Jesus' trial
before the Sanhedrin in Mark's Gospel, Jesus boldly states to the high
priest, "You will see the Son of Man seated at the right hand of power

and coming with the clouds of heaven" (Mark 14:62). That is, the end would come and the high priest would see it. Luke, writing many years later, after the high priest was long dead and buried, changes the saying: "from now on the Son of Man will be seated at the right hand of the power of God" (Luke 22:69). No longer does Jesus predict that the high priest himself will be alive when the end comes.

Here, then, is a later source that appears to have modified the earlier apocalyptic sayings of Jesus. You can see the same tendency in the Gospel of John, the last of our canonical accounts to be written. In this account, rather than speaking about the Kingdom of God that is soon to come (which is never spoken of here), Jesus talks about eternal life that is available here and now for the believer. The Kingdom is not future, it is available in the present, for all who have faith in Jesus. Those who believe experience a "heavenly birth" (John 3:3, 5); they already have eternal life, and do not have to face any prospect of judgment in the future, for good or ill (5:24). In this Gospel, Jesus does not utter his apocalyptic message at all except in a couple of older traditions, like the one found in 5:28–29. In fact, the older view—that there will be a day of judgment and a resurrection of the dead at the end of the age—is here debunked in view of the newer view, that in Jesus a person can already be raised into eternal life. For example, when Mary, the sister of the dead man Lazarus, tells Jesus that her brother will "be raised on the last day," Jesus corrects her by saying that he, Jesus himself, is "the resurrection and the life," and that anyone who believes in him "though he die, yet shall live" (John 11:23–26).

There is no longer an apocalyptic message about the coming Son of Man. The emphasis now is on faith in Jesus who gives eternal life in the present. This world is not going to enter a crisis at the end of the world before being redeemed. Believers are saved *out of* this world.

This "de-apocalypticizing" of Jesus' message continues into the second century. In the Gospel of Thomas, for example, written somewhat later than John, there is a clear attack on anyone who believes in a future Kingdom here on earth. In some sayings, for example, Jesus denies that the Kingdom involves an actual place but "is within you and outside you" (saying 3); he castigates the disciples for being concerned about the end (saying 18); and he spurns their question about when the Kingdom will come, since "the Kingdom of the Father is spread out on the earth and people do not see it" (saying 113). For these Gnostic sayings, the Kingdom of God is not a future reality that will come to earth in a cataclysmic break in history at the end of the age. It is a salvation from within, available now to all who know who they really are and whence they have come.

If we were to tally up these data to this point, we'd have a fairly compelling subtotal. Early traditions record apocalyptic teachings on the lips of Jesus. Later traditions generally mute this emphasis. And the latest of our early sources explicitly argue against it. I'd say we have a trend.

Two Prominent Counterproposals

This information is old hat to historians of the New Testament. But how then can scholars contend that Jesus was not an apocalypticist? There are several strategies that have been used, some of them marvels of ingenuity. Two of these strategies are widely enough known among the reading public that I should say something about them. Both involve ways of reconceptualizing our sources so that, strikingly, it is the *earlier* ones that are nonapocalyptic.

SEEKING THE LOST.   Since one cannot very well deny that our earliest surviving sources portray an apocalyptic Jesus (after all, one only has to read Mark and *bam!*, there he is), one interesting approach is to claim that the earliest *non*surviving sources did not portray him this way. It's a clever view.

I've pointed out that we don't have the Q source. Since we don't have it, you might expect that scholars would be fairly cautious in what they say about it. But nothing is further from the truth. Books on Q have become a veritable cottage industry in the field. One of the most popular proposals that has fueled enormous speculation about all sorts of things is that not only can Q be reconstructed, but its entire prehistory and the social histories of the Christian communities lying behind it can be reconstructed as well. Not bad for a nonexistent source!

The most important aspect of this proposal relates to the undeniable fact that if Q was the source for the materials in common between Matthew and Luke that are not found in Mark, then it was loaded with apocalyptic traditions. How to get around this problem? By arguing that Q in fact came out in multiple editions. According to this line, the original edition of Q didn't have these traditions. They were added when the document was edited by later followers of Jesus with too much end-time on the brain. Thus Q as we have it (well, even though we don't have it) may be an apocalyptic document. But in fact it provides evidence of a nonapocalyptic Jesus.

This is the kind of proposal that tends to appeal to people who are already inclined to be persuaded.[3] But it's easy to see its drawing power: in the earliest edition of this nonexistent source, Jesus is said to have delivered a lot of terrific one-liners, but uttered not a word about a coming Son of Man, sent from heaven in judgment.

Still, the proposal is enormously problematic. Let me repeat: Q is a source that *we don't have*. To reconstruct what we think was in it is hypothetical enough. But at least in doing so we have some hard evidence, since we do have traditions that are verbatim the same in Matthew and Luke (but not found in Mark), and we have to account for them in *some* way. But to go further and insist that we know what was *not* in the source, for example, a Passion narrative, what its multiple editions were like, and which of these multiple editions was the earliest, and so on, really goes far beyond what we can know—however appealing such "knowledge" might be.

In fact, the proposal looks too convenient by half, once you realize the pattern of thought behind it all. Suppose you are sure, for some reason or another, that Jesus was not an apocalypticist. You have an obvious dilemma, then, since the earliest surviving account, Mark, portrays him that way. So you look for an earlier account that does *not* survive, and find it in Q. But Q also portrays him as an apocalypticist. And so you claim that even though Q *is* apocalyptic, it wasn't *always* that way. And what evidence exists to disprove your claim? Well, strictly speaking, none: the document doesn't exist!

We'll see that there are still other problems with this kind of approach when we get to the end of this chapter. For now, though, I'd like to mention a second, somewhat related counterproposal.

GETTING A DATE. One of the most prominent and interesting scholars engaged in studying the historical Jesus is the witty and indomitable John Dominic Crossan, whose books on Jesus have sold in the hundreds of thousands.4 Crossan does not think Jesus was an apocalypticist. What does he do with the fact that our earliest sources, Q, Mark, M, and L, portray Jesus as an apocalypticist? He denies that these are our earliest sources.

Crossan engages in a detailed analysis to argue that *other* sources not found in the New Testament are earlier than the sources that are. These others include such documents as the "Egerton Gospel," a fragmentary text from the second century that contains four stories about Jesus; the "Gospel of the Hebrews," which no longer survives, but is quoted a bit by some church fathers in the late second to the early fifth centuries; and parts of the Gospel of Peter, which survives again only in fragments. Such sources, Crossan claims, provide more reliable access to Jesus than the New Testament Gospels, which everyone, including Crossan, dates to the first century.

At best, the argument strikes most other scholars as ingenious but odd; at worse it's an argument driven by the ultimate goal. For if in fact the

JESUS

Gospel of the Hebrews, to pick one example, is older than the Gospel of
Mark, even though it's never mentioned or even alluded to until 190 CE
or so—and is seen by nearly everyone else, therefore, as a second-century
production—then Mark's apocalyptic Jesus could well be a later creation
formed from the nonapocalyptic Jesus of the Gospel of the Hebrews!
This strikes most scholars as a case of special pleading. Most recognize
clear and certain reasons for dating the New Testament Gospels to the
first century. But giving yet earlier dates to noncanonical Gospels that
are, in most cases, not quoted or even mentioned by early Christian writers until many, many decades later seems overly speculative.

Before moving on to a consideration of the specific criteria that historians use with the Gospel traditions, let me stress again here, in conclusion, my simple point about our rules of thumb. The earliest sources
that we have consistently ascribe an apocalyptic message to Jesus. This
message begins to be muted by the end of the first century (e.g., in
Luke), until it virtually disappears (e.g., in John), and begins, then, to
be explicitly rejected and spurned (e.g., in Thomas). It appears that
when the end never did arrive, Christians had to take stock of the fact
that Jesus said it would and changed his message accordingly. You can
hardly blame them.

Considering the Specific Criteria

Does this judgment hold up when we scrutinize the surviving sources in
view of the various criteria we've discussed for establishing historically
reliable material? Given some of the things I've already said, I can keep
this part of the discussion reasonably short. Probably the easiest way to
proceed is by taking our criteria in reverse sequence.

Contextual Credibility

There is absolutely no trouble seeing Jesus as an apocalypticist in terms
of contextual credibility. We know that there were apocalyptic Jews—
in fact lots and lots of apocalyptic Jews—in first-century Palestine, that
is, in precisely his time and place. A number of these Jews have left us
writings. The Dead Sea Scrolls, for example, are chock-full of apocalyptic materials. Writings of this kind date from the latest book of the
Hebrew Bible—Daniel, composed probably during the Maccabean
revolt in the second century BCE—up until at least the second century
CE (e.g., 2 Baruch). Others of these apocalyptic Jews were written
about—for example, John the Baptist (in the New Testament accounts)

and various other prophets at the time who were mentioned by Josephus (see my brief references to Theudas and the Egyptian in chapter 7; we'll be meeting these fellows again later). If Jesus was an apocalypticist expecting the imminent end of his age, he didn't stand out as a sore thumb at all during his own time. Scores of other people—teachers, prophets, and just regular ole folk—thought something similar.

Dissimilarity

In some respects, there isn't a whole lot that we can say about the various traditions of Jesus as an apocalypticist from the standpoint of the trickiest of our criteria to use, the criterion of dissimilarity.[5] Most of his followers, as I've already pointed out, *were* his followers precisely because they agreed with him, and if the burden of his message was that the end of the world was coming soon through the appearance of the Son of Man, we might expect them to have said something fairly similar. But there are a couple of aspects of the apocalyptic traditions that make them look authentic, even given the difficulties of the case. That is to say, some of the ways Jesus talks about the coming end do *not* coincide with the way his followers later talked about it, suggesting that these particular sayings are not ones they would have invented.

As an example, consider one that I quoted above: Mark 8:38. "Whoever is ashamed of me and of my words in this adulterous and sinful generation, of that one will the Son of Man be ashamed when he comes in the glory of his Father with the holy angels." Now we know that the earliest Christians believed that Jesus himself was the Son of Man (cf. Rev. 1:13). For that reason, when Jesus talks about *himself* as the Son of Man in the Gospels—as he frequently does—there's no way to know, in view of this criterion, whether that's the way he actually talked or if that's how Christians—who believed he was the Son of Man—"remembered" him talking. But in sayings like Mark 8:38, there is no indication that he is talking about himself. In fact, if you didn't know in advance the Christian idea that Jesus was the Son of Man, there'd be no way you would infer it from this saying. On the contrary, just taking the saying on its own terms, Jesus appears to be referring to someone else. To paraphrase the saying: "whoever doesn't pay attention to what I'm saying will be in big trouble when the Son of Man arrives." That is, at the end of this age, the cosmic judge from heaven will punish those who reject Jesus' message.

My point is that since Christians thought *Jesus* was the Son of Man, it seems unlikely that they would make up a saying in such a way as to leave it in question whether he was referring to himself. That means Jesus probably did say the words now found in Mark 8:38.

Or take a second example. At the end of Matthew 25 is Jesus' famous description of the final judgment, in which the "Son of Man comes in his glory, and all the angels with him, and he sits on his glorious throne" (Matt. 25:31). There appear before the Son of Man all the nations, and he separates them into two groups, as a shepherd would separate the sheep from the goats. He welcomes those on his right hand, the "sheep," and invites them to "inherit the Kingdom prepared for you from the foundation of the earth." Why are they entitled to the Kingdom? Because, says the king, "I was hungry and you gave me food, I was thirsty and you gave me drink, I was a stranger and you welcomed me, I was naked and you clothed me, I was sick and you visited me, I was in prison and you came to me." These righteous ones, though, don't understand, since they had never laid eyes on this glorious divine figure, let alone done anything for him. And so they ask, "When did we see you hungry and feed you, or thirsty and give you drink? And when did we see you a stranger and welcome you...?" And the king replies to them: "as you did it to one of the least of these, my brothers, you did it to me" (25:34–40).

He then turns to the group on his left, the "goats," and curses them, telling them to "depart into the eternal fire prepared for the devil and his angels." Why? Because "I was hungry and you gave me no food, I was thirsty and you gave me no drink, I was a stranger and you did not welcome me, naked and you did not clothe me, sick and in prison and you did not visit me." These, though, are equally surprised, for they too have never seen this king of kings. But he then informs them, "Truly I say to you, insofar as you did not do it to the least of these, my brothers, neither did you do it to me." And he then sends them "away into eternal punishment," whereas the righteous enter "into eternal life" (Matt. 25:41–46).

What is striking about this story, when considered in view of the criterion of dissimilarity, is that there is nothing distinctively *Christian* about it. That is to say, the future judgment is not based on belief in Jesus' death and resurrection, but on doing good things for those in need. Later Christians—including most notably Paul (see, e.g., 1 Thess. 4:14–18), but also the writers of the Gospels—maintained that it was belief in Jesus that would bring a person into the coming Kingdom. But nothing in this passage even hints at the need to believe in Jesus per se: these people didn't even *know* him. What matters is helping the poor, oppressed, and needy. It doesn't seem likely that a Christian would formulate a passage in just this way. The conclusion? It probably goes back to Jesus.[6]

There are other apocalyptic materials that pass this criterion, as we'll see in the next several chapters; for now it's enough to have shown that not only are the traditions about Jesus as an apocalypticist contextually credible, some of them also appear to pass the criterion of dissimilarity.

Independent Attestation

Luckily (for you *and* me!) I don't need to say much about the independent attestation of the apocalyptic traditions, given what I already pointed out at length earlier in this chapter. Not only are these traditions early, they permeate our independent sources. We find Jesus portrayed as an apocalypticist in Mark, Q, M, and L; and as I pointed out, fragments of the tradition are found even in John (e.g., 5:28-29) and are argued *against* in our later Gospel of Thomas (why argue against something unless someone else subscribes to it?). All of these sources were independent of one another; all of them to a greater or lesser extent— the earlier the greater, as it turns out—portray Jesus apocalyptically.

On the grounds of these criteria alone I should think that we would be justified in thinking that Jesus must have been an apocalypticist in some sense of the term. (We haven't *begun* to explore yet, of course, what he specifically said and did; but we can probably rest assured that it was something apocalyptic!) But I've actually saved what I consider to be the strongest argument for last, a final coup d'état. The argument is both simple and compelling. I wish I had thought of it myself.

In a nutshell, the argument is that we know beyond any reasonable doubt what happened at the very beginning of Jesus' public ministry and we know what happened in its aftermath. The continuity between the two is Jesus' public ministry itself. This ministry began on a decidedly apocalyptic note; its aftermath continued apocalyptically. Since Jesus is the link between the two, his message and mission, his words and deeds, must also have been apocalyptic. That is to say, the beginning and end are the keys to the middle.

The Beginning and End as Keys to the Middle

There is little doubt about how Jesus began his ministry. He began by being baptized by John. As I have already indicated in the previous chapter, the story is independently attested by multiple sources: Mark, Q, and John all begin with Jesus' associating with the Baptist. Nor is it a story the early Christians would have been inclined to invent, since it was commonly understood that the one doing the baptizing was spiritually superior to the one being baptized. That is, Jesus' baptism by John passes the criterion of dissimilarity. Moreover, in view of our discussion in the previous chapter, we can see that the event is contextually credible. John appears to have been one of the "prophets" who arose during the first century of the Common Era in Palestine. Somewhat like Theudas and the Egyptian, he predicted that God was about to destroy his enemies and reward his people, as he had done in the days of old.

John the Baptist appears to have preached a message of coming destruction and salvation. Mark portrays him as a prophet in the wilderness, proclaiming the fulfilment of the prophecy of Isaiah that God would again bring his people from the wilderness into the Promised Land (Mark 1:2–8). When this happened the first time, according to the Hebrew Scriptures, it meant destruction for the nations already inhabiting the land. In preparation for this imminent event, John baptized those who repented of their sins, that is, those who were ready to enter into this coming Kingdom. The Q source gives further information, for here John preaches a clear message of apocalyptic judgment to the crowds that have come out to see him: "Who warned you to flee from the wrath to come? Bear fruits worthy of repentance.... Even now the ax is lying at the root of the trees; every tree therefore that does not bear good fruit is cut down and thrown into the fire" (Luke 3:7–9). Judgment is imminent: the ax is at the root of the tree. And it will not be a pretty sight. In preparation, Jews can no longer rely on having a covenantal relationship with God: "Do not begin to say to yourselves, 'We have Abraham as our ancestor'; for I tell you, God is able from these stones to raise up children to Abraham" (Luke 3:8). Instead, they must repent and turn to God anew, doing the things he requires of them.

There can be little doubt that Jesus went out into the wilderness to be baptized by this prophet. But why would he go? Since nobody compelled him, he must have gone to John, instead of to someone else, because he agreed with John's message. Jesus did not join the Pharisees, who emphasized the scrupulous observance of the Torah, or align himself with the Sadducees, who focused on the worship of God through the Temple cult, or associate with the Essenes, who formed monastic communities to maintain their own ritual purity, or subscribe to the teachings of the "fourth philosophy," which advocated a violent rejection of Roman domination. He associated with an apocalyptic prophet in the wilderness who anticipated the imminent end of the age.

That was how Jesus began. Is it possible, though, that he changed his views during the course of his ministry and began to focus on something other than what John preached? This is certainly possible, of course, but it would not explain why so many apocalyptic sayings are found on

Jesus' own lips in the earliest sources for his life, sayings that came to be muted later on. Even more seriously, it would not explain what clearly emerged in the aftermath of his ministry. I have argued that we are relatively certain about how Jesus' ministry began; we are even more certain concerning what happened in its wake. After Jesus' death, those who believed in him established communities of followers throughout the Mediterranean. We have a good idea what these Christians believed, because some of them have left us writings. What is striking is that these earliest writings are imbued with apocalyptic thinking. The earliest Christians were Jews who believed that they were living at the end of the age and that Jesus himself was to return from heaven as a cosmic judge of the earth, to punish those who opposed God and to reward the faithful (see, e.g., 1 Thess. 4:13–18; 1 Cor. 15:51–57—writings from our earliest Christian author, Paul). The church that emerged in Jesus' wake was apocalyptic.

This means that Jesus' ministry began with his association with John the Baptist, an apocalyptic prophet, and ended with the establishment of the Christian church, a community of apocalyptic Jews who believed in him. The only connection between the apocalyptic John and the apocalyptic Christian church was Jesus himself. How could both the beginning and the end be apocalyptic, if the middle was not as well? My conclusion is that Jesus himself must have been a Jewish apocalypticist.

This does not mean that Jesus was saying and doing exactly what every other Jewish apocalyptist was saying and doing; indeed, no two people are ever exactly alike, and we are still interested in learning specifically what Jesus taught and did during his life. But it helps to know his general orientation before going into the details, because if we know that his overall message was apocalyptic, it will assist us in understanding the other aspects of the tradition about him that can be established as authentic.

nine

the apocalyptic teachings of jesus

SO, JESUS WAS EVIDENTLY AN APOCALYPTICIST. WHAT, THOUGH, DID HE ACTUALLY SAY AND DO? THESE ARE THE KEY QUESTIONS, THE GOALS TOWARDS WHICH WE'VE BEEN DRIVING SINCE word one. And now that we've passed through the preliminaries we can put the pedal to the floor. In this chapter and the one that follows we'll consider teachings of Jesus that appear to go directly back to him (as opposed to those that his later followers put on his lips—for example, many of the ones found in the Gospel of Thomas). In this chapter, we'll consider teachings that are most obviously apocalyptic in nature; in chapter 10 we'll look at other teachings, for example, those involving Jesus' "ethics," that are rooted in this apocalyptic context. In subsequent chapters we'll go on to consider Jesus' deeds, controversies, and experiences in a similar light. Throughout these discussions you should recall that we are trying to reconstruct what the *historical* Jesus himself actually said, based on the various criteria that I mapped out in Chapter 6 and in light of the context of his life as discussed in Chapter 7.

A Preliminary Overview: Jesus and the Kingdom

The very first thing that Jesus is recorded to have said in our very earliest surviving source involves an apocalyptic pronouncement of the coming Kingdom of God. In Mark's Gospel, after being baptized by John and tempted by Satan in the wilderness, in neither of which is he recorded as having said anything, Jesus comes into Galilee with an urgent message:

> The time is filled up and the Kingdom of God is almost here; repent and believe in the good news! (Mark 1:15).

I take this to be an adequate summary of what Jesus himself actually preached. The saying about "time being filled up" is an apocalyptic image. Recall that for apocalypticists there were two ages of history—the present evil age that was running along its predetermined course and the glorious age to come in which God would establish his sovereignty once and for all. For Jesus, the time of this age was all but complete; the bottom of the sand clock was virtually filled. This age was near its end and the new Kingdom was almost here. People needed to prepare by turning to God and accepting this good news.

Later Christians, of course, took this very term "good news" and applied it to the accounts of Jesus' life itself—especially the accounts of his death and resurrection. The same Greek word that I've rendered "good news" is translated "gospel" elsewhere. But obviously Jesus wouldn't be urging people to believe in his own death and resurrection when he had just started his ministry—hence my translation. He is urging people to accept the message of the good news, that now, very soon, God is going to intervene in history and bring in his Kingdom. What does Jesus *mean* when he speaks of God's coming Kingdom?

This is a question that has plagued New Testament scholars since—well, since there have been New Testament scholars. I won't go into all the ins and outs of the debates here, but instead simply emphasize a couple of the significant points. For one thing, almost all scholars today would agree that when Jesus talks about the Kingdom of God, he is *not* referring to "heaven"—in the sense of the place that your soul goes, God willing, when you die. To be sure, the Kingdom of God has *some* relationship to "heaven" as the place where God is enthroned; but when Jesus talks about the Kingdom, he appears to refer principally to something here on earth—where God will at some point *begin* to rule as he already *does* rule up above. This is in full keeping with the Jewish background to Jesus' life and thought. For throughout the Hebrew Bible, there is constant talk of the God of Israel being the King of all people and establishing his rule for them.

> God is the king of all the earth; sing praises with a psalm.
> God is king over the nations; God sits on his holy throne (Ps. 47:7–8).

> The LORD is king, he is robed in majesty;
> The LORD is robed, he is girded with strength ...
> Your throne is established from of old;
> you are from everlasting (Ps. 93:1-2).

Moreover, when Jesus refers to this coming Kingdom, in which God will reign, he does not appear to be thinking in purely symbolic terms about God becoming the ruler of your heart. For he often describes the Kingdom with graphically tactile language. Jesus talks about the Kingdom of God "coming in power," about people "entering into" the Kingdom, about people "eating and drinking in the Kingdom" with the Jewish ancestors, about his disciples serving as "rulers" of the Kingdom, sitting on actual "thrones" in the royal court.

> Truly I say to you, in the renewed world, when the Son of Man is sitting on the throne of his glory, you (disciples) also will be seated on twelve thrones, judging the twelve tribes of Israel (Matt. 19:28; cf. Luke 22:30).[1]

> And there will be weeping and gnashing of teeth when you see Abraham and Isaac and Jacob and all the prophets in the kingdom, but you are cast out; and people will come from east and west and from north and south and recline at table in the kingdom of God (Q: Luke 13:23–29; cf. Matt. 8:11–12).

Such references are scattered throughout the tradition, and rather than writing them off—for example on the grounds that we ourselves don't imagine that God will actually, literally, establish a kingdom here on earth—we should take them seriously. Jesus, like other apocalypticists living before him and afterwards, evidently thought that God was going to extend his rule from the heavenly realm where he resides down here to earth. There would be a real, physical kingdom here, a paradisal world in which God himself would rule his faithful people, where there would be eating, drinking, and talking, where there would be human co-regents sitting on thrones and human denizens eating at banquets.

This future kingdom stands over against the present evil kingdoms to which God's people are now subjected, kingdoms of hatred, want, and oppression. In the future kingdom, God's people will be rewarded with a utopian existence. No wonder Jesus proclaimed the coming Kingdom as "good news" to those who would listen. But it wasn't good news for everyone—not, for example, for those who were *already* in power. For when the coming kingdom arrived those who were in power now would be overthrown. And the day of judgment was soon.

The Coming Judgment

Throughout his teachings, Jesus warns of the coming judgment and the need to prepare for it. As I've already intimated in chapter 8, this judgment was to be brought by someone Jesus called the Son of Man, a cosmic judge sent from heaven who would destroy all that is opposed to God and reward those who were faithful to him. Consider the following sayings, found in independent parts of the tradition.

> Whoever is ashamed of me and of my words...of that one will the Son of Man be ashamed when he comes in the glory of his Father with the holy angels (Mark 8:38).

> And in those days, after that affliction, the sun will grow dark and the moon will not give its light, and the stars will be falling from heaven, and the powers in the sky will be shaken; and then they will see the Son of Man coming on the clouds with great power and glory. And then he will send forth his angels and he will gather his elect from the four winds, from the end of earth to the end of heaven (Mark 13:24–27).

> For just as the flashing lightning lights up the earth from one part of the sky to the other, so will the Son of Man be in his day.... And just as it was in the days of Noah, so will it be in the days of the Son of Man. They were eating, drinking, marrying, and giving away in marriage, until the day that Noah went into the ark and the flood came and destroyed them all. So too will it be on the day when the Son of Man is revealed (Luke 17:24; 26–27, 30; cf. Matt. 24:27, 37–39).

> Whoever acknowledges me before others, the Son of Man will also acknowledge before the angels of God; but the one who denies me before others, will be denied before the angels of God (Luke 12:8–9; cf. Matt. 10:32–33).[2]

> Be alert at all times, praying to have strength to flee from all these things that are about to take place and to stand in the presence of the Son of Man (Luke 21:34–36).

These dire warnings about the coming Son of Man in judgment are scattered throughout our early sources: Mark, Q, M, and L. Sometimes they occur in graphic parables of Jesus, such as the parable of the weeds among the wheat in Matthew 13:24–30; 36–42, which concludes with the fearful prospect that

> Just as the weeds are gathered and burned with fire, so will it be at the culmination of the age. The Son of Man will send forth his angels, and they will gather from his kingdom every cause of sin and all who do evil, and they will cast them into the furnace of fire. In that place there will be weeping and gnashing of teeth. Then the righteous will shine forth as the sun, in the kingdom of their father (Matt. 13:40–43).

Or the parable of the fishnet, found in both Matthew and Thomas. Its oldest surviving form reads as follows:

> Again, the kingdom of heaven is like a net which was thrown into the sea and gathered fish of every kind. When it was full, they hauled it ashore, and sitting down chose the good fish and put them into containers, but the bad fish they threw away. That's how it will be at the completion of the age. The angels will come and separate the evil from the midst of the righteous, and cast them into the fiery furnace. There people will weep and gnash their teeth (Matt. 13:47–50).

As can be seen, Jesus calls this coming agent of judgment who is regularly accompanied by angels, the "Son of Man."

The Coming Son of Man

Among the most heated, and least enlightening, debates among New Testament scholars has been the question of the origins of the phrase "the Son of Man" in the teachings of Jesus. Everyone agrees—since it's plain for all to see—that in the Gospels Jesus uses the phrase in a variety of ways, sometimes to talk about his present ministry ("the son of man has no where to lay his head"; Luke 9:58; Matt. 8:20), sometimes to predict his future suffering ("the son of man must suffer many things and be rejected by the elders and the chief priests and the scribes and be killed, and after three days rise again"; Mark 8:31; Luke 9:22), and sometimes to refer to a cosmic judge from heaven, whom we've now met on several occasions (for example, Mark 8:38). Hence the questions: Did Jesus—that is, the historical Jesus, the actual man himself (not Jesus as portrayed in the later Gospels) use the phrase in all of these ways? Did he always use it in reference to himself? Did he ever use it in reference to himself? Was it a common phrase in first-century Aramaic? Would his hearers have understood what he meant by it? These and related questions have occupied scholars and led to mixed results. And as I've suggested, some of the debates have been less than scintillating.

For example, one of the most hotly contested questions is whether the phrase "Son of Man" was a widely-used (or *ever*-used!) title among Jesus' contemporaries to refer to a future cosmic judge of the earth. The assumption behind the question seems to be that if no one else used it this way, Jesus wouldn't have either. This kind of assumption strikes me not only as unreflective but also as demonstrably false. People make up words, or generate new uses of words, all the time. Anyone who thinks otherwise simply hasn't spent enough time with high school and college kids. And the fact is that there are lots of places in our tradition—independently attested all over the map—that Jesus himself does use the phrase in this way, as a title for a future cosmic judge from heaven. *Someone* coined the phrase; it would be pretty bizarre to think that it couldn't have been Jesus, the one to whom all of these sayings are attributed in independent sources, or someone living before him.

So point one: in multiply attested traditions Jesus did use the phrase to refer to a cosmic judge of the earth. Point two has already been made: when he does so, he seems to be referring to someone other than himself. Moreover, these are sayings that Christians themselves would not have been likely to invent, since Jesus' later followers naturally assumed that he *was* the Son of Man.[3] These particular Son of Man sayings, at least, have a good chance of going back to Jesus on the grounds of dissimilarity. The same is not true of the other kinds of Son of Man sayings, since they presuppose that Jesus, like his later followers, *did* use the term to refer to himself. That is, they can't be shown to have been said by Jesus on the grounds of dissimilarity.

Moreover, as we've seen, the apocalyptic sayings are multiply attested. Where did the idea come from, though, that a future cosmic judge of the earth would be called the Son of Man? Almost everyone agrees that the phrase, used in this apocalyptic way, ultimately comes from our oldest surviving apocalypse, the book of Daniel in the Hebrew Bible. In a fascinating passage in Daniel 7, the prophet is shown the future course of history in one of those ghoulish nightmares that you're glad was inflicted on someone else. He first sees a series of beasts arising out of the sea, one after the other. There are four beasts, each worse than the preceding. These trample the earth, wreak havoc, and devastate the people of God. But then, in contrast to these grotesquely formed beasts, Daniel sees "one like a son of man" coming from heaven on the clouds. Unlike the beastly ravagers of earth, this figure is human-like, humane. To him is given an eternal kingdom, the perpetual rule over the earth, with dominion, power, and praise forever, as the beasts are robbed of their power and done away with (Dan. 7:2–14).

In an angelic interpretation of the dream, we're told that the beasts represent kingdoms that will take over the earth and assert their oppressive control over its peoples. These evil powers will remain until the coming of the one like a son of man, who will bring destruction to the forces opposed to God but eternal dominion to God's people (Dan. 7:17–27).

When Jesus refers to the Son of Man, he appears to be alluding to this vision in Daniel 7. Like other apocalypticists from his time that we know about, Jesus maintained that there will be an actual cosmic judge sent from God to overthrow the forces of evil and bring in God's good kingdom. Consider the following Jewish apocalyptic texts of the first century:

And they [the people of God] had great joy, and they blessed and praised and exalted because the name of that Son of Man had been revealed to them. And he sat on the throne of his glory, and the whole judgment was given to the Son of Man, and he will cause the sinners to pass away and be destroyed from the face of the earth. And those who led astray the world will be bound in chains, and will be shut up in the assembly-place of their destruction, and all their works will pass away from the face of the earth. And from then on there will be nothing corruptible, for that Son of Man has appeared and has sat on the throne of his glory, and everything evil will pass away and go from before him (1 Enoch 69).

As I kept looking the wind made something like the figure of a man come up out of the heart of the sea. And I saw that this man flew with the clouds of heaven; and everywhere he turned his face to look, everything under his gaze trembled.... After this I looked and saw that an innumerable multitude of people were gathered together from the four winds of heaven to make war against the man who came up out of the sea... When he saw the onrush of the approaching multitude, he neither lifted his hand nor held a spear, or any weapon of war; but I saw only how he sent forth from his mouth something like a stream of fire, and from his lips a flaming breath...[which] fell on the onrushing multitude that was prepared to fight, and burned up all of them, so that suddenly nothing was seen of the innumerable multitude but only the dust of ashes and the smell of smoke (4 Ezra 13:1–11).

Jesus appears to have shared this basic apocalyptic vision and called the coming judge the "Son of Man." In his view, at the judgment that this one will bring, those who are at present oppressed will be vindicated, and those who are in power will be vanquished. This in fact is a general theme of Jesus' apocalyptic teaching: there is to be a major set of reversals when the kingdom comes. Those who are suffering now will be rewarded then; those who are in control now will be overthrown. And this coming reversal should affect how people live, and want to live, in the present.

The Reversal of Fortunes

Among Jesus' most widely attested sayings are those that indicate that everything will be turned on its head when the Son of Man arrives in judgment. Many of these sayings have lost their apocalyptic edge over the years, as Christians began using them almost as clichés—as even today, when someone wryly remarks that "the first shall be last and the last first" (for example, when standing in an aggravatingly long line) without reflecting on what, actually, the saying means. For Jesus, it means that those who are on the top of the socio-politico-economic heap now are actually going to be displaced at the end of this age by those who are underneath them. There will be a radical set of reversals in the coming kingdom.

Reversals in the Kingdom

The logic behind this system of reversals should be pretty clear, given what we've already seen. The present age is governed by the forces of evil. Those who prosper and succeed and rule in this age are therefore, of necessity, empowered by these evil forces (or else they wouldn't prosper, succeed, and rule!). But in the age that is coming, evil will be overthrown and God will reassert himself. Those who are in charge now will be dethroned and debunked, and those who are suffering and oppressed now—the people of God who are opposed by his enemies, the devil and his minions—will take their place. The first really will be last and the last really will be first.

Notice that on Jesus' lips, the saying occurs in the context of the coming Kingdom. This can be seen in Mark's version:

> Truly I tell you, there is no one who has left a house or brothers or sisters or mother or father or children or lands for my sake and the

sake of the good news, who will not receive them all back a hundred fold in this present time—houses, brothers, sisters, mothers, children, and lands, along with persecutions—and in the age that is coming, life that never ends. But many who are first will be last and the last will be first (Mark 10:29–31).

And in L's:

And people will come from east and west and from north and south and recline in the kingdom of God; and behold, those who are last will be first and the first will be last (Luke 13:29–30; this may be Q—cf. Matt. 20:16).

The reality of this future reversal should affect the way people seek to live in the present, as we'll see more fully in chapter 10. They should, in fact, be willing to give up their lives in the service of others, rather than seek to dominate and control others through power or money. It is in this apocalyptic sense that Jesus told his followers that "whoever wants to save his life will destroy it, and whoever will destroy his life for my sake and the sake of the good news will save it" (Mark 8:35; notice that Jesus goes on to talk, then, about the coming Son of Man in 8:38). Destroying one's life now does not mean committing suicide. It means giving up one's own desires and quests for power and prominence for the sake of others. Those who do so will enter into the Kingdom and find true life. Those who refuse to do so, who only grasp for what *they* can get out of this life, will lose their life when the Son of Man arrives in judgment.

Serving Others

That's why, repeatedly throughout our traditions, Jesus insists that his followers become the slaves of others, living lives of service, rather than asserting themselves like domineering masters who constantly seek power and control. Thus, from our earliest surviving source, Jesus is recorded as saying:

If anyone wishes to be first, he will be last of all and the servant of all (Mark 9:35).

And also:

You know that those who are thought to rule over the nations exercise full power over them and their mighty rulers utilize their great authority over them. But it will not be so among you. But whoever wishes to be great among you will be your servant, and the one who wishes to be first among you will be the slave of all (Mark 10:42–44).

Or from the L materials: "For whoever is least among you, this one in fact is great" (Luke 9:48).

What all this means for the way one lives should be obvious. Rather than seeking to be exalted one ought to debase oneself, seeking to serve others rather than dominate them. And Jesus himself regularly draws this conclusion in apocalyptic terms. Thus, from Q: "For whoever exalts himself will be humbled (= brought low), and those who are humble (= lowly) will be exalted" (Luke 18:14; Matt. 23:12); from L: "whoever exalts himself will be humbled, and the one who humbles himself will be exalted" (Luke 14:11); and from M: "Whoever humbles himself as this small child, this is the one who is great in the Kingdom of heaven" (Matt. 18:4).

What I am claiming here is that Jesus really meant these sayings— they weren't simply clichés. When the Kingdom comes, those who have debased themselves in order to serve others will be rewarded, and those who have vaunted themselves over others will be punished.

Becoming Like Children

Relatedly, the earliest traditions sometimes portray Jesus as speaking about receiving the Kingdom "as a child" (as in the passage just quoted from Matt. 18:4). People have engaged in lots of speculation concerning what he might have meant by that, but since the sayings are commonly found in the context of humility and self-abasement, perhaps that should be our clue. For ancient Jews, children had no legal standing to speak of; they had no power, no prestige, nothing that could elevate them above others. To enter into the Kingdom, one should become like that—not like a powerful ruler of an empire, but like a lowly and seemingly unimportant child. For when the Son of Man arrives, there will be a radical reversal in which the lowly will be exalted and the high and mighty brought down low.

Salvation for Sinners

Among those who were sometimes seen as particularly lowly in Jesus' world, or at least among the least likely candidates to enter into the Kingdom, were, of course, the people who did not go out of their way to maintain appearances of strict religiosity. In chapter 11, I'll look further into the companions of Jesus—the "tax collectors and sinners" who were so scorned by many of the religious elite in our early accounts of Jesus' life. At this point, though, I should say at least a brief word about who such "sinners" were, to make sense of the surprising fact (it's surprising to most people still today, who in fact refuse to believe it!) that Jesus maintained that it was *they*, rather than the devout religious folk, who would enter into the Kingdom when it arrived.

Contrary to what is often said—even by scholars—the category "sinners" does not refer simply to "prostitutes," on the one hand (even though prostitutes would no doubt have been considered sinners; but not every sinner was a prostitute), nor is it a shorthand term for non-Pharisees on the other (it is sometimes claimed that everyone who did not follow Pharisaic traditions was mocked as a sinner; in reality, that's not true). In the Hebrew Bible, sinners are people who make no attempt to follow God's law, the Law of Moses itself. They are people that most reasonably religious folk would see as beyond the pale, corrupt, evil, mean-spirited, selfish, self-centered, godless SINNERS. Jesus appears, as we'll see, to have attracted more than his share of such people to be his followers. And he insisted that they were the ones who would inherit the Kingdom.[4]

Consider the following independently attested types of traditions. (a) In Mark, when asked why he associated with such people, Jesus replied "Those who are well have no need of a physician, but those who are sick; I came to call not the righteous, but sinners" (Mark 2:17). (b) In Q and the Gospel of Thomas is the parable of the shepherd who leaves his ninety-nine sheep to seek after the one that was lost; when he finds it, he calls his friends and says, "Rejoice with me, for I have found my sheep which was lost." Jesus concludes the parable by saying, "So there will be more joy in heaven over one sinner who repents than for the ninety-nine who don't need repentance" (Luke 15:1–7; Matt. 18:12–14; cf. G.Thom. 107). (c) In L: after a parable about a woman who finds a coin that was lost, Jesus says: "So there will be joy before the angels of God over one sinner who repents" (Luke 15:8–10).

All of these sayings seem to indicate that Jesus is particularly concerned in bringing those who are lost and in need into the Kingdom. What is even more striking, though, is that there is an independently attested strain of his teaching that indicates that in contrast to such sinners, people who are otherwise righteous (that is, who do what is right before God) will *not* necessarily enter into the Kingdom. And so, in a saying found in M, Jesus tells a group of Jewish leaders who did not heed the call of John the Baptist: "Truly I say to you that tax collectors and prostitutes will go before you into the Kingdom of God; for John came to you in the path of righteousness, and you did not believe him; but the tax collectors and prostitutes believed him" (Matt. 21:31–32). So too, in a parable found only in Luke, we're told that a tax collector who recognized and regretted his own sinfulness was "right before God" (= justified), instead of a righteous Pharisee who was proud of his religious devotion (Luke 18:9–14).

It is a little difficult to know what to make of these traditions. One particularly competent recent interpreter has argued that Jesus proclaimed that such wicked people would enter into the Kingdom without repenting—and that it was precisely this teaching that caused such a scandal.5 But we've already seen in independent traditions that Jesus urged people to repent (for example, Mark 1:15; 2:17; Luke 15:7), and I'd assume that when he speaks about them "hearing" John the Baptist he doesn't simply mean that the sound waves emitting from John's mouth impacted their ears. They actually took his words to heart and began to live differently in view of the coming Kingdom. Moreover, this seems to be the point of the sayings about the sick in need of the physician and the lost sheep: those who are sick but recover have experienced a change in their lives, and the sheep that was lost does return to its fold.

Jesus appears, then, to have taught that people needed to repent and live in ways God wanted them to in light of the coming Kingdom. In the next chapter we'll consider more fully what that might have entailed. For now we should return to the central theme of this chapter, Jesus' apocalyptic message of the coming Kingdom of God. In this context, Jesus' point about the wicked inheriting the Kingdom makes perfect sense. There will be a complete reversal in which the high and mighty are brought low and the low and oppressed are lifted up. This includes those who were widely discounted by the religious establishment as beyond reach. The worst of sinners will be exalted in the coming Kingdom.

The Lowly Who Get Lifted: Jesus' Beatitudes

This theme of reversal gets played out in some of Jesus' most familiar teachings, the so-called Beatitudes, which tend, unfortunately, to be ripped out of their original apocalyptic contexts by people who quote them. The beatitudes are a group of sayings attributed to Jesus in a variety of our sources in which he pronounces "blessings" on certain groups of people (the term "beatitude" itself comes from the Latin "beatus"— blessed). The best known of these sayings are found in Matthew's Sermon on the Mount, which begins:

Blessed are the poor in spirit, for theirs is the Kingdom of heaven; blessed are those who mourn, for they will be comforted; blessed are those who are meek, for they will inherit the earth; blessed are those who hunger and thirst for righteousness, for they will be satisfied (Matt. 5:3–6).

What many readers evidently haven't noticed in these sayings is the verb tenses. They describe what certain groups of people are experiencing in the present and what they *will* experience in the future. *Will* experience? When? Not in some vague, remote, and uncertain moment—sometime in the sky by and by; it will happen when the Kingdom arrives. Those who are lowly, poor, and oppressed now will have their reward then.

A number of these Matthean sayings are actually derived from Q. Interestingly, in Luke's version they tend to emphasize physical hardship more than internal struggles. For instance, rather than blessing the "poor in spirit," in Luke Jesus blesses "you who are poor" (i.e, those who are literally impoverished). Rather than speaking of those who "hunger and thirst for righteousness," in Luke Jesus speaks of those who "hunger and thirst." There are good reasons for thinking that in these instances Luke's version is closer to what Jesus himself may have said. For one thing, we find a very similar form of the sayings independently attested in the Gospel of Thomas:

Blessed are the poor, for yours is the kingdom of heaven (G.Thom. 54).

Blessed are those who are hungry, for the belly of the one who desires will be filled (G.Thom. 69).

Blessed are you when you are hated and persecuted; no place will be found where you are persecuted (G.Thom. 68).

Interestingly, in Luke's version of the beatitudes, these various apocalyptic blessings are followed by their counterparts, a set of apocalyptic woes:

But woe to you who are wealthy, for you have your comfort (now); woe to you who are full now, for you will go hungry. Woe to you who are rejoicing now, for you will mourn and weep. And woe when everyone speaks well of you; for so too did your ancestors treat the false prophets (Luke 6:24–26).

These particular apocalyptic judgments are not independently attested in our other sources, but they certainly coincide with the major themes we've already seen in this chapter. Jesus taught that a day of judgment was coming with the appearance of the Son of Man, who would bring a radical reversal: those who were presently well-off would be condemned and those who were suffering would be blessed. Included in this apocalyptic message was a warning of imminent destruction for all who did not heed Jesus' words and turn to God as he wished.

The Coming Destruction

We have already seen that the coming judgment was to involve an act of destruction, as individuals who have failed to heed Jesus' message will be condemned when the Kingdom arrives. This kind of tradition is multiply attested in independent sources.

1 In Mark, Jesus warns:

   If your eye should cause you to sin, pluck it out; for it is better to enter into the Kingdom with a single eye than to be cast with two eyes into Gehenna [a place of torment], where their worm does not die and the fire is not quenched (Mark 9:47–48; picked up also in Matt. 18:9).

2 In Q, Jesus says:

   There will be weeping and gnashing of teeth, when you see Abraham, Isaac, Jacob, and all the prophets in the kingdom of God, but you are cast out (Luke 13:28; Matt. 8:11–12).

3 In M, Jesus speaks of the last judgment as a separation of the sheep and the goats, the latter of whom are told:

   Go away from me, you who are cursed, into the eternal fire that is prepared for the Devil and his angels (Matt. 25:41).

None of this is a pretty prospect. And the coming destruction of those opposed to God doesn't stop here, with the judgment of individuals. It also entails the demolition of governments (as the new Kingdom replaces older ones) and institutions. In particular—and this appears to have been a particular emphasis of his proclamation—Jesus maintained that the coming judgment of God would engulf the most holy place of the Jewish people, where God himself was believed to dwell, the Jerusalem Temple itself. This was the locus of Jewish worship and praise for the God of Israel. Jesus claimed that in the coming judgment sent by God, the Temple would be destroyed.

No surprise that Jesus' message was not heartily welcomed by the leaders among his people. As we will see at greater length in chapter 11, it was this aspect of Jesus' proclamation in particular that got him into some serious hot water, especially among the Jewish aristocracy charged with running the Temple and conducting its services. Jesus insisted that all they held dear and cherished was soon to be destroyed by God himself. This was the message that provoked the Jewish leaders into turning Jesus over to the Roman governor, Pilate, for prosecution.

The Demise of the Temple

The Temple in Jerusalem

The Jerusalem Temple was built on instruction from God in the Hebrew Bible. It was the place that Jewish worshipers could come to perform sacrifices of animals and foodstuffs to him in fulfillment of the Jewish Law found in the Hebrew Bible. For most Jews, it was the only place on earth where such sacrifices (commanded by God) could be performed.

The Temple was known to be one of the grandest buildings in the world of antiquity, spoken of with praise and admiration even by those who were not among its devotees. In the days of Jesus, the Temple complex was immense, encompassing an area roughly 500 yards by 325 yards—large enough to accomodate twenty-five (American) football fields, including the end zones. From the outside, its stone walls rose 100 feet from the street, as high as a modern ten-story building. No mortar had been used in its construction; instead, the stones—some of them 50 yards in length—had been carefully cut to fit together neatly; the gates into the temple were 45 feet high by 44 feet wide (with two doors, 22 feet wide, in each). One ancient source indicates that 200 men were required to close them each evening. From all of our ancient descriptions, the Temple complex appears to have been a fantastically beautiful set of buildings with the best materials money could buy, extensive portions of it overlaid with gold. As you might imagine, its construction was an immense feat. When it was completed in 63 CE, 18,000 local workers were reportedly left unemployed. It was destroyed just seven years later at the climax of the Jewish war against Rome, never to be built again.[6]

One of the things that made the Jerusalem Temple unique in the Greco-Roman world is that, as I've indicated, for most Jews of the period it was to be the only temple for the God of Israel. Whereas numerous temples could be devoted to any of the pagan gods, this God would receive sacrifices only in the Temple in Jerusalem. It is striking that Jews from around the world paid an annual tax to help defray the costs of its upkeep and administration—even Jews who never managed to set foot inside. In no small measure, this special reverence for the place derived from the belief that God himself dwelt there, in the Temple, in a special room called the Holy of Holies. The belief that a god might actually be present in a holy place was widespread throughout antiquity. In most ancient temples, however, the deity was present in the cult image, or "idol," kept in a sacred room. The sacred room in the Jerusalem Temple, on the other hand, was completely empty. Since the Jewish God was so holy, unlike all else that is, he explicitly forbade any images to be made of him.

No one could enter this holiest of rooms except the Jewish High Priest, and that came only once a year on the Day of Atonement (Yom Kippur), when he performed a sacrifice for the sins of the people. The Holy of Holies was thus the most sacred spot in the Temple and the rest of the building complex was structured so as to emphasize the holiness that emanated from its center. Around the Holy of Holies was the sanctuary, into which only certain priests could go; further removed still was the court of the priests, which allowed only priests and their assistants, the Levites. Yet further removed was the court of the Israelites, in which only Jewish men could come to bring their offerings to the priests; beyond that was the court of (Jewish) women, who were not allowed any nearer to the inner sanctum (Jewish men could assemble there as well). And finally beyond that came the court of the Gentiles, where even non-Jews could congregate.

Jesus and the Temple

It was this most sacred place, the dwelling of God himself, that Jesus predicted would be destroyed in the coming judgment—of this very God. Evidence is found in multiply attested traditions. The earliest surviving account is Mark 13:2:

> And as [Jesus] was coming out of the temple, one of his disciples said to him, "Teacher: see what great stones and what great buildings are here." And Jesus said to him, "Do you see these great buildings? Not one stone will be left upon another that will not be destroyed."

In later traditions, Jesus himself is said to have threatened to destroy the place. For example, at his trial, false witnesses reputedly claimed, "We have heard him saying, 'I will destroy this temple that is made with hands and after three days build another made without hands" (Mark 14:58); and on the cross he was allegedly mocked: "Look at the one who would destroy the temple and rebuild it in three days!" (Mark 15:29). Something similar is independently stated in John, where Jesus tells his Jewish opponents, "Destroy this temple and I will raise it up in three days" (John 2:19). And from an unrelated source, a speech found in the book of Acts, at the martyrdom of Stephen, false witnesses again arose to say that they had heard Stephen claim that "this Jesus the Nazarene will destroy this place and revamp the customs that Moses gave to us." Even the Gospel of Thomas gets in on the act, as Jesus there says, "I will destroy this house and no one will be able to rebuild it" (G. Thom. 71).

Thus the tradition that Jesus spoke about the destruction of the Temple is widely spread. Moreover, most of these traditions indicate that Jesus himself will have something to do with it. The idea that he would personally destroy the Temple is difficult to get past the criterion of dissimilarity: Christians who considered him the all-powerful Lord may well have given the sayings that twist in order to show that after his death, he "got even" with Jews by destroying their temple. Nor does it do well by the criterion of contextual credibility: How could a single man claim to be able to demolish an enormous set of buildings like this? Similarly problematic is the notion found only in John, that when Jesus talked about the temple being destroyed and raised in three days, he was actually speaking of his body (John 2:21).

Did Jesus then speak at all about the coming destruction of the Temple? One might be tempted to push the criterion of dissimilarity a bit further, and claim that since the Temple was in fact destroyed by the Romans in 70 CE, none of the predictions of Jesus can be safely trusted as actually going back to him—that is, that later Christians put predictions of its destruction on his lips to show his prophetic powers. Most scholars, though, consider this an extreme view, since the predictions of the destruction on one level or another pass all of our criteria: (a) They are obviously multiply attested (Mark, John, Acts, and Thomas!). (b) Moreover, in one respect, at least, the earliest form of these sayings appears to pass the criterion of dissimilarity, since Jesus' claim in Mark that not one stone would be left upon another did not in fact come true, as you can see yourself by visiting the Western Wall in Jerusalem today; if anyone actually knew the details of the destruction, they wouldn't have invented this verse. (c) And, just as importantly, the sayings are completely contextually credible. For we know of other prophetic figures throughout the history of Israel who had maintained that the Jewish people had so strayed from God that he would enter into judgment with them by destroying their central place of worship. Of particular relevance are the words of the Hebrew prophet Jeremiah, living in the sixth century BCE, before the destruction of the first Jewish Temple in 568. Jeremiah maintained that since the people of Israel had sinned so thoroughly, they could no longer trust God to deliver them or their sacred temple. In fact, despite their trust in the sanctuary to provide them protection, God was soon going to destroy both it and them. Jeremiah's words are worth quoting at some length:

> Thus says the Lord of hosts, the God of Israel: Amend your ways and your doings, and let me dwell with you in this place. Do not trust in these deceptive words: This is the temple of the LORD, the temple of the LORD, the temple of the LORD.... Will you steal, murder, commit adultery, swear falsely, make offerings to Baal, and go after other gods that you have not known, and then come and stand before me in this house which is called by my name, and say 'We are safe!'—only to go on doing all these abominations? Has this house, which is called by my name, become a den of robbers in your sight?...And now because you have done all these things... therefore I will do to the house that is called by my name, in which you trust, and to the place that I gave to you and to your ancestors, just what I did to Shiloh (that is, destroy it). And I will cast you out of my sight, just as I cast out all your kinsfolk. ... And I will bring to an end the sound of mirth and gladness, the voice of the bride and bridegroom in the cities of Judah and in the streets of Jerusalem; for the land shall become a waste" (Jer 7:3–4, 9–11, 14–15, 34).

The prediction that God would enter into judgment with his people, destroying them and their sacred places, is as old as the Hebrew prophets that Jesus heard read as a child in the synagogue in Nazareth.

And the tradition was kept alive, not just in literary texts, but among living, breathing people down through his own day. Recall the prophet named "Theudas" and the unnamed one called, simply, "the Egyptian" whom I mentioned in chapter 7. Both of them, in their own ways, predicted that God would bring about a destruction of Jerusalem and a salvation of the remnant of his people who remained faithful to him (and to his prophetic servants).

And consider the proclamation of yet another prophet of the first century, another Jew who was, by an odd coincidence, also named Jesus, the son of an otherwise unknown Ananias. Some thirty years after Jesus' death, according to the Jewish historian Josephus, this other Jesus went through the city of Jerusalem crying out: "A voice from the east, a voice from the west, a voice from the four winds, a voice against Jerusalem and the sanctuary, a voice against the bridegroom and the bride, a voice against all the people" (*Jewish War*, 6.5.3). Jesus son of Ananias spent seven and a half years proclaiming the doom and destruction of Jerusalem and its Temple. As with his better-known namesake, he too was arrested and placed on trial before the Roman governor as a trouble maker. In this instance, though, the accused was found to be innocent on grounds of insanity, and was released after being scourged. But his mistreatment didn't retard his proclamation: he continued lamenting the coming destruction until he was accidentally killed by a catapulted stone during the seige of Jerusalem, a couple of years before his predictions came true.

To return now to our own Jesus. As part of his prediction of the coming judgment of God, he too urged—as Jeremiah and other prophets had done before, and several lesser lights were to do after—that destruction was at hand, and that not only individuals but also social institutions and structures would be brought low when the Son of Man arrived on the clouds of heaven with the angels of glory and the power of God.

A Judgment That Is Universal

Unlike some of his prophetic confreres (for example, Jeremiah), Jesus did not think that the coming judgment would be limited in scope. It didn't apply, that is, only to the individual Jew or to Jewish institutions like the Temple. For Jesus, as for most apocalypticists, judgment was to be universal. Recall: apocalypticists were concerned not just with the godless activities of their own people. They believed in forces of evil that had been unleashed in the world. For them, the entire created order had become corrupt. And God the Creator was going to clean house and start anew. Judgment would affect everyone and everything.

Everyone. Note that in a number of the apocalyptic sayings of Jesus that we've considered, there is talk of non-Jews coming into the Kingdom. He speaks, for example, of people (whom I take to be Gentiles) coming from east and west, north and south to enter the Kingdom and dine with the Jewish ancestors Abraham and Co., while Jews are left outside. And he discusses the final judgment of the nations—the same word as "Gentiles," that is, non-Jews—in the story of the future separation of the sheep and the goats. The coming of the Son of Man is not an event to be beheld only by Jews, but by the whole world.

Moreover, his coming will have a universal effect. Sometimes this effect is spelled out in language that heightens its cosmic nature: "the sun will be darkened, and the moon will not give its light, and the stars will be falling from heaven and the powers in the heavens will be shaken" (Mark 13:24–25). It's not clear here whether these signs in the heavens are to be thought of as temporary markers of the new world—eclipses and falling stars—or whether Jesus, like his apocalyptic follower who later wrote the book of Revelation, envisioned an entirely new created order, a "new heaven and new earth" (Rev. 21:1)—complete with a new sun, moon, and stars—for the coming Kingdom. What is clear is that this kingdom will be universal in scope. The present world and all its powers will be overcome, prior to the arrival of the new realm in which God will rule his people and, through them, the entire world.

The Imminence of the End

Jesus appears to have thought that this coming judgment of God through the cosmic Son of Man is imminent. It is right around the corner. In fact, it is to happen within his own generation. The stress on the imminent end is independently attested in all of our earliest sources. The end will come suddenly and unexpectedly, and people need to be alert:

1 Mark

Whoever is ashamed of me and of my words in this adulterous and sinful generation, of that one will the Son of Man be ashamed when he comes in the glory of his Father with the holy angels. Truly I tell you, *some of those who are standing here* will not taste death before they see that the Kingdom of God has come in power (8:38–9:1).

Truly I tell you, *this generation* will not pass away until all these things have taken place (13:30).

Be awake, keep alert. For you don't know when that time is. It is like a man on a journey, who leaves his house and gives his slaves authority over their own work, and orders the doorkeeper to watch. Watch therefore—for you don't know when the master of the house is coming, whether in the evening, at midnight, at the crack of dawn, or in the morning—lest when he comes suddenly he finds you sleeping. But what I say to you I say to everyone: Watch! (Mark 13:33–37).

2 Q

But you should realize that if the homeowner knew the hour when the thief was coming, he would not allow him to dig a hole through the wall of his house; and you also, be prepared, for the Son of Man is coming in an hour that you are not expecting (Luke 12:39–40; Matt. 24:43–44).

If a servant [whose master has left town for a time] says to himself, "My master is not coming for awhile," and begins to beat the servants, both men and women, and to eat, drink, and carouse, the master of that servant will come on a day he is not expecting and in an hour he does not know, and he will cut him to shreds (Luke 12:45–46; Matt 24:48–50).

3 M (at the conclusion of the story of the ten maidens waiting for their master, five wise who were prepared and five foolish who were not)

Watch therefore, for you do not know the day or the hour. (Matt. 25:13).

4 L

Let your loins be girded and keep your lamps burning, like people who are waiting for their master to return home from a wedding feast (Luke 12:36).

What matters for my purposes here is not whether Jesus spoke each and every one of these sayings exactly as they are recorded. What matters is that these themes are resounded repeatedly and independently in our earliest surviving sources. Jesus appears to have anticipated that the coming judgment of God, to be brought by the Son of Man in a cosmic act of destruction and salvation, was imminent. It could happen at any time. But it would certainly happen within his own generation.

Conclusion

In many ways, as I've indicated, this message was like that proclaimed throughout the writings of the prophets in the Hebrew Bible. Judgment was coming, people needed to repent in preparation or they would be condemned. Those who turned to God, though, would be saved. At the same time, Jesus' message was different, for his was framed within an apocalyptic context. As a first-century Jew, Jesus lived when many Jews expected God to intervene once and for all for his people, to overthrow the forces of evil that had gained ascendancy in the world and to bring in his good Kingdom on earth. There would then be no more war, poverty, disease, calamity, sin, hatred, or death. This kingdom would arrive in power, and all that was opposed to it would be destroyed and removed.

I do not want to leave the impression that these warnings of the coming judgment were the *only* things Jesus taught about during his public ministry. As we'll see in the next chapter, that's not the case at all. But it's important to understand fully the framework within which his other teachings are to be fitted. Many people—Christian and non-Christian alike—think of Jesus as a great moral teacher whose ethical views can help produce a better society for those of us who are determined to make our lives together as just, peaceful, and enjoyable as possible. On one level, I think that's probably right. But it's also important to realize that Jesus himself did not see it that way. He did not propound his ethical views to show us how to create a just society and make the world a happier place for the long haul. For him, there wasn't going to *be* a long haul. The judgment of God was coming soon with the arrival of the Son of Man—and people needed to prepare for its coming by changing the way they lived. Preparation for the Kingdom—*that's* what ultimately lies at the heart of Jesus' ethics, as we'll see now in the chapter that follows.

ten

a place for everything:
jesus' other teachings in their apocalyptic context

CONTEXT MAY NOT BE EVERYTHING, BUT IT'S NOT FAR OFF. THE WORDS "JUST KIDDING" MEAN SOMETHING PRETTY DIFFERENT IF SPOKEN BY THE SELF-APPOINTED COMEDIAN WHO LIVES across the hall from you, a sheep farmer in the barn of his Wyoming ranch, or the president of the United States speaking into a red phone in the Oval Office.

And so I've tried as best I can to set the context within which Jesus' teachings were delivered. As I indicated at the end of the previous chapter, Jesus taught about a lot of things other than the coming judgment of God to be brought by the Son of Man. In this chapter, we'll be looking at some of these other teachings in light of the overarching framework of his apocalyptic message. In particular, I'll be examining Jesus' "ethical" teachings to show how they relate to his proclamation of the Kingdom. In short, Jesus' followers were to live in ways that prepared for this coming Kingdom and that embodied the values that would be manifest completely and finally when it arrived.

I should emphasize that I won't be able to discuss each and every word found on Jesus' lips in our earliest sources, but only sayings that I think can reasonably be established as going back to him (in most instances I'll be giving the grounds for this judgment). Even among these, though, I'll need to be a bit selective, since I don't mean this to be an exhaustive study. I hope I won't overlook any of your favorites.

Jesus and the Jewish Law

To this point in my discussion of Jesus as a Jewish apocalypticist, I've focused more on the noun than the adjective. Now it's time to shift focus. Jesus was Jewish. Realizing the Jewishness of Jesus is critical if we are to make sense of his teachings. For despite the fact that the religion founded in his name quickly came to be filled with non-Jews—and eventually, in fact, became itself *anti*-Jewish (on ugly occasions, violently so)—it was founded by a Jewish teacher who taught his Jewish followers about the Jewish God who guided the Jewish people by means of the Jewish Law. Jesus kept and discussed Jewish customs like prayer and fasting, he worshiped in Jewish places of worship like the synagogue and the Temple, and he kept Jewish festivals like the Passover. Like just about every other Jew that we know about from the ancient world, Jesus believed in the one Creator God of Israel and insisted that his people were to worship no other gods. He understood that this one God had made a special pact with Israel from the beginning, to be their God in exchange for their exclusive worship and devotion. He maintained that God's will was revealed in the books written by Moses, especially in "the Law" that was delivered to Moses on Mount Sinai, as recounted in these books (the first five books of the Hebrew Bible: Genesis, Exodus, Leviticus, Numbers, and Deuteronomy). And he believed that when the people of Israel violated the Law, God punished them.

Most of Jesus' teachings, in fact, relate in one way or another to his understanding of this Jewish Law.

The Jewish Law, of course, included the Ten Commandments, but it contained much more besides. The Law consisted of stories of the ancient Jewish ancestors, from the time of Adam and Eve up to the death of the law-giver himself, Moses. Perhaps more important, it contained the other laws God had given to his people—laws pertaining to how they should worship and honor him, for example, by observing kosher food laws and requirements for tithing all produce, and laws pertaining to how they should relate to one another, for example, by not destroying one another's property. The Law was central to Jewish life. Jewish teachers taught this Law, Jewish lawyers were expert in this Law, Jewish scribes copied this Law.

Jesus was neither a scribe nor a lawyer. But he was a Jewish teacher who taught about the Law. Evidence of Jesus' attachment to the Jewish

Law is evident in multiple layers of our traditions, scattered throughout a range of independent traditions. Consider some of the following (this list simply gives examples; it is by no means exhaustive):

1 Mark

   When a man runs up to Jesus and asks him what he must do to "inherit eternal life," Jesus' immediate response is to list some of the Ten Commandments. (In Matthew's version of this story, he actually tells the man: "if you want to enter into life, keep the commandments" (Mark 10:17–22; Matt. 19:16–22; see also Luke 18:18–23).

2 Q

   Jesus states that it is easier for heaven and earth to pass away than for a single dot of the Law to pass away (Luke 16:16; Matt. 5:18).

3 M

   Jesus states that he came to fulfill the Law and that his followers must keep the Law even better than the scribes and Pharisees if they want to enter into the Kingdom of heaven (Matt. 5:17, 19–20).

4 John

   Jesus argues with his opponents about the Law, and points out to them that "the Scripture cannot be broken" (John 10:34–35).

In fact, throughout the Gospels Jesus spends his time arguing and debating aspects of the Law—teaching his followers what God really wants and disagreeing with his opponents about it. In Mark he claims that Pharisees violate God's commandment in order to preserve their own traditions (Mark 7:8–9); in M he attacks his opponents for never considering what is written in the Law about the Sabbath (Matt. 12:5); and even in John he claims that Moses gave the Law but none of his opponents keeps it (John 7:19).

My point is not that each and every one of these accounts must be historically accurate exactly as it's reported, but that the idea that Jesus was principally concerned about understanding and teaching the real meaning of the Jewish Law, often in opposition to other Jewish teachers, is thoroughly rooted in our tradition. It is therefore to be trusted as historical.

What, though, did Jesus teach about the Law? Perhaps it is easiest to explain his views by setting them in contrast with other perspectives that we know something about. Unlike certain Pharisees, Jesus did not think that what really mattered before God was the scrupulous observance of the laws in all their details. Going out of one's way to avoid doing anything questionable on the Sabbath or to tithe all produce, whether bought or sold, was of very little importance to him. Unlike some Sadducees, Jesus did not think that it was of the utmost importance to adhere strictly to the rules for worship in the Temple through the divinely ordained sacrifices. Unlike some Essenes, he did not think that people should seek to maintain their own ritual purity in isolation from others in order to find God's ultimate approval. For Jesus—as for some other Jews from his time about whom we are less well informed (see, e.g., Mark 12:32–34)—what really mattered were the commandments of God that formed, in his opinion, the very heart of the Law, the commandments to love God above all else and to love one's neighbor as oneself.

This emphasis on the dual commandments to love is found in our earliest surviving Gospel, in a passage that deserves to be quoted at length:

> And one of the scribes who came up heard them arguing, and noticing that [Jesus] was giving good answers, he asked him: "What is first among all the commandments?" Jesus answered, "The first of all is this, 'Hear, O Israel, the Lord our God is one Lord, and you shall love the Lord your God with your whole heart and your whole soul and your whole understanding and your whole strength.' [Deut. 6:4–5] This is the second: 'you shall love your neighbor as yourself.' [Lev. 19:18] There is no other commandment greater than these." And the scribe said to him: "You are right, teacher; you speak the truth, because 'He is one and there is none other than him,' and 'to love him with all one's heart and understanding and strength' and 'to love one's neighbor as oneself" is much more than all of the burnt offerings and sacrifices." And when Jesus saw that he replied intelligently, he said: "You are not far from the Kingdom of God" (Mark 12:28–34).

Notice: the Kingdom of God again. Earlier when someone had asked Jesus how to have eternal life (which was to come in the Kingdom), Jesus told him to keep the commandments of God (Mark 10:17–22). Here when someone agrees that the chief commandments, above all others, were those of Deuteronomy 6:4–5 (love the Lord your God) and Leviticus 19:18 (love your neighbor as yourself—a commandment, I should perhaps emphasize, that Jesus himself did not come up with! He was simply citing one of the laws of Moses), Jesus tells him that he is near to entering God's Kingdom.

The commandment to love is at the heart of the Law for Jesus, and keeping it is an apocalyptic necessity, as people prepare for the coming Kingdom.

The Value of the Kingdom

It could easily be argued, in fact, that all of Jesus' injunctions to love others, to give oneself to others, to serve others, and so on were instructions on how to inherit the Kingdom that was soon to appear. For Jesus, everything else paled in comparison. People should eagerly wait for the Kingdom and sacrifice all to its appearance. According to parables found in M (and attested independently in the Gospel of Thomas), the Kingdom is like a treasure that a man discovers in a field; he goes out and sells everything he owns to purchase the field (Matt. 13:44; cf. G.Thom. 109). The treasure of the Kingdom, in other words, is more valuable than the sum total of everything else a person owns. And it's like a merchant in search of fine pearls; when he finds the pearl he really wants, he sells everything (everything!) in order to buy it (Matt. 13:45–46; G.Thom. 76). It may seem bizarre and radical to sell all one's possessions in order to get a solitary pearl. What does one do with it, but sell it to regain what one sold to get it? But as odd as it might seem to others, that is what the Kingdom is worth—everything one has. It's worth more, in fact, than one's entire life: "for what does it profit a person to gain the entire world but to forfeit his life? And what will a person give in exchange for his life?" (Mark 8:36–37). For Jesus, the answer is obvious. One should give up everything.

That's why, for Jesus, the present life holds no real attractions. Life in the present age should be at best a matter of indifference. One shouldn't be concerned about such trivial matters as what kind of clothes to wear or what kind of food to eat. As he says in the Q source, "seek first the Kingdom of God, and all its right way of living, and all these things will be added to you" (Matt. 6:33). What does its "right way of living" entail? It entails loving God, the one who brings the Kingdom, and one's neighbor as oneself. All else should be completely secondary in importance. If thieves want to take your clothes—let them! If bullies want to force you to do their work for them—let them! If the government wants to take your money—let them! If thugs want to beat you— let them! If enemies want to kill you—let them! None of these things matters. You should give away your shirt as well as your coat, you should go an extra mile, you should render unto Caesar the things that are Caesar's, you should turn the other cheek, you should not fear the one who can destroy your paltry body. The Kingdom is coming, and the concerns of this life are trivial by comparison (see Matt. 5:39–42; 10:28; Mark 12:17; Luke 6:29–30; 12:4–5).

Your focus instead should be on God (the first great commandment) and taking care of others (the second). No one who is tied to the things of this world can put God above it. As Jesus is reported to have said in early and independent sources: "No one is able to serve two lords; he will either hate the one and love the other or be devoted to the one and despise the other. You can't serve God and material things" (from Q: Luke 16:13; Matt. 6:24).[1] And serving God means serving one's fellow human being. At the root of the second commandment, to love one's neighbor as oneself, is the so-called "Golden Rule," as found, for example, in Q: "Just as you want people to do for you, do for them" (Luke 6:31). Matthew adds the line that seems entirely appropriate for Jesus' own views: "for this is the Law and the Prophets" (Matt. 7:12)— that is, treating your neighbor as you want yourself to be treated is the point of the entire Scriptures. So, too, the words of Jesus in the Gospel of Thomas: "Love your brother as your own soul, keep him as the apple of your eye" (G.Thom. 25). Even traditions preserved only in the Gospel of John agree: "This is my commandment, that you love one another as I have loved you. Greater love has no one than this, that a person lay down his life for his friends"; "By this everyone will know that you are my disciples, if you love one another" (John 15:12–13; 13:35).

In sum, the coming Kingdom should be the complete focus of one's attention. The charms of this age have no allure, the present life is a matter of indifference. Jesus' hearers were to give up their entire lives for the coming Kingdom, loving God above all else and sacrificing their lives for the sake of others. Recall the passages we discussed earlier in chapter 9, for example, those that deal with the reversals to be brought in the coming judgment. Those who make themselves lowly servants now will be exalted then, those who tend the needs of others now will be rewarded then. In the judgment of the sheep and the goats this involves feeding the hungry, clothing the destitute, visiting the sick and imprisoned (Matt. 25:31–46).

As a corollary, people should give all they have for the sake of others. In our earliest accounts Jesus not only urges indifference to the good things of this life (which, when seen from an apocalyptic perspective, are actually not all that good—since they too will be destroyed in the coming Kingdom), he rails against them, telling his followers to be rid of them. And thus, when a rich person comes to Jesus to ask about inheriting eternal life, upon finding out that he has already observed the commandments of God found in the Law—he hasn't murdered, committed adultery, stolen, or borne false witness, for example—Jesus tells him, "You still lack one thing: go, sell everything you have and give to the poor, and you will have treasure in heaven" (Mark 10:17–21).

The man is said to have gone away crestfallen because he was rich. Ever since, readers of the story have gone away crestfallen as well, especially those who suspect that Jesus meant what he said, and that his injunction wasn't limited to this one particular fellow. Interpreters have tried to get around the problem since it was first written (especially interpreters who weren't willing to give away everything for the coming Kingdom); but doing so ignores its logic. *Everyone* who saves his life will lose it. Jesus' demands were simple, in that they weren't that difficult to figure out; but they were also radical. The Kingdom required an absolute commitment. No one should look for it without considering what it would cost (cf. Luke 14:28–33)—for it will cost everything.

No wonder it's easier for a camel to go through the eye of a needle than for a rich person to inherit the Kingdom. What person with wealth has really, actually, loved others as himself or herself? If there are people starving on the doorstep—and there are always people starving on the doorstep—how can one keep one's possessions and claim to have followed the Golden Rule or kept the second great commandment? This wasn't a matter of debate and nuance for Jesus, but of clear pronouncement. Anyone who adhered to this teaching would be like a person who built his house on a rock. The house would withstand the beating of the wind and rain when a violent storm arose (the coming judgment!). But anyone who held back would be like a person who built his house on sand—the shifting sands of this world and what it has to offer—who would experience great loss when the storm came (Q: Matt. 7:24–27; Luke 6:47–49). And the Kingdom would not come to those who simply paid lip service to his commands to give up everything in this world, but to those who had actually done what he said (cf. Q: Matt. 7:21; Luke 6:46).

Such people would be willing to cut off a hand or foot rather than hurt someone else (Q: Matt. 5:28–30; Luke 9:46–48). Such people would become like little children who own nothing and can lay claim to nothing (Mark 10:13–16). Such people would become slaves who do the bidding of others (Mark 10:42–44; cf. John 13:12–17). It is people like these who will enter into the Kingdom, not the powerful, wealthy, and important. And just about everyone is powerful, wealthy, and important in comparison to toddlers and slaves.

That's why Jesus' own disciples evidently gave up everything they had and held dear in order to follow him. As Simon Peter allegedly said, "See, we have left everything behind and followed you." Jesus' reply, as we have seen already, seems consistent with his entire message:

> Truly I tell you, there is no one who has left a house or brothers or sisters or mother or father or children or lands for my sake and the sake of the good news, who will not receive them all back a hundredfold in this present time—houses, brothers, sisters, mothers, children, and lands, along with persecutions—and in the age that is coming, life that never ends. But many who are first will be last and the last will be first (Mark 10:29–31).

The Family and the Kingdom

Does, then, seeking the Kingdom above everything else also mean leaving even one's *family* behind? Yes indeed. The common sense shared by modern proponents of "family values" notwithstanding, Jesus was quite unambiguous that even parents, siblings, spouses, and children were to be of no importance in comparison with the coming Kingdom. Consider the words preserved in Q: "If anyone comes to me and does not hate his own father and mother and wife and children and brothers and sisters and even his own life, he is not able to be my disciple" (Luke 14:26; Matt. 10:37).[2] A person must *hate* his or her family? The same word is used, strikingly, in the saying independently preserved in the Gospel of Thomas: "The one who does not hate his father and mother will not be worthy to be my disciple" (G.Thom. 55). If we understand "hate" here to mean something like "despise in comparison to" or "have nothing to do with," then the saying makes sense. And it helps explain Jesus' reaction to his own family, as we'll see in greater length in chapter 11. For there are clear signs not only that Jesus' family rejected his message during his public ministry, but that he in turn spurned them publicly (independently attested in Mark 3:31–34 and G.Thom. 99).

Jesus clearly saw the familial rifts that would be created when someone became committed to his message of the coming Kingdom:

> You think that I have come to bring peace on earth; not peace, I tell you, but division. For from now on there will be five people in one house, divided among themselves: three against two and two

against three; a father will be divided against his son and a son against his father, a mother against her daughter and a daughter against her mother; a mother-in-law against her daughter-in-law and a daughter-in-law against her mother-in-law (Luke 12:51–53; Matt. 10:34–46; independently attested in G.Thom. 16).

And family tensions would be heightened immediately before the end of the age, when "a brother will betray his brother to death, and a father his child, and children will rise up against their parents and kill them" (Mark 13:12).

These "antifamily" traditions are too widely attested in our sources to be ignored (they are found in Mark, Q, and Thomas, for example), and show that Jesus did not support what we today might think of as family values. But why not? Evidently because, as I've already emphasized, he wasn't teaching about the good society and about how to maintain it. The end was coming soon, and the present social order was being called radically into question. What mattered was not, ultimately, the strong family ties and social institutions of this world. What mattered was the new thing that was coming, the future Kingdom. It was impossible to promote this teaching while trying to retain the present social structure. That would be like trying to put new wine into old wineskins or trying to sew a new piece of cloth to an old garment. As any winemaster or seamstress could tell you, it just won't work. The wineskins will burst and the garment will tear. New wine and new cloth require new wineskins and new garments. The old is passing away and the new is almost here (Mark 2:18–22; G.Thom. 47).

Some "Ethical" Corollaries

This new thing that was coming, then, required a complete commitment to love God and one's neighbor as oneself, even to the point of abandoning all else—including one's own family and home—in order to do so. Jesus appears to have maximized the commandment to love and minimized, in comparison to it, everything else. It is difficult to know whether the so-called antitheses preserved in Matthew's Sermon on the Mount (Matt. 5:21–48) are authentic sayings of Jesus—they aren't independently attested, for instance. But they certainly bear out this theme that is found throughout our earliest traditions. The Law says not to murder, and Jesus, in light of the commandment to love others as oneself, radicalizes it to say that one shouldn't even express anger. The logic: if anger leads to murder, then you shouldn't be angry. The

Law says not to take someone else's wife; Jesus radicalizes it to say that you shouldn't passionately desire her. The logic: if desiring her leads to taking her (and thereby taking her away from the one to whom you are to be showing love), then you shouldn't desire her. The Law says to show mercy in judgment, so that the penalty you mete out fits the crime ("an eye for an eye, a tooth for a tooth"); Jesus radicalizes it to say that you should show complete mercy, by turning the other cheek.

The supreme importance of love is probably what led Jesus to minimize the importance of other aspects of the Law that other Jewish teachers emphasized. As we'll see more in the next chapter, for example, Jesus probably did not disagree with the Pharisees in principle that the Sabbath should be observed. *Of course* it should be—it's part of God's Law. But if abstaining completely from work on the Sabbath means letting someone else suffer, then it's not what God wants, since God is ultimately concerned with humans and their welfare. "Sabbath was made for humans, not humans for the Sabbath!" (Mark 2:27). So, too, Jesus may well have agreed with the Pharisees that it's a good thing to tithe agricultural produce—doing so, after all, is commanded in the Law. But to focus on tithing while ignoring more important things, like human needs, is against God's Law. And so, in a tradition preserved in Q: "Woe to you Pharisees, because you tithe mint, and rue, and every herb, and you bypass justice and the love of God. True, you should have done those things, but not passed by these others" (Luke 11:42; cf. Matt. 23:23).

Similarly, Jesus agreed that one should worship in the Temple and, evidently, perform the proper sacrifices there. That *is* part of the Law given to Moses, and Jesus does, for example, keep the Passover in Jerusalem. But the sacrificial cult in the Temple was not nearly as important as meeting human needs: "for I desire mercy and not sacrifice," says Jesus, quoting the Hebrew prophet Hosea twice in the M traditions (Matt. 9:13; 12:7; see Hos. 6:6).[3] And he completely agrees that love of God and neighbor is much more important than "burnt offerings and sacrifices," according to Mark (12:33).

Some of Jesus' best-known ethical teachings relate directly to this radicalization of the love command as the heart of the Law. We have already seen that those who are wealthy should give what they have for those in need. Consider as well the following ethical corollaries.

Divorce

As today, the grounds for divorce were hotly debated in Jesus' day, some Jewish teachers claiming that a man could dismiss his wife for just about any reason he chose, others insisting that the grounds be weighty. Jesus' own sayings on divorce come down to us in several different forms. Probably the most familiar today (in part because it fits more closely with a *modern* common sense) states that one has no right to get divorced *except* in cases of adultery (Matt. 5:31–32). But in Mark and the earliest form of Q (as preserved in Luke) Jesus forbids divorce altogether (Mark 10:4–12; Luke 16:18). In fact, anyone who divorces his wife and marries another commits adultery—since the Law itself indicates that when a man and woman join together, they are one flesh, not two. And that which God has united should not be separated.

Divorce leads to serious hardship still today, of course. But throughout history things have been, as a rule, even worse. In Jesus' time, when women were not able to go out to find a second job, but were for the most part reliant, by necessity, on the men in their lives (fathers, husbands, and sons), divorce could lead to abject poverty and misery. Jesus' understanding of the Law (with love as the guiding principle) forbade the practice altogether—even though the Law itself allowed it! Thus love for others means radicalizing the Law. Rather than providing documented grounds for a divorce by giving a certificate (as in Deut. 24:1–4), you shouldn't get divorced at all.

Forgiveness

The Law taught that anyone whose property was stolen or damaged by another could expect full restitution plus an additional 20 percent as a penalty (see, e.g., Lev. 6:1–5). For Jesus, though, the material things of this world were a matter of indifference, and the love you show another should be manifest in your willingness to forgive whatever was owed you. Just as everyone is eager for God to overlook the ways they've mistreated him (by breaking his laws, for example) so, too, they should be willing to overlook the ways others have mistreated them.

This, in fact, is one of the most widely attested teachings of Jesus. For example, in Mark Jesus says, "When you stand praying and have anything against someone, forgive it, so that your Father in heaven may forgive your trespasses" (Mark 11:25). In the Lord's Prayer, given in Q, God is asked to "forgive us our sins, just as we have forgiven everyone indebted to us" (Luke 11:4; cf. Matt. 6:12). Also in Q Jesus tells his disciples to forgive anyone who repents (Luke 17:3; Matt. 18:15); in L Jesus specifies that you should do so as many as seven times in a single day (Luke 17:4); in M he says you should do it seventy times seven (Matt. 18:22). Moreover, both M and L tell parables that stress the need to forgive in light of God's own forgiveness (Matt. 18:23–35, the parable of the unforgiving servant; and Luke 7:40–43, the parable of the two debtors).

Judging Others

If following the heart of the Law meant forgiving one another's debts, it makes sense, as a corollary, that one should not stand in judgment on the faults, shortcomings, and misdeeds of others. Another constant refrain of Jesus' teaching is summed up nicely in Q: "Don't judge, so that you won't be judged" (Luke 6:37; Matt. 7:1). I probably don't need to add that the teaching is clearly linked to an apocalyptic notion of the future comeuppance; in Matthew, for example, the saying continues: "for you will be judged [i.e., in the coming judgment!] with the measure that you yourself use to judge" (Matt. 7:2). Luke moves in a similar direction: "Don't condemn and you won't be condemned; forgive, and you will be forgiven" (Luke 6:37–38).

This teaching appears to relate closely to Jesus' general condemnation of those who don't practice what they preach, who condemn the faults and deeds of others while paying no heed to their own. The Pharisees in his acquaintance were not the only ones liable to the charge. As again he says in Q, in one of the most memorable and witty of his metaphorical gems,

> And why do you see the speck that is in your brother's eye, but pay no attention to the log stuck in yours? How can you say to your brother, "Brother, let me get that speck out of your eye," without even noticing the log that's in your eye? Hypocrite! First get rid of the log in your eye, and then you'll see clearly to get the speck out of your brother's (Luke 6:41–42; Matt. 7:3–5; independently attested in G.Thom. 26).

Love of Enemy

Jesus insisted that people love not only their friends but even their enemies. This is another of those teachings that some who call themselves Jesus' followers have wanted to explain away over the years. Some of us like to have enemies, and others realize that our enemies' acts of hatred and violence are inexcusable and unforgivable. Nonetheless, it appears that Jesus maintained that one should forgive even the most senseless and cruel acts of others and pray to God on their behalf. And why not? This world that provides our sworn enemies with all their power and authority is to pass away; they will soon be faced with the wrath of God and their humiliation will be complete. Better to try to turn them now to the right path than to hate and despise them. If they don't turn, they will soon pay the price, quite independently of our enmity. Thus in Q, for example, Jesus tells his followers to "love your enemies" and to "pray for those who abuse you" (Luke 6:27; Matt. 5:43–44), in L materials he says to "do well to those who hate you and bless those who curse you" (Luke 6:27–28).

Care for the Underprivileged and Oppressed

Jesus' insistence on the love for others was particularly manifest in his concern for the destitute of society, those who were impoverished, terminally ill, mentally diseased, and socially outcast. It was people like this who would inherit the Kingdom when the Son of Man arrived. Possibly their suffering now was a direct result of the forces of evil rampant here at the end of the age. God, though, would overthrow these forces in the end and vindicate those they had overpowered. In the meantime, anyone awaiting his Kingdom was to show the same kind of love for them. This is evident throughout the sayings materials of our earliest sources. Jesus pays particular heed to those with little or no standing in his society (e.g., women and children) and to those who were oppressed and suffering (e.g., the poor and the weak).

We have already seen Jesus' particular interest in children, as those who have no standing, position, wealth, or claim. Throughout first-century society, children were viewed as imperfect adults who would eventually mature into full human beings with rights and privileges. For the time being, though, they were obviously weak, dependent, and inferior.

Women, for their part, were often restricted to doing work in the home—and grueling work it was, for the most part. Just raising a family was a drain. Childbearing women of that era had to produce on average five babies just to keep the population *constant*. Women did the domestic chores—washing, cooking, teaching the children, and so on. In the poorer homes (such as those of most of Jesus' followers), they did so with no help. How draining was the work? Just take a solitary example. Today it takes just a few seconds to toss a loaf of bread into the shopping cart at the store. In Jesus' world, it took around three hours for a woman to grind enough grain for the next day's bread. There wasn't a lot of time for the finer things in life. Most women were illiterate and worn out. No wonder then that in daily prayers attested later, Jewish males thanked God that they were neither a child nor a woman.

Jesus, though, had a special place for both children and women. In our earliest Gospel, he claims that anyone who welcomes a child in his name welcomes him; and whoever welcomes him welcomes the Father (Mark 9:37; Matt. 18:5; Luke 9:48). And he may have had children in mind when he later says that anyone who causes "one of the least of these who believe in me to stumble" would be better off drowning in the sea (Mark 9:42). Perhaps most memorably, when some young children were kept from him, he rebuked the disciples, "Let the small children come to me, don't forbid them. For the Kingdom of God belongs to such as these" (Mark 10:14). Note: the Kingdom of God again. The theme recurs independently in the Gospel of Thomas, where Jesus is said to have seen some infants being nursed, and to have commented to his disciples, "These little ones who are being nursed are like those who enter into the Kingdom" (G.Thom. 22).

These various traditions appear to pass the criterion of dissimilarity. We know that at a later time Christians were mocked for being attractive to unsophisticated and uneducated children. Christianity was widely thought, then, to be a religion of ignorant nobodies. Not everyone, of course, disdained kids on principle; presumably, most parents more or less liked their own. But given the general disdain of children in that society it seems unlikely that someone would make up the idea that Jesus was especially keen on them.

Jesus was at least as concerned with the status of women. The sayings traditions are more scattered here, but Jesus does speak with women in public and instructs them one on one (something unusual for a reputed teacher; see the independent traditions in Mark 7:27–28; John 4:7–26; 11:20–27); he urges at least one woman to be more concerned with hearing his teaching than doing womanly duties about the house (Luke 10:38–42); he publicly praises one for an act of kindness (Mark 14:6–9); and so on. And as we'll see more fully in chapter 11, women were clearly a central part of his mission.

Finally, we have already seen Jesus' concern for the poor and oppressed. When he tells those with material goods to give them away to the poor, he doesn't seem to be concerned only that those with ties to this world remove them—else he could have told them simply to toss their stuff into the sea. The destitute should be cared for. Nowhere are Jesus' concerns for such people more clear than in the Beatitudes, as discussed in chapter 9. Those who were poor, hungry, thirsty, oppressed, and in mourning would be lifted up in the coming Kingdom. No wonder Jesus called this message "good news." In the short meantime, such people should be cared for by those willing to abandon everything for God, in accordance with the Law he's given his people.

I Can See It Already! The Foretaste of the Kingdom

As I've already intimated, since Albert Schweitzer published his *Quest of the Historical Jesus* in 1906, scholars have wrangled over the meaning of the Kingdom of God in the teachings of Jesus (they were actually wrangling about it before, but the issue became focused after Schweitzer). Some have basically agreed with Schweitzer that for Jesus, the Kingdom was a future, actual rule of God on earth. Others have urged that the apocalyptic language of the Gospels was completely metaphorical, and that the Kingdom was, for Jesus, already present on earth in his ministry. Those who have argued this latter view point to such verses as Luke 17:21, where Jesus reportedly said, "The Kingdom of God is among you." Unfortunately for this view, as most of its opponents have been quick to point out, the verse is found only in Luke (i.e., it is not multiply attested), a Gospel, as we have seen, that went some way to tone down the apocalyptic dimensions of our earlier sources. The fact is that there are apocalyptic pronouncements throughout all of our earliest accounts of Jesus' teachings, predictions of the coming judgment, of the imminent arrival of the Son of Man, of the future Kingdom on earth—and these pronouncements need to be taken seriously.

At the same time, there *are* other indications, even in these earlier sources, that in some sense Jesus and his followers thought they were already enjoying aspects of the future Kingdom in the present. As a result, probably the majority of scholars have been content to say that Jesus talked about the Kingdom as both future and present.

I think this general view (and as stated, it *is* very general!) is right, even though I'm not confident that most scholars have understood in what *sense* it's right. It should be quite clear by now that Jesus' predictions about the coming Kingdom cannot be watered down, compromised, Milquetoasted to death. For they form the very core of his teachings. His entire proclamation consisted in a call to prepare for the coming Kingdom, which would be brought in by a final judgment through the imminent appearance of the Son of Man. Jesus' teaching of what we might call "ethics" was advanced to show people how they could be ready.

At the same time, since the end represented an act of God to reclaim his creation for himself, Jesus understood that God was even now, in the present, ultimately sovereign over this world, notwithstanding the fact that the forces of evil had been unleashed against it. God was still, in the final analysis, in control, and could act, even in the present, on behalf of those who followed his will. Moreover, those who followed his will in the present—who would, then, inherit the Kingdom that was coming in the future—were in some sense practicing the ethics of the future Kindom. In that sense, they were experiencing a kind of foretaste of what life in the Kingdom would be like.

God's Care for His Children in the Present

The fact that God is sovereign over this world is what allows people the freedom to give themselves completely to others in preparation for the coming Kingdom. When Jesus says, "Seek first the Kingdom and all these things will be added to you" (Matt. 6:33; Luke 12:31), he is referring specifically to food and clothing: "Don't be concerned about your life, what you shall eat, nor about your body, what you should wear. For your life is more than food and your body more than clothing." And so, since God will provide what is needed to live in the present, people should give completely of what they have for others: "Sell what you own and give it away; make for yourselves wallets that don't grow old, a treasure that will never forsake you.... For where your treasure is, there also is your heart" (Q: Luke 12:22–34; Matt. 6:19–21, 25–34).

That is why, even in the present age, people can trust God as a good parent who will give his children what is necessary. All they need to do is ask, and they will receive it:

> Ask and it will be given to you, seek and you will find, knock and the door will be opened. For everyone who asks receives, and the one who seeks finds, and to the one who knocks it will be opened. For what father among you has a son who asks for a fish, and he gives him a serpent instead; or who asks for an egg, and he gives him a scorpion? If then you who are evil know to give good gifts to your children, how much more will your Father in heaven give good things to those who ask him? (Q: Matt. 7:7–11; Luke 11:9–13; cf. G.Thom. 2, 92, and 94).

Thus a central element of Jesus' teaching involved trust in God to give what is needed to his children. In particular, those who follow Jesus' words can trust that God will give them the Kingdom that is soon to come. But trust in God—or "faith," as it is usually translated—is related not just to the future but to the present as well. This can be seen in the multiply attested sayings about faith attributed to Jesus in our earliest sources. Thus, for example, when Jesus heals a person (see chapter 11), he indicates that "your faith has made you well" (Mark 5:34); he tells his would-be followers that everything is possible to the one who has faith (Mark 9:23); he tells his disciples that faith can (literally) move mountains (Mark 11:23); even faith the size of a tiny mustard seed is enough to uproot an enormous sycamore tree (Q: Matt. 17:20; Luke 17:6).

Those who anticipate God's act of judgment and salvation in the future can trust that he will care for them and do what they need now, even in the present evil age. And what is more, those who live lives of

faith and love (i.e., trusting God to bring the Kingdom and loving others as themselves in preparation) have already begun to experience a
bit of what that Kingdom will be like.

Growing into the Kingdom

Some of Jesus' best-known parables suggest that in some sense the
Kingdom is already being experienced in the present, leading some
scholars to make the mistake of thinking that there was nothing radically new to come in the future. That this is a misreading of these parables should be obvious by now. And it should be emphasized that even
these parables themselves stress the enormous difference between the
small and inauspicious experience of the Kingdom in the present and
the enormous and cataclysmic coming of the Kingdom in the future.

Most of these parables have to do, in one way or another, with illustrating this immense difference. For example, in a parable independently attested in Mark and Thomas, Jesus likens the Kingdom to a
mustard seed, that begins as a tiny seed (the "smallest on earth,"
according to Mark) but then becomes a huge shrub, large enough for
birds to nest in ("the greatest of all," Mark 4:30–32). Scholars have had
a field day with this parable, trying to make it mean all sorts of things.
Most recently in vogue is the view that since the mustard plant was
seen as a completely undesirable weed, the image was meant to shock
Jesus' hearers into realizing that the Kingdom wasn't at all what they
hoped for or wanted, but would be something completely unexpected.[4]
A clever reading, but not at all what the text itself emphasizes: in both
Mark and Thomas, the point is that something with a tiny beginning
has such a huge result. Jesus and his followers had not exactly taken the
world by storm! But when the Son of Man arrives, as they anticipate, a
storm will be the least of the world's problems. Thus the Kingdom was
like a mustard seed: a small beginning in Jesus' ministry, but an
immense outcome on the day of judgment.[5]

So, too, in the parable of the woman putting leaven in three batches
of dough (Q: Matt. 13:33; Luke 13:20). The leaven is hidden at first,
but it eventually permeates all three batches in their entirety. The
Kingdom of God is like that: inauspicious beginnings with enormous
consequences.

Other images are more directly horticultural. In our earliest source,
Mark, Jesus speaks of the kingdom as seed that someone sows on the
ground. The farmer doesn't really know how the seed grows, but it does:
"On its own, the ground brings forth fruit: first the blade, then the ear,
then the full grain in the ear." The parable ends with an ominous note
of judgment: "And when the fruit has become ripe, immediately the

farmer sends forth his sickle, because the harvest arrived" (Mark 4:26–29). The inauspicious sowing of the seed will lead to a time of harvest (not by human effort!), in which the good fruit will be saved and all else destroyed.

Finally, one of the most famous parables of all, found in both Mark (along with Matthew and Luke) and Thomas, the parable of the sower, whose seed falls on different kinds of ground: on the path, on rocky soil, among thorns, and—thank goodness—on good soil. Only the seed on good soil produces a crop, and what a crop it is! Not due to the efforts of the sower (who doesn't appear to have been overly scrupulous in where he sowed his precious seed), but to the mysterious workings of nature, the seed sown on the good soil brings forth a huge harvest, multiplying itself many times over (according to Mark, thirty-, sixty-, and a hundredfold; according to Thomas, sixty- and a hundred-twenty fold; Mark 4:26–29; G.Thom. 9).

The seed of God's coming Kingdom is being sown on the earth. Most of those who hear of its coming fail to act. They are like the beaten earth of a pathway, or rocky or thorny soil. But some who hear give up everything they have in order to prepare. And they indeed will bear fruit worthy of the coming harvest.

The Foretaste of the Kingdom

In what sense, though, is it true to say that those who heard Jesus' proclamation were already participating—even in a small and seemingly insignificant sense—in the Kingdom that would be brought in a major cataclysmic way by the appearance of the Son of Man? In what sense had the Kingdom already begun, if even in a feeble and largely unnoticed way, to make its appearance on earth?

It's important to remember what the coming Kingdom would bring. In the Kingdom the forces of evil would be eliminated. The demonic powers in control of this age would be overthrown. There would be no more death or war or disease or sin or oppression or injustice or hatred. And Jesus' followers who were preparing for the Kingdom had already begun to implement the ideals of the Kingdom in the present. Jesus himself had allegedly begun to overcome the forces of evil that would be annihilated in the imminent appearance of the Son of Man (as we'll see in the next chapter). In the Kingdom, there would be no more demonic powers; Jesus allegedly cast out the demons that haunted people and shattered their lives. In the Kingdom there would be no more disease; Jesus allegedly healed the sick. In the Kingdom there would be no more death; Jesus allegedly raised the dead. These were not simply acts of kindness. They were parables of the Kingdom.

In the Kingdom there would be no more war. Jesus' disciples were not to engage in acts of violence *now*. In the Kingdom there would be no more poverty. Jesus' disciples were to give away all they had and give to the poor *now*. In the Kingdom there would be no more oppression or injustice. Jesus' disciples were to treat all people equally and fairly *now*—even the lowest classes, the outcasts, the destitute; even women and children. In the Kingdom there would be no more hatred. Jesus' disciples were to be living examples of God's love *now*, giving of themselves completely in the service of others.

The ways Jesus' disciples were to live in the present in preparation for the coming Son of Man reflected life as it would be when the Kingdom fully arrived. They had not, obviously, yet begun to experience the Kingdom in its fullness. But they had experienced a foretaste of the glories that lay ahead, in a world in which there would be no demonic powers, disease, or death, a world in which no one would suffer from poverty or oppression, where no one engaged in acts of violence or malice, no one hurt another, hit another, or hated another. In a small way—a very small way—they had begun to see what it would be like when God once and for all established his Kingdom on earth.

No wonder that Jesus saw this coming Kingdom as good news and invited his hearers to join him in preparing for it, implementing its ideals in the present, seeking to turn others away from the anxieties and pains of this life in expectation of the new life that was coming. For Jesus, the news of the Kingdom was a bright light that couldn't be hid under a basket, a secure city that couldn't be obscured, built high on a hill (cf. Mark 4:21; Matt. 5:14–16; G.Thom. 33). Those who saw the light and beheld the city needed to abandon everything and take up the message, so that all might be prepared for what was soon to take place. These beginnings may have seemed inconsequential, but the harvest would be great, and there was need of many laborers (Q: Matt. 9:37; Luke 10:2; cf. John 4:35; G.Thom. 73). And Jesus himself was leading the charge into the fields.

eleven

not in word only:
the associates, deeds, and controversies
of jesus in apocalyptic context

WE HAVE SEEN THAT WORDS ARE ALWAYS BOUND TO CONTEXTS THAT HELP DETERMINE THEIR MEANING. CONTEXTS AFFECT NOT ONLY WORDS, BUT EVERYTHING WE SEE, DO, AND experience as well—every gesture, action, and activity, every natural event, every movement, every tactile substance. Everything has a context, and when you change the context, you change what it means.

What does it mean if you see a person avidly raising an arm straight over his head with index finger pointed upward? It depends. Is it a football fan celebrating in the end zone after the last game of the season, an excited Pentecostal convert at a tent revival, a terrified spectator at an aerial show, or a distressed first-grader in the back row, an hour after drinking too much orange juice for breakfast? Actions are intelligible only in context.

Not just Jesus' words, but also his deeds, experiences, and personal interactions were set in a context. We can't, of course, reconstruct his context in toto. But we can have a general idea about it, and that general idea is far better than nothing—better, for example, than thinking that something Jesus did can make sense *without* a context. In fact, when we examine the things Jesus is reputed to have done in light of the criteria we have already discussed, and consider the results in light of the apocalyptic context that we have already established, we find a very nice confluence between his sayings that we have already considered and his actions that we will consider now. I might add that some other historical reconstructions of Jesus falter on just this score, making it appear that what he said and what he did had no relationship to one another. But as it turns out, if we accept the evidence cited at some length earlier that Jesus was an apocalypticist, we can make good, coherent sense not just of his sayings, but also of his deeds and experiences.

Jesus' Baptism

As we have seen, our first solid information about Jesus as an adult comes in the traditions about his baptism. We don't know exactly how old he was at the time; only Luke claims that he was "about thirty" (Luke 3:23) and there's no way to track down his source of information. Still, if Jesus was in fact born during the reign of Herod the Great (as both Matthew and Luke attest), and if he was executed when Pilate was the prefect of Judea (26–36 CE), then he must have been at least in his thirties at the time of his baptism.

We have already seen that there is overwhelming evidence that Jesus was baptized by and became a follower of John the Baptist. The baptism itself is described in our earliest narrative, Mark, followed by the other Synoptics; it is alluded to independently by John (Mark 1:9–11; Matt. 3:13–17; Luke 3:21–22; John 1:29–34). The Q source gives a lengthy account of John's apocalyptic preaching, evidently at the very outset of its account of Jesus' teaching (see Luke 3:7–18; Matt. 3:7–12).

Moreover, throughout his teachings, Jesus refers back to his former leader, John. For example, in Q he asks the crowds who they thought John really was and states that John was the greatest man ever to live (Matt. 11:7–19; Luke 7:24–35; also G.Thom. 46); in Mark he confronts his opponents by asking them about John's authority: "Was the baptism of John from God or humans?" (Mark 11:30); and in the Fourth Gospel he claims that John testified to his own message (John 5:31–36). It's striking that Luke associates Jesus and John while both are still in their mothers' wombs (Luke 1:39–45—this is not multiply attested, of course, but it shows that the tradition of their association was very strong). Somewhat more plausibly, the Fourth Gospel explicitly shows that Jesus' own earliest followers were former disciples of John the Baptist (John 1:35–42; cf. Acts 1:21–22). This is a tradition that is supported, to some extent, by the independent account in the book of

Acts, which indicates that even long afterward some of John's followers became Christian followers of Jesus (Acts 19:1–7). It's interesting to note that, like John, Jesus' followers practiced baptism; at one point in the Fourth Gospel even Jesus himself is said to have gotten into the act (see John 3:22; 4:1–3).

We have seen that John was an apocalypticist. The fact that Jesus associated with him early on, prior to his own ministry, and then continued to speak of him with fondness later, shows that whatever their differences in emphasis—many interpreters have seen John more as a fiery preacher of repentance in the face of the terrible onslaught soon to come and Jesus more as a proclaimer of the good news that God will soon right the wrongs in the world for all those who practice his will by loving one another—the two saw eye to eye on the coming judgment of God and the need to prepare for it.

So the first thing to note about Jesus' activities is that he began by associating with and showing his devotion to an apocalyptic preacher of repentance, John the Baptist. With whom else did he associate, and how can one make sense of these associations in an apocalyptic context?

Jesus' Associates

Some of the best-attested traditions about Jesus are that he had a number of followers. Most of these followers appear to have been lower-class, illiterate peasants, not known for their scrupulous observance of the Law. Some of them were women and people of dubious moral reputation. Many appear to have been social outcasts—for example, the impoverished and diseased. If you're known by the company you keep, it's no wonder that the pious religious leaders and members of the Jewish aristocracy did not, as a rule, think much of Jesus. Still, these associations make sense, given Jesus' apocalyptic message. In the coming judgment, the first will be last and the last first. Most of his followers could hope to be at the very top of the new heap.

Jesus' Followers

The fact that Jesus sought people out to follow him—a somewhat unusual practice in the ancient world—is multiply attested in the tradition, with accounts of the call of his first disciples preserved in independent narratives of Mark (1:16–20; see Matt. 4:18–22), L (Luke 5:1–11; this is a different account from Mark and Matthew), and John (1:35–51). All of these accounts, despite their many differences, portray these first followers as lower-class fishermen, engaged in sea-to-hand-to-mouth operations. They evidently left their jobs behind (along with their houses and families, as we saw in chapter 10) to follow Jesus, ministering with him in expectation that the end would soon arrive and they would receive back many times over that which they had forsaken (see, e.g., Mark 10:28–31).

The Twelve

One of the best-attested traditions of our surviving sources is that Jesus chose twelve of his followers to form a kind of inner circle. It is interesting that all three Synoptics list the Twelve, but some of the names differ in Luke's list (Mark 3:14–19; Matt. 10:1–4; Luke 6:12–16). This may suggest that everyone knew that there were twelve of these people, but not everyone knew who they were. The "twelve" are also mentioned independently by Paul (1 Cor. 15:5), John (6:67; 20:24), and Acts (e.g., 6:2). Moreover, some of the traditions involving the Twelve pass the criterion of dissimilarity. For example, in the Q source Jesus says to his twelve disciple: that in the "age to come, when the Son of Man is seated upon his glorious throne, you also will sit upon twelve thrones judging the twelve tribes of Israel" (Matt. 19:28; cf. Luke 22:30). This is not a tradition that was likely to have been made up by a Christian later, after Jesus's death—since one of these twelve had abandoned his cause and betrayed him. No one thought that *Judas Iscariot* would be seated on a glorious throne as a ruler in the Kingdom of God. The saying, therefore, appears to go back to Jesus, and indicates, then, that he had twelve close disciples whom he predicted would reign in the coming Kingdom.

That final point should perhaps be emphasized. Why did Jesus choose *twelve* disciples? Why not nine, or fifteen? The selection of twelve was not, in fact, an arbitrary act. It wasn't that Jesus happened to like the number, or that he just picked the fellows he most wanted to hang around with. In view of the Q statement cited above, it appears that the twelve were chosen as a representative number with apocalyptic significance. Just as the nation of Israel whom God had called to be his people was originally comprised of twelve tribes, so too in the new age, when God once more ruled his people, they would again comprise twelve tribes. The twelve disciples represent the true Israel, the people of God who would enter into his glorious Kingdom when the Son of Man arrives. This would be a real kingdom, with real rulers; and they would be Jesus' close followers. Those who were obedient to his words would enter into this Kingdom. Jesus' choice of twelve disciples, in other words, was a symbolic action meant to convey a concrete lesson about the coming Kingdom.

Jesus evidently taught his disciples about their roles in the Kingdom (see, e.g., the Q quotation given above)—which may account for another firmly rooted tradition, that the message had gone to some of the disciples' heads. For they are occasionally depicted as arguing among themselves over which of them would be the greatest when the Kingdom arrived. Nothing like a vision of glory to raise a lower-class peasant into an egomaniacal, if imaginary, despot. The disputes are found explicitly in our earliest source (e.g., Mark 9:34; 10:35–37, 41). Moreover, they appear to lie implicitly behind Jesus' constant reminders to his disciples that only the least will become great, only the last will become first, only those like children will enter the Kingdom, only those who enslave themselves to others will rule over all. These were lessons that the future lords of the earth evidently needed to learn.

Jesus, the Wicked, and the Outcast

Jesus associated with others, of course, besides the Twelve. Best-attested are the "wicked" and "outcast" of various stripe. Unlike most upright religious leaders among the Jews of his day (and most upright Christians among his followers ever since!), Jesus chose to spend his time with people who were widely seen as beyond the pale. It is multiply attested all over the map, for example, that Jesus associated with "tax collectors and sinners" (Mark 2:15–16; Q [Matt. 11:19; Luke 7:29]; M [Matt. 21:31–32]; L [Luke 15:1]; see also Mark 2:13–17 and Luke 19:1–10). Moreover, this is not the sort of tradition—our Master particularly enjoyed the lowlifes and hookers—that later Christians would be likely to invent.

Who were these people? "Tax collectors" were probably employees of the large tax-collecting corporations that milked the Galilean population for tribute that would be paid to Rome for the upkeep of the country and the protection of its borders. When Galilee was ruled by a Jewish king in those days, he would pay the tribute to Rome directly; taxes that were collected, then, would come straight to him. It's never spelled out directly in our early traditions just *why* lower-level tax collectors were so widely despised (do *you* need to explain why you dread an IRS audit?). But scholars have made plausible guesses: such people may have been notoriously dishonest, greedy, and hard-nosed, collecting excessive funds with the threat of imperial force in order to line their own pockets, all in the service of a foreign power that had taken over the land that God had promised to the Jews themselves. Even if some individual tax collectors bucked the trend and were reasonably honest (not *every* American politician is a bald-faced liar), as a group they were widely despised as misanthropic and godless. The term "sinners," as I've mentioned earlier, did not designate a particular kind of sinner (e.g., "prostitutes"), but a general class of people who made little or no effort to do what God commanded in the Law of Moses.

These are the people—the despised and the irreligious—that Jesus appears to have associated with. How does one make sense of this? Did Jesus simply exercise poor judgment, as some of his opponents, and even his own followers, occasionally charged (see Mark 2:13–17 and Q, Matt. 11:19; Luke 7:24)? Did he prefer the dregs of society to the socially respectable? Or were his associations somehow related to his apocalyptic message?

Recall: the Kingdom is not coming for the high and mighty, but for the low and outcast ("tax collectors and prostitutes will go before you into the Kingdom of God," Matt. 21:31; cf. Luke 7:29–30). And Jesus did not see himself as needing to minister to the well, but to the sick (Mark 2:17).

Indeed, there were others besides those blanketed with the term "sinners" who appear constantly in Jesus' company. He befriends wild demoniacs whom no one else will come near (Mark 5:1–20). He converses with and touches outcast lepers (Mark 1:40–46; Luke 17:11–19). He speaks with and (favorably) about Samaritans (who were hated by many Jews as kind of illegitimate half-breeds and heretics; Luke 10:29–37; John 4:4–42). Here again, my point is not that every one of these stories is historically accurate on its own. But they all do point to the well-established tradition that Jesus associated with those who were viewed widely as "undesirables."

Jesus' Women Followers

Jesus associated with women and ministered to them in public. To be sure, his twelve closest disciples were almost certainly men, as one would expect of a first-century Jewish rabbi. It is largely for this reason that the principal characters in almost all of the Gospel traditions are men. But not all of them are. In fact, the importance of women for Jesus' ministry is multiply attested in our earliest traditions. Both Mark and L (Luke's special source), for example, indicate that Jesus was accompanied by women in his travels (Mark 15:40–41; Luke 8:1–3), a tradition corroborated by the Gospel of Thomas (G. Thom. 114). Mark and L also indicate that women provided Jesus with financial support during his ministry, evidently serving as his patrons (Mark 15:40–41; Luke 8:1–3). In both Mark and John, Jesus is said to have engaged in public dialogue and debate with women who were not among his immediate followers (John 4:1–42; Mark 7:24–30). Both Gospels also record, independently of one another, the tradition that Jesus had physical contact with a woman who anointed him with oil in public (Mark 14:3–9; John 12:1–8). In Mark's account this is an unnamed woman in the house of Simon, a leper; in John's account it is Mary the sister of Martha and Lazarus, in her own home.

In all four of the canonical Gospels, women are said to have accompanied Jesus from Galilee to Jerusalem during the last week of his life and to have been present at his crucifixion (Matt. 27:55; Mark 15:40–41; Luke 23:49; John 19:25). The earliest traditions in Mark suggest that they alone remained faithful to the end: all of his male disciples had fled. Finally, it is clear from the Synoptics, John, and the Gospel of Peter that women followers were the first to believe that Jesus' body was no longer in the tomb (Matt. 28:1–10; Mark 16:1–8; Luke 23:55–24:10; John 20:1–2; G. Pet. 50–57). These women were evidently the first to proclaim that Jesus had been raised.

There are other interesting traditions about Jesus' contact with women that do not pass the criterion of multiple attestation, including the memorable moment found only in Luke's Gospel when Jesus encourages his friend Mary in her decision to attend to his teaching rather than busy herself with "womanly" household duties (Luke 10:38–42).

What about the contextual credibility of these traditions? It is true that women were generally viewed as inferior to men in the ancient world. But there were exceptions: philosophical schools like the Epicureans and the Cynics, for example, advocated equality for women. Of course, there were not many Epicureans or Cynics in Jesus' immediate environment of Palestine, and our limited sources may suggest that women, as a rule, were generally even more restricted in that part of the empire with respect to their abilities to engage in social activities outside the home and away from the authority of their fathers or husbands. Is it credible, then, that a Jewish teacher would have encouraged and promoted such activities?

We have no solid evidence to suggest that other Jewish rabbis had women followers during Jesus' day. But we do know that the Pharisees were supported and protected by powerful women in the court of King Herod the Great. Unfortunately, the few sources that we have say little about women among the lower classes, who did not have the wealth or standing to make them independent of their fathers or husbands. One consideration that might make the traditions about Jesus' association with women credible, however, is the distinctive burden of his own apocalyptic message. Jesus proclaimed that God was going to intervene in history and bring about a reversal of fortunes. The last would be first and the first last. Those who were rich would be impoverished and the poor would be rich. Those who were exalted now would be humbled and the humble would be exalted. Jesus associated with the outcasts and downtrodden of society, evidently as an enactment of his proclamation that the Kingdom would belong to such as these. If women were generally looked down upon as inferior by the men who made the rules and ran the society, it does not seem implausible that Jesus would have associated freely with them, and that they would have been particularly intrigued by his proclamation of the coming Kingdom.

Some recent scholars have proposed that Jesus in fact did much more than this, that he preached a "radically egalitarian society"—that is, that he set about to reform society by inventing a new set of rules to govern social relations, creating a community in which men and women were to be treated as absolute equals.[1] This, however, may be taking the evidence too far and possibly in the wrong direction. For as we have seen, there is little to suggest that Jesus was concerned with pushing social "reform" in any fundamental way in this evil age. In his view, present-day society and all its conventions were soon to come to a screeching halt, when the Son of Man arrived from heaven in judgment on the earth. Far from transforming society from within, Jesus was preparing people for the destruction of society. Only when God's Kingdom arrived would an entirely new order appear, in which peace, equality, and justice would reign supreme. This Kingdom, though, would not arrive through the implementation of new social reform programs. It would arrive with a cosmic judge, the Son of Man, who would overthrow the evil and oppressive forces of this world.

To this extent (and, I would stress, *only* to this extent), even though Jesus may not have urged a social revolution in his time, his message had radically revolutionary implications. In particular, we should not forget that Jesus urged his followers to begin to implement the ideals of the Kingdom in the present in anticipation of the coming Son of Man. For this reason, there may indeed have been some form of equality practiced among the men and women who accompanied Jesus on his itinerant preaching ministry—not as the first step toward reforming society from the grass roots, but as a preparation for the new world that was soon to come, when the present age would be brought to its climactic end with the arrival of the Kingdom.

That, in fact, appears to be the message—often unspoken but sometimes stressed—behind all of Jesus' best-known associations. From the outside, Jesus may appear to be nonreligious and unclean, but in fact the people he befriended and taught represented the outcasts, the lowly, and the despised who would be rewarded when the Son of Man arrives, bringing with him judgment and a Kingdom, to be enjoyed by the unlikelies.

Jesus' Early Ministry in Galilee

Throughout our earliest surviving sources, it is quite clear that Jesus spent most of his ministry, if not virtually all of it, in the towns, villages, and rural areas of Galilee (in the northern part of what is now Israel). We don't know how long this ministry lasted. If you were simply to read Mark's Gospel, you would probably assume that it took just under a year, from the early summer when grain had become ripe enough to be eaten from the fields (2:23) until the Passover the following spring (14:12). John's Gospel, though, records three Passover feasts (2:13; 6:4; 11:55), so that here the ministry is assumed to have lasted somewhat over two years.

In any event, even if the dates aren't set in stone, some of the places are. We've seen that Jesus was raised in the small rural village of Nazareth. He appears to have spent nearly all of his time prior to his fateful trip at the end of his life to the big city (Jerusalem) in similar places—either out in the country itself or in villages and small towns (Mark 1:45; 3:7; 4:1; 6:6, 31; etc.). Even though there was a major city within easy walking distance of Nazareth—the much-discussed city of Sepphoris—it is never mentioned in any of our ancient Gospel records. This should perhaps give us pause when considering the widespread claim today among certain scholars (including a number of those associated with the "Jesus Seminar") that Jesus would have been intimately familiar with Greek philosophical traditions, especially those associated with the Cynics, from his many trips to Sepphoris. *What* trips to Sepphoris? Nor is Jesus ever said to have visited the other major city of the region, Tiberias. Jesus was a small-town-and-rural person. His followers, too, were drawn from such places.

Possibly because it was *so* small and unknown, or possibly because he was not well received there, Jesus did not use Nazareth as the base for his mission, but chose nearby Capernaum instead. This is attested throughout our sources, for example, Mark (1:21; 2:1; 9:33), M (Matt. 4:13), and John (2:12; 6:59). And it is not the sort of thing that later Christians would have had any clear reason to invent—that is, it passes the criterion of dissimilarity—especially since there *were* traditions that people in Capernaum, on the whole, did not take kindly to Jesus' message (Q: Matt. 11:23; Luke 10:15). Capernaum, like Jesus' hometown of Nazareth, was relatively small—archaeologists put its population at the time at around two thousand or less. But it had the advantage of being on the Sea of Galilee, so that to get around one could hop a boat as well as walk. It is from there that Jesus began to engage in an itinerant ministry throughout the region (see, e.g., Q: Matt. 8:20; Luke 9:58; 10:1; G.Thom., 14; etc.) visiting local synagogues on the Sabbath (e.g., Mark 1:21; 6:1–6; Matt. 4:23; John 6:59; etc.), teaching any who had the time and leisure to come to hear him speak on other days. Principally he taught Jews, according to almost all of our early sources, with such isolated exceptions as the Syrophoenician woman of Mark 7 and the Samaritan woman of John 4. He also reportedly performed amazing feats that kept the crowds coming.

Among other things, this basic sketch of Jesus' activities during his ministry shows yet again how thoroughly Jewish his mission and message were. He was speaking to Jews, often in their own synagogues about their own Scriptures. His own interpretations of these Scriptures caused some surprise, especially, as we'll see momentarily, among those who knew him when he was younger. When not offering interpretations of the Scriptures, he was teaching in parables, using, for example, agricultural and fishing imagery that these Galilean peasants could readily relate to (seeds, weeds, soils, harvests, sheep, shepherds, fish, fishnets, etc.). These teachings, as we have seen repeatedly, related to the coming end of the age.

Intimately connected with this message were the amazing feats that Jesus was widely reported to have done.

Jesus' Miraculous Deeds

Most of the accounts of Jesus' deeds involve the miraculous. Everywhere you turn in our Gospels he is healing the sick, casting out demons, raising the dead, multiplying the loaves, walking on the water, calming the storm, and so on. These miraculous deeds cause special problems for historians, but I want to address a general problem before trying to discuss any of the specifics.

A lot of modern people, of course, believe that miracles are strictly speaking impossible—that is, that they never happen—and that people who think they happen are either deluded or naive. For such people, there is no reason, by definition, to discuss Jesus' miracles, since if miracles don't happen, then Jesus didn't do any. This is sometimes called the "philosophical" problem of miracles.

I do *not* want to address this particular issue here. For the sake of the argument, I'm willing to grant that miracles—that is, events that we cannot explain within our concepts of how "nature" normally works—can and do happen. There still remains a huge, I'd even say insurmountable, problem when discussing Jesus' miracles. Even if miracles *are* possible, there is no way for the historian to show that they have ever happened.

I'll call this the "historical" problem of miracle. Let me explain the problem at some length.

An Interlude: The Historical Problem of Miracle

I'll begin by considering what people in the modern world mean when they use the term "miracle," in contrast to what people in antiquity meant by it.[2]

"Miracles" in the Modern World and in Antiquity

People today typically think of miracles as supernatural violations of natural law, divine interventions into the natural course of events. I should emphasize that this popular understanding does not fit particularly well into modern scientific understandings of "nature," in that scientists today are less confident in the entire category of natural "law" than they were, say, in the nineteenth century. For this reason, it is probably better not to speak of supernatural violations of "laws," but to think of miracles as events that contradict the normal workings of nature in such a way as to be virtually beyond belief and to require an acknowledgment that supernatural forces have been at work.

As we will see momentarily, this understanding is itself the major stumbling block for historians who want to talk about miracles, since the historian has no access to "supernatural forces" but only to the public record, that is, to events that can be observed and interpreted by any reasonable person, of whatever religious persuasion. If a "miracle" requires a belief in the supernatural realm, and historians by the very nature of their craft can speak only about events of the natural world, events that are accessible to observers of every kind, how can they ever certify that an event *outside* the natural order—that is, a miracle—occurred?

Before pursuing the question, I should point out that in the ancient world, "miracles" were *not* understood in the quasi-scientific terms that we use today, terms that have been available to us only since the advent of the natural sciences during the Enlightenment. Even in antiquity, of course, people understood that nature worked in certain ways. Everyone knew, for example, that iron ax heads would sink, and people would too, if they tried to walk on water in the middle of a lake. But in the ancient world, almost no one thought that this was because of some inviolable "laws" of nature, or even because of highly consistent "workings of nature" whose chances of being violated were infinitesimally remote. The question was not whether things happened in relatively fixed ways; the question was who had the power to do the things that happened.

For people in Greco-Roman times, the universe was made up of the material world, divine beings, humans, and animals, with everyone and everything having a place and a sphere of authority. A tree could not build a house, but a person could. A person could not make it rain, but a god could. A normal human being could not heal the sick with a word or a touch, or cast out an evil demon, or bring the dead back to life; but a divine human could, one who was in a special relation to the gods, like Jesus or some other holy man, of whom we know several by name. For such a person to heal the sick or raise the dead was not a miracle in the sense that it violated a "law"; it was "spectacular" in the sense that such things did not happen very often, since few people had the requisite power. And when they did happen, they were a marvel to behold.

This means that for most ancients the question was not whether miracles were possible. Spectacular deeds happened all the time—it was spectacular when the sun came up or the lightning struck or the crops put forth their fruit. It was also spectacular when a divine man healed the blind or cured the lame or raised the dead. These occurrences did not involve an intrusion from outside of the natural world into an established nexus of cause and effect that governs the way things work. For these people there *was* no "closed system" of cause and effect, a natural world that was set over against a supernatural realm. Thus, when spectacular deeds, which people today might call "miracles," occurred, the only questions for most ancient persons were (a) who was able to perform these deeds, and (b) what was the source of their power? Was a person like Jesus, for example, empowered by a god or by black magic?

To agree with an ancient person, therefore, that Jesus healed the sick, walked on water, cast out demons, or raised the dead is to agree first that there were divine men (or magicians) walking the earth who could do such things, and second that Jesus was one of them. In other words, from a historian's perspective, anyone who thinks that Jesus did these miracles has to be willing in principle to concede that other people did them as well, including the pagan holy man Apollonius of Tyana, the Roman emperor Vespasian, and the Jewish miracle worker

Hanina ben Dosa—all of whom were reputed to be miracle workers. The evidence that is admitted in any one of these cases must be admitted in the others as well.

But what evidence could there be? Here is where we get into our problem.

The Historian and Historical Method

One way to approach the question is by reflecting for a moment on the ways in which historians engage in their craft, in contrast, say, to the ways natural scientists engage in theirs. The natural sciences operate through repeated experimentation, as they seek to establish predictive probabilities based on past occurrences. To illustrate on the simplest level: suppose I wanted to "demonstrate" that a bar of iron will sink in a tub of lukewarm water, but a bar of Ivory soap will float. I could perform a relatively simple experiment by getting several hundred tubs of luke warm water, several hundred bars of iron, and several hundred bars of Ivory soap. By tossing the bars of iron and soap into the tubs of water, I could demonstrate beyond reasonable doubt that one will sink and the other will float, since the same result will occur in every instance. This does not necessarily prove that in the future every bar of iron thrown into a tub of lukewarm water will sink, but it does provide an extremely high level of what we might call presumptive probability. In common parlance, a "miracle" would involve a violation of this known working of nature: it would be a miracle, for example, if a preacher prayed over a bar of iron and thereby made it float.

The historical disciplines are not like the natural sciences, in part because they are concerned with establishing what has happened in the past, as opposed to predicting what will happen in the future, and in part because they cannot operate through repeated experimentation. An occurrence is a one-time proposition; once it has happened, it is over and done with. Since historians cannot repeat the past in order to establish what has probably happened, there will always be less certainty. It is much harder to convince people that John F. Kennedy was the victim of a lone assassin than to convince them that a bar of Ivory soap will float.

And the farther back you go in history, the harder it is to mount a convincing case. For events in the ancient world, even events of earth-shattering importance, there is sometimes scant evidence to go on. All the historian can do is establish what probably happened on the basis of whatever supporting evidence happens to survive.

This is what makes alleged miracles so problematic. On one level, of course, everything that happens is improbable. Suppose you were in a minor car accident last night. The chances of that happening were probably not very great, maybe even remote. But it's not so unlikely as to defy the imagination. And if fifteen years from now someone wanted to show that you did have that accident last night, they could appeal to certain kinds of evidence (newspaper articles, police reports, eyewitness accounts) and demonstrate their historical claim to most people's satisfaction. They could do this because there is nothing improbable about the event itself. People have accidents all the time, and the only issue would be whether you had one on the night in question.

What about events that do not happen all the time? As events that defy all probabilities, miracles create an inescapable dilemma for the historian. Since historians can only establish what probably did happen in the past, and the chances of a miracle happening, by definition, are infinitesimally remote, they can never demonstrate that a miracle *probably* happened.

This is not a problem for only one kind of historian—for atheists or agnostics or Buddhists or Roman Catholics or Baptists or Jews or Muslims; it is a problem for all historians of every stripe. Even if there are otherwise good sources for a miraculous event, the very nature of the historical discipline prevents the historian from arguing for its probability. Take a hypothetical example. Suppose that three otherwise credible eyewitnesses claimed to see Reverend Jones of the Plymouth Baptist Church walk across his parishioner's pond in 1926. The historian can certainly discuss what can be known about the case: who the eyewitnesses were, what they claimed they saw, what can be known about the body of water in question, and so forth. What the historian cannot claim, however, at least when discussing the matter as a historian, is that Reverend Jones actually did it. This is more than we can know, using the canons of historical knowledge. The problem of historical probabilities restrains our conclusion. The fact is that we all know several thousand people, none of whom can walk across pools of water, but all of whom at one time or another have been mistaken about what they thought they saw, or have been misquoted, or have exaggerated, or have flat out lied. To be sure, such activities may not be probable, especially for the upstanding members of the Plymouth Baptist Church. But they would be more probable than a miracle that defies the normal workings of nature. Thus if we as historians can only say what probably happened, we cannot say—as historians—that the good Reverend probably performed a miracle.

I should emphasize that historians do not have to deny the possibility of miracles or deny that miracles have actually happened in the past. Many historians, for example, committed Christians and observant

Jews and practicing Muslims, believe that they have in fact happened. When they think or say this, however, they do so not in the capacity of the historian, but in the capacity of the believer. In the present discussion, I am not taking the position of the believer, nor am I saying that one should or should not take such a position. I am taking the position of the historian, who on the basis of a limited number of problematic sources has to determine to the best of his or her ability what the historical Jesus actually did. As a result, when reconstructing Jesus' activities, I will not be able to affirm or deny the miracles that he is reported to have done.

Jesus' Reputation as an Exorcist

There can be little doubt that whether or not there exist supernatural evil spirits that invade human bodies to make them do all sorts of vile and harmful things, Jesus was widely thought to be able to cast them out, restoring a person to health. Scholars who believe in demons, of course, may well think that Jesus actually did exorcise them. Scholars who don't believe in them have come up with their own explanations—for example, that these were all psychosomatic illnesses, or that they represent internalized conflicts created through a sense of personal helplessness in the face of Roman colonialization of the land.3 And indeed, there have been some very interesting cross-cultural studies of demon possession and exorcism in our own time that lend support to one or another of these views.4 In my judgment, though, it is not really possible to know exactly what happened. As I've pointed out, the historian cannot say that demons—real live supernatural spirits that invade human bodies—were actually cast out of people, because to do so would be to transcend the boundaries imposed on the historian by the historical method, in that it would require a religious belief system involving a supernatural realm outside of the historian's province. But we *can* say that Jesus was widely recognized by people of his own time—who *did* believe that demons existed and could be exorcised—to have the powers to do just this.

In fact, Jesus' exorcisms are among the best-attested deeds of the Gospel traditions. Individual accounts are scattered throughout the first part of Mark (1:21–28; 5:1–20; 7:24–30; 9:14–29); in M (Matt. 9:32–34; cf. Luke 11:14—this may be Q); and L (Luke 13:10–14; cf. 8:2). Moreover, the sources themselves consistently summarize Jesus' activities as involving exorcisms (e.g., Mark 1:32–34, 39; 3:9–12; see also Acts 10:38), and the theme that Jesus could and did cast out demons is documented in multiply attested forms throughout the sayings materials, for example, Mark, Q, and L (Mark 3:22; Matt.

12:27–28; Luke 11:15, 19–20; 13:32). Such traditions cannot pass the criterion of dissimilarity, of course, since Christians who thought that Jesus had overcome the powers of evil might well have wanted to tell stories to show that he did. But they are contextually credible, to the extent that we know of other persons, both pagan and Jewish, who were said to have had power over demons, including, for example, the great pagan holy man, Apollonius of Tyana, who lived a bit later in the first century (see also Mark 9:38).

In sum, without making a faith claim, historians can't say that Jesus actually cast evil spirits out of people. But we can say that he probably did have some pretty amazing encounters with people believed to be demon-possessed, and that his ability to cast the demons out was seen as a characteristic aspect of his ministry. Moreover, the controversy over him was not about whether he had this ability but whether he had this power from God or the devil. As reported in our earliest surviving Gospel:

> And the scribes who came down from Jerusalem were saying that "He has Beelzebub, and by the ruler of the demons he casts out demons" (Mark 3:22).

Jesus' response to the charge is telling, especially in the version preserved in the Q source:

> If I cast demons out by Beelzebub, by whom do your sons cast them out?... But if I cast demons out by the spirit of God, behold the Kingdom of God is come upon you. Or how is anyone able to enter into the house of a strong man and steal his property, if he does not first bind the strong man? Only then can he plunder his house (Matt. 12:27–30; cf. Luke 11:19–23).

Note that everyone—Jesus and his opponents together—admits not only that Jesus can cast out demons, but that other Jewish exorcists can do so as well. Moreover, for Jesus, casting out demons signified the conquest over the forces of evil (the "strong man," in this case, would represent the main power opposed to God, Satan). And most important, Jesus' exorcisms are interpreted apocalyptically. They show that the Kingdom of God was at the doorstep. Just as Jesus' followers had begun to experience the life of the Kingdom by following his teachings, so too they understood that he himself had begun to manifest God's power in the present over the forces of evil, which would be completely destroyed at the coming of the Son of Man. Strikingly, this apocalyptic view is the earliest understanding of the widespread tradition that Jesus could cast out demons.

Jesus' Reputation as a Healer

Much the same can be said about Jesus' reputation as a healer. On numerous layers of our traditions Jesus is said to have healed those with various ailments—fever, leprosy, paralysis, hemorrhaging, lameness, blindness, and so on—and even to have raised some who had already died (see Mark 5:35–43 and John 11:38–44). Whatever you think about the philosophical possibility of miracles, it's clear that Jesus was widely reputed to have done them.

Let me add that he was also known to have performed other miracles not associated with healing physical ailments, though dealing still with the "natural" world—for example, multiplying the loaves, walking on water, stilling the storm. Such miracles, too, are attested in multiple sources. Like the exorcisms, they cannot, of course, pass the criterion of dissimilarity.

They are contextually credible to the extent that there were other persons from the ancient world—lots of them, in fact—who were also known to be able to do some fairly miraculous things, either through prayer—as in the case of some other Galilean Jews from about that time, such as Hanina ben Dosa and Honi the circledrawer, who were reputed to have had God's ear about matters of particular concern—or directly because of their own holiness, for example, Apollonius of Tyana. It may be worth noting that many of the healing and nature miracles of Jesus in fact are closely related to miracles described in the Hebrew Bible of other Jewish prophets, and invariably, Jesus comes off looking even better than his prophetic predecessors. The prophet Elijah, for example, had to engage in some real personal theatrics to raise a child from the dead (1 Kings 17:17–24); Jesus could do it with just a word (Mark 5:35–43). Elijah's successor, Elisha, allegedly fed a hundred people with just twenty barley loaves (2 Kings 4:42–44); Jesus fed over five thousand (not counting the women and children!) with just five (Mark 6:30–44). Elisha was able to make an ax head float on the water (2 Kings 6:1–7); Jesus could *himself* walk on the water (Mark 6:45–52).[5]

Interestingly enough, these activities were not taken in our earliest sources to be signs that Jesus was himself God. They were the sorts of things that Jewish prophets did. Jesus simply did them better than anyone else. Moreover, the earliest traditions again assign an apocalyptic meaning to these acts. Recall: in the Kingdom there would be no more disease or death. Jesus healed the sick and raised the dead. In a small way, then, the Kingdom was already becoming manifest. And there was not much time before the end finally arrived. According to an account in Q, when John the Baptist wanted to know whether to expect another one to come or whether Jesus was himself the final prophet before the end, Jesus reportedly replied:

> Tell John the things you have seen and heard: the blind are regaining their sight, the lame are starting to walk, the lepers are being cleansed, the deaf are starting to hear, the dead are being raised, and the poor are hearing the good news! (Luke 7:22; Matt. 11:4–5).

The end has come, and the Son of Man is soon to appear in the climactic act of history, after which there will never again be any who are blind, lame, leprous, deaf, or poor. Jesus represented the final prophet before the end, who was already overcoming the forces of evil in the world.

The Reception of Jesus

You would think that Jesus would have been one popular fellow. Someone who could cast out demons, heal the sick, and raise the dead would be handy to have around in a pinch. Remarkably though—really, this is one of the most remarkable things about our earliest accounts—the traditions about Jesus are quite unified that he was not at all well received. Even though some of his followers were completely devoted to him, and in fact had great hopes for him, he was rejected by the vast majority of the people who heard of him or saw him in person and squarely opposed by the religious leaders of his own people.

Widespread Rejection

There is no doubt that Jesus' closest followers were firmly committed to him—at least until the end, when one of them betrayed him and all the others abandoned him, possibly for fear of their own lives. At this stage of our discussion, though, I want to stress the flip side of the coin. The devotion of his closest followers notwithstanding, throughout his public ministry Jesus was regularly and consistently subjected to rejection and scorn. He was rejected by his own family, by people living in his hometown, by those living in other villages and towns throughout Galilee, by the Jewish crowds, by the Jewish religious leaders, by the Jerusalem aristocracy, and eventually, of course, by the Roman overlords.

For those who know about the annunciation story in the Gospel of Luke (where the angel Gabriel informs Mary who her son will be) it may seem odd that Jesus was rejected by his own family. But the theme is attested in multiple and independent traditions, and is not the sort of thing later Christians would be likely to make up. That is, it passes our criteria. Early in his ministry, according to our first account, his family tried to seize him from the public eye because they thought he had gone mad (Mark 3:21); he in turn spurned them when they came to see him (Mark 3:31–35). His brothers are said in a later source not to have believed in him (John 7:5), and it is striking that he had no relatives among his closest followers. Paul may imply that it was only after his resurrection that Jesus' brother James became a believer (1 Cor. 15:7). It is difficult to know what his mother actually thought about him; it is only in our latest Gospel, John, that she is said to be with him until the end, although the book of Acts indicates that she was one of the early believers immediately after the resurrection (John 19:25–27; Acts 1:14).

Jesus was clearly rejected in his own hometown in Nazareth, as shown not only by the rejection scene recorded in Mark 6:1–6 (cf. Matt. 13:53–58) and amplified by independent traditions in Luke 4:16–30, but even more by his widely attested saying that "a prophet is not without honor except in his own country" (Mark 6:4; John 4:44; "in his own village," G.Thom. 31). In the earliest form of the saying, Jesus indicates that the prophet is also dishonored "among his own relatives and in his own house," suggesting yet again that he was not well received in the Joseph and Mary household.

It is clear from the Q materials (which are early and here pass the criterion of dissimilarity), that other towns and villages of Galilee rejected Jesus:

> Woe to you Chorazin, woe to you Bethsaida. For if the great deeds that have been done among you had been done in Tyre and Sidon, they would have repented long ago and sat in sackcloth and ashes. But it will be more tolerable for Tyre and Sidon in the day of judgment than for you. And you Capernaum, you will not be exalted up to heaven will you? No, you will descend into hell (Luke 10:13–15; Matt. 11:20–24).

It is worth observing that Jesus' response to his own rejection is couched in such clear apocalyptic terms of judgment, condemnation, and destruction.

There are indications throughout our traditions that Jesus was by and large rejected more generally by most of the people who either heard him or heard of him. Not only in his own town and the surrounding areas, but also in a place like Gergesa on the other side of the Sea of Galilee, he is clearly not welcomed, at least according to our earliest

Gospel (Mark 5:17). This would make sense of (a) Jesus' multiply attested lament that even though foxes and birds have places to stay, he has nowhere (Matt. 8:20; Luke 9:58); (b) the implication of many of his parables that the *reason* the Kingdom has such a small and inauspicious beginning is that most of his proclamation is falling on deaf ears (e.g., the parable of the sower: Mark 4:1–9; G.Thom. 9); and (c) his claims, in a completely independent source, that he is "hated by the world" (John 15:18). As we'll see, this rejection by the crowds who heard him becomes nearly complete during his final days.

Above all, of course, Jesus was rejected by the religious leaders of his own people. At the end of his life, as we'll see, it was his rejection by the aristocracy that ran the Temple—the Sadducees and the chief priests—that ultimately led to his execution by the Romans. During his itinerant ministry in Galilee, though, Jesus did not much concern himself or tangle with the priests in far-off Jerusalem. Most of his controversies were with local Jewish authorities, including the Pharisees and the experts in the Law known as scribes, who thought that his teachings were wrong, that he misunderstood what God wanted, that he and his followers profaned the Law, and that, as a result, his powerful deeds could not come from God but were from the devil.

Controversies with the Pharisees

I should emphasize that the controversies Jesus had with other Jewish teachers were *not* over whether the Law of God should be followed. Everyone agreed on that. Jesus and his disciples kept Jewish customs, observed Jewish festivals, and followed the Jewish Law. The disputes instead were over the proper interpretation of the Law. These were internal Jewish debates, no more harsh or vitriolic than those going on between other Jewish groups, for example, between the Essenes and the Pharisees.

Some of Jesus' disagreements with Pharisees involved moral decisions that a person had to make (many of which continue to be debated by religious persons today) based on some rather incomplete instructions given in the Law or involving matters not directly mentioned in the Law. As an example of the former: the Law made provision for a man divorcing his wife (cf. Deut. 24:1–4). Even among the Pharisees there were disputes concerning legitimate grounds for divorce; Jesus himself, taking a fairly radical stand, insisted that the legal grounds provided by Moses were simply a makeshift measure and that God preferred people never to divorce.[6] As an example of the latter: Should one support a corrupt civil government? For Jesus, since the end of the present order was imminent, taxes were a matter of indifference: "Render unto Caesar the things that belong to Caesar" (i.e., the money Caesar minted that bore his own impression; Mark 12:13–17; G.Thom. 100). Such principles were widely debated among different Jewish leaders.

More vitriolic were the disputes Jesus had with Pharisees over the proper interpretation of laws that both sides agreed were given by God and were to be followed. I won't give a complete inventory here, but briefly mention just two: the laws about Sabbath and tithing. Even today, readers of the New Testament, including some scholars committed to examining the question, often think that Jesus violated the Mosaic proscription of work on the Sabbath and urged his followers not to keep the Sabbath. It's true, of course, that his Pharisaic opponents *charged* Jesus with breaking Sabbath. But in fact it's difficult to find any place in the Gospel traditions where Jesus actually does anything in violation of the Sabbath laws found in the Hebrew Scriptures themselves. In nearly every instance that Pharisees accuse him of breaking Sabbath, Jesus has broken *their interpretation* of the Sabbath laws—for example, by healing on the Sabbath or allowing his disciples to pluck some grain to eat on the Sabbath. But healing on the Sabbath is nowhere forbidden in the Law itself, and Jesus himself is not said to have plucked grain on the Sabbath. For Jesus, there is in fact an overarching principle that determines what is appropriate to do on the Sabbath: "Sabbath was made for humans, not humans for the Sabbath" (Mark 2:27). In other words, the Sabbath is a great good—it's a much needed day to rest from other weekly activities. But it is not to pose an inordinate burden on anyone. And since the Law of God is meant to help, not hurt humans, then it is always right to do what helps, not what hurts, others on the Sabbath (Mark 3:4).

To some extent the Pharisees agreed with this judgment. We know, for example, that Pharisees judged that if a farmer had an animal that fell into a pit in the Sabbath, it was all right to pull it out (in contrast, the Essenes claimed that this ruling was far too lax, as known now from the Dead Sea Scrolls).[7] Jesus himself alludes to the Pharisaic view in both Q (Luke 14:5; Matt. 12:11) and L (Luke 13:15), but takes it a step further: humans are worth more to God than animals, and so it's perfectly acceptable to do something that might benefit someone on the Sabbath. Moreover, it is multiply attested that Jesus cited biblical precedent for such views, pointing out that even in the Hebrew Bible God extends his approbation of certain activities on the Sabbath (Mark 2:25–26; John 7:22–23). And so, it would be a mistake to think that Jesus abrogated the laws about the Sabbath: he kept the Sabbath day himself and interpreted the laws about Sabbath in view of his overarching notion of what God ultimately wanted, which was for people to live completely for the sake of others. Any interpretation of the Law that violated that principle was automatically ruled out of court. What put the Pharisees at odds with Jesus—just as it put them at odds with the Essenes and others—was how the Law was to be interpreted, not whether it should be kept.

Consider a second example, already mentioned in chapter 10: tithing. In Jesus' words on the Pharisaic practice of tithing he does not condemn the idea of giving 10 percent of all produce *purchased* as well as *grown* to God. He simply thinks that this policy—devised in order to guarantee that the Mosaic laws of tithing be applied to all produce that an upright person had to do with—is of less importance than what he calls "the weightier matters of the law." Anyone insisting that what really mattered was the amount of mint and cumin God had been offered was completely missing the point. What God wanted was a people committed to loving him above all else and loving their neighbors as themselves (Q: Matt. 23:23; Luke 11:42).

It may be that at times Jesus pushed his emphasis on love to such an extreme that it seemed to others that he discounted the Law. In some parts of the tradition, for example, he seems to spurn some of the laws of purity that are so central to the Hebrew Bible. At one point, for example, he denies the necessity of the Pharisaic practice of washing one's hands before a meal. This kind of ritual washing was done not to get rid of germs—these people didn't know about germs—but to become "ritually clean" before God. In our earliest tradition about the matter, though, Jesus says: "There is nothing outside a person that can bring defilement by entering into him; but it is the things that are outside of a person that bring defilement" (Mark 7:16). In Mark's account, Jesus is then said to explain:

> Nothing that enters into a person from the outside can defile the person because it doesn't enter into his heart but into his stomach and then into the toilet.... It is what goes out from a person that defiles him, evil thoughts, sexual perversions, thefts, murders, adulteries, illicit longings, evil deads, deceit, wild living, evil glances, blasphemy, pride, foolishness. All these evil things proceed out of a person and bring defilement (Mark 7:19–23; cf. G.Thom. 14).

Some people—even those who passed along the traditions—understood Jesus to mean that it didn't matter what kind of food a person ate, so that, for example, there was no reason to keep the kosher food laws of the Hebrew Bible. Indeed, this is the interpretation given by the author of Mark himself, who adds a parenthetical comment indicating that Jesus, by saying this, "declared that all foods were clean" (Mark 7:19). This, though, would be an odd thing for a Jewish teacher to proclaim—that the Jewish Law is no longer valid. And there are reasons for thinking that this is simply the interpretation given later, *after* Jesus' day, especially to Gentiles in the Christian congregations. In context, Jesus himself is not abrogating the Mosaic food laws, but denying the need to wash hands before eating. Cleansing the outside (the hands) isn't really going to make clean the inside (the person). And what matters is what is within.

Thus, following narrow and clear-cut prescriptions about how to keep Sabbath, what to tithe, and how to eat is not really what matters before God. Anyone who keeps the Sabbath, tithes the produce, and washes the hands, but then commits murder or adultery, or deceives or slanders another, or exalts oneself over or oppresses others, has completely missed out on what God wants. The Pharisees, in other words, have emphasized the wrong things. In Jesus' words from Matthew, they "strain out the gnat but swallow the camel" (Matt. 23:24).

It's clear that harsh rhetoric between Jesus and the Pharisees cut both ways. That is to say, not only was Jesus the object of attack by Jewish teachers who objected to his interpretations; he himself also went on the attack. This is evidenced in multiple traditions scattered throughout all of our earliest sources, where Jesus calls some of his opponents "blind leaders of the blind" (Q: Matt. 15:14; Luke 6:39; G.Thom. 34), insisting that they are intent simply to draw attention to themselves. And we know what Jesus thinks of those who exalt themselves (see Mark 12:38–40; Matt. 23:5; Luke 11:43; 20:45–47). Elsewhere he claims that they place people under heavy demands that they cannot (or at least do not) meet themselves (Q: Matt. 23:4; Luke 11:46). And he insists that their rules are in fact a hindrance to those who want to do God's will (Q: Matt. 23:13; Luke11:52; G.Thom. 39, 102), warning that they will be subject to the wrath of God when the day of judgment arrives (Mark 12:40; Matt. 23:12, 33, 36).

I should reemphasize in conclusion that these heated disagreements with the Pharisees were not particularly out of place in Jesus' world of first-century Palestinian Judaism. There were lots of internal disputes among Jewish teachers—sometimes teachers within the same party (though these tended to be not quite so heated)—as Essenes vehemently disagreed with Sadducees and Pharisees, Sadducees with advocates of the violent "fourth philosophy" mentioned by Josephus, the prophetic followers of John the Baptist with the proponents of the status quo among the scribes, and so on. It was *not*, as is sometimes thought among Christian readers, a case of Jesus against everyone else.

There were lots of views that all contended with one another, each group insisting that it was right and that the others were, tragically, wrong.

Moreover, it was not these legal disputes with the Pharisees that ultimately led to Jesus' execution. As I mentioned at an earlier stage in chapter 7, the Pharisees were not the power players in Jesus' day. Though they may have been widely respected for their great piety (even this is somewhat hard to establish on the basis of the surviving evidence) they had no political clout, civil authority, or legislative jurisdiction. Their disputes with Jesus could not, in themselves, have led to his crucifixion, any more than your own local Baptist preacher's firm and outspoken disdain of the Jesuit priest across town can lead to his arrest and imprisonment today. It is striking that when Jesus went to Jerusalem, it was not the Pharisees who had him arrested and who bore witness against him at his trial. It was the Sadducees and chief priests. It was only when Jesus left the familiar rural environs of his childhood and took his apocalyptic message of the coming judgment of God to the capital city of Jerusalem that he aroused the opposition of those who were powerful enough to silence him. Once he offended them by proclaiming that they, too, would face God's coming wrath, his own days became numbered.

twelve

the last days of jesus

TO UNDERSTAND THE DEATH OF SOCRATES, IT'S NOT
ENOUGH TO KNOW THAT HE DRANK HEMLOCK IN HIS PRISON
CELL WHILE TALKING TO A GROUP OF HIS ADMIRERS. YOU NEED TO KNOW
something about the social and political situation in Athens and about
Socrates' teachings—both those that his enemies found dangerous and
those that enabled him to take his own life philosophically and cheer-
fully, with a clever witticism on his lips before breathing his last. To
understand the death of Martin Luther King Jr., it's not enough to know
that he was shot on the balcony of a motel in Memphis. You need to
know something about the social and political turmoil in the United
States during the Civil Rights Movement and about his message, which
inspired his followers and terrified his enemies. To understand the
death of Jesus, it's not enough to know that he was flogged and then
crucified outside the walls of Jerusalem. You need to know something
about the social and political world of first-century Palestine and about
the message that he delivered, a message that brought hope of deliverance to the powerless but a fear of uprising to the powerful.

It is not that the people in power actually feared that Jesus' words
would come true. They were by no means quaking in their sandals at
the thought that the Son of Man might arrive soon and destroy their
government, their institutions, their base of power, and their very lives.
But they did know what rabble-rousers like Jesus could do to a crowd,

and keeping the peace sometimes meant resorting to violence. In this case it was, all things considered, a rather limited act of violence. They had the preacher of this incendiary message of the imminent end of the age nailed to a cross, to silence his message forever. Or so they thought.

The link between Jesus' message and his death is crucial, and historical studies of Jesus' life can be evaluated according to how well they establish that link. This in fact is a common weakness in many portrayals of the historical Jesus: they often sound completely plausible in their reconstruction of what Jesus said and did, but they can't make sense of his death. If, for example, Jesus is to be understood as a Jewish rabbi who simply taught that everyone should love God and be good to one another, why did the Romans crucify him? It wasn't a crime to teach love and kindness. Or if Jesus was mainly interested in opposing the materialistic world that he found himself in, urging his followers to give up their possessions to live simple, natural lives, apart from the trappings of society, why would he have been sentenced to death? It wasn't a capital offense to share your goods with others.

Sometimes scholars do try to make connections between their reconstructions of Jesus' life (e.g., as a loving rabbi or a countercultural Cynic) and his death, and these proposed connections need to be looked at carefully. Often they are rather tenuous. Let me explain in a nutshell, here at the outset, what I think the connection is between the apocalyptic message and mission of Jesus and his execution by the Romans. The rest of this chapter will go into more of the details.

At the end of his life Jesus brought his apocalyptic message of the coming judgment to Jerusalem. This judgment, he declared, would be inflicted by the Son of Man, who would destroy all those opposed to God and bring in the Kingdom. This would be a Kingdom for the poor and oppressed, as well as for all who heard Jesus' message and turned completely to God, determining in their hearts to love God above all else and to love their neighbors as themselves. Those who refused to accept this message were to be condemned—even if they, like the Pharisees, followed the Torah of God to the "t," or maintained the purity regulations of the Essenes, or remained faithful to the sacrificial cult of the Temple promoted by the Sadducees. In fact, religious leaders among these various groups, and the institutions they represented, would be destroyed at the coming of the Son of Man. So, too, would the Temple itself.

Jesus not only preached this message upon arriving in Jerusalem, he acted it out, entering the Temple and engaging in a kind of symbolic action of destruction as a warning of what was to come, overturning some tables and causing a mild ruckus. This public display and its accompanying message angered some of the chief priests on the scene, who recognized how explosive the situation could become during the Passover, given the tendency of the celebration to become a silent protest that could always erupt into something far worse, as we saw in chapter 7. Fearing a possible uprising, the priests conferred with one another, had Jesus arrested, and questioned him about his words against the Temple. Realizing that it would be dangerous to let him run loose, they decided to have him taken out of the way. They could not handle the matter themselves, however, because the Romans did not allow Jewish authorities to execute criminals. And so they delivered him over to Pilate, who had no qualms at all about disposing of yet one more troublemaker who might cause a major disturbance. Jesus was then executed by the Romans on political charges. We will see what these charges were, along with other details of these various points that I've just raised, in the more thorough sketch that follows.

For such information about Jesus' last days we are better informed than for any other period of his life. This is because for the Gospel writers, his life was by and large seen as a preparation for his death. These authors were, after all, Christians, producing their accounts several decades later, after the church had spread its message of salvation throughout the major urban areas of the Roman Empire and had developed its theological understanding of the meaning of Jesus. His life itself was, to be sure, important. The Gospels do, after all, recount the spectacular things Jesus did and the inspiring teachings he delivered. But the focus of these earliest surviving accounts is instead on Jesus' last days. Mark devotes five of his sixteen chapters to Jesus' last days, and John devotes ten out of twenty-one. It's no stretch to say that the Gospels are principally concerned about Jesus' Passion, that is, the accounts of his suffering and death, or, as some scholars have put it, that the Gospels are Passion narratives with long introductions.

The Trip to Jerusalem

Jesus spent most, if not all, of his adult life in the rural towns and villages of Galilee. But his life ended in the city of Jerusalem, the capital of Judea, during an annual Passover feast. This is the unified testimony of all our early sources.

It's not clear why, exactly, Jesus went with his disciples to Jerusalem. A theologian, of course, might say that it was in order to die for the sins of the world. This view, though, is based on Gospel sayings (such as Jesus' predictions of his own Passion in Mark 8:31; 9:31; 10:33–34) that cannot pass the criterion of dissimilarity, in that they portray Jesus as being fully cognizant of the details of his own fate. From a strictly historical perspective—that is, restricting ourselves to what we can show on historical grounds—perhaps we should recall what we saw in chapter 7, that Passover was a popular festival and that the size of Jerusalem swelled during its celebration. It may be, then, that Jesus went to Jerusalem, like so many thousands of other Jews at the time, simply in order to celebrate the Passover feast.

On the other hand, Jesus' actions in Jerusalem appear to have been well thought-out. When he arrived, he entered the Temple and caused a disturbance. He then evidently spent several days, in the Temple, teaching his message of the coming Kingdom. Given Jesus' understanding that this Kingdom was imminent and the urgency with which he taught others that they needed to repent in preparation for it, perhaps it is best to conclude that he went to Jerusalem precisely in order to proclaim this message in the heart of Israel itself—in the Temple on Passover, when faithful Jews from around the world would be gathered to worship the God who saved them from their oppressors in the past and who was expected to do so once more. If so, then Jesus came to the Temple to tell his people how this salvation would occur and to urge them to prepare for it by repenting of their sins and accepting his teachings. For this salvation also involved judgment and massive destruction, including the destruction of the Temple.

The Gospels indicate that Jesus entered Jerusalem in a particularly spectacular fashion, riding a donkey to the shouts of acclamation of the crowds, in fulfilment of a prophecy of Hebrew Scripture about the coming Messiah: "Tell the daughter of Zion, Look, your king is coming to you humble, and mounted on a donkey, and on a colt, the foal of a donkey" (see Isa. 62:11; Zech. 9:9, cited in Matt. 21:5).[1]

Even though this account is multiply attested (see Mark 11:1–10; John 12:12–19), it is very difficult to accept it as historically accurate. The days before Passover were a tense and potentially dangerous time in the view of the Roman authorities. This was the one time of the year that the Roman governor, who normally stayed in Caesarea on the coast, would come to the capital with troops in tow in order to quell any possible uprisings. If Jesus actually entered the city with such fanfare, crowds shouting their support for him as their new ruler, the king who fulfills the prophecies (who would, therefore, need to overthrow the present ruler and his armies!), it's nearly impossible to understand why he wasn't arrested and taken out of the way immediately.

Probably the most we can say is that Jesus actually did enter Jerusalem (!), that he was one of the pilgrims coming for the feast, and that he may well have entered on a donkey. Possibly others in the crowds along the roads into town preferred not to walk as well. Moreover, it's possible that at a later time, looking back on his last days, Jesus' disciples read more into the donkey than was originally there.

It is also possible, of course, that some of the crowds in Jerusalem had already heard about Jesus' teachings and remarkable deeds and, when he came to the city, wondered aloud if this could be the Messiah. There would have been nothing extraordinary about some such speculation. We know of other Jews both before Jesus' day and afterward who were thought by some to be the future ruler of Israel. And we know what typically happened to such potential threats to the Roman authorities. They were normally executed.[2]

The Temple Incident

We are on more solid ground when determining what Jesus did once he arrived in Jerusalem. Like many pilgrims for the Passover, he appears to have arrived a week before the feast. According to the Hebrew Bible, a person needed to be ritually cleansed from any contact with dead bodies before celebrating the feast. This purification required a week, and was normally performed in Jerusalem (see Num. 9, 19). For most people, this may have been a welcome requirement: it guaranteed a bit more of a vacation in the big city. Jesus, though, had somewhat more serious plans.

Upon his arrival, Jesus entered the Temple and caused a disturbance. According to our earliest source, Mark, he drove out people who were buying and selling in the Temple, he overturned the tables of those who were exchanging money and the seats of those who were selling sacrificial animals, and he would not allow anyone to carry anything through the Temple (Mark 11:15). According to John, who places the event at the beginning of Jesus' ministry instead of its end, he did this with a whip of cords (John 2:15). In both places his violent acts were matched by his "fightin' words":

Is it not written, "My house will be called a house of prayer for all the nations"? But you have made it into a den of thieves! (Mark 11:17).

Take these things away! Don't make my Father's house a place of business!" (John 2:16).

To help unpack these accounts, I should perhaps give a bit of background. I have already discussed the grandeur of the Jerusalem Temple and the importance of its sacrificial cult for Jewish worship, as instituted by God himself in the Hebrew Bible (see chapter 10). But what's with these money changers and sellers of animals? Since most Jews no longer lived in Jerusalem, but had to make a trip—sometimes a very long trip—to Jerusalem in order to worship in the Temple, some kind of provision had to be made in order to allow them to participate in the sacrificial cult. Someone coming from Egypt couldn't very well be expected to load a lamb up on his shoulders and start walking, especially since the sacrificial animals had to be completely free from injury and blemish. And so animals had to be provided for pilgrims near, or within, the Temple precincts themselves. How, though, was a person to purchase such an animal? It wouldn't be right to use the Roman currency: it bore an image of Caesar, who was thought by some in the empire to be himself divine. The God of Israel disallowed images of any kind in his cult—especially images of other so-called gods. And so, those traveling to Jerusalem needed to exchange their money for Temple currency to participate in the Temple cult. This was to keep the Temple pure from idolatrous influences. Surely all this was to the good. How else could the Temple cult function?

Jesus, though, allegedly entered the Temple, overturned the tables of the money changers, and drove out those who were selling sacrificial animals. What did he actually do and what did it mean?

Most scholars recognize that some aspects of our accounts appear exaggerated, including Mark's claim that Jesus completely shut down the operation of the Temple (if no one could carry any vessels, it would have been impossible to sacrifice and butcher the animals—which was after all what the Temple was for). As we have seen, the Temple complex was immense, and there would have been armed guards present to prevent any major disturbances. Moreover, if Jesus had actually created an enormous stir in the Temple, it's nearly impossible to explain why he wasn't arrested on the spot and taken out of the way before he could stir up the crowds. For these reasons, it looks as if Mark's account represents an exaggeration of Jesus' actions. But exaggerations aside, it is almost certain that Jesus did something that caused a disturbance in the Temple—for example, overturned some tables and made at least a bit of a ruckus. As I've noted, the event is multiply attested in independent sources.[3]

Moreover, it coincides with Jesus' predictions about the Temple, that it would soon be destroyed. For this reason, a good number of scholars have begun to recognize that Jesus' actions in the Temple represented a symbolic expression of his proclamation. We should recall that Jesus sometimes engaged in symbolic acts that illustrated his apocalyptic message: for example, he associated with tax collectors and sinners (illustrating his message that the Kingdom was for the outcast and lowly), and he chose twelve disciples (illustrating that those who adhered to his message would be those who enter the Kingdom). In view of Jesus' overarching message of the coming destruction when the Son of Man arrives, perhaps then it is best to see Jesus' action in the Temple as a kind of prophetic gesture, an enacted parable, in which he demonstrated on a small scale what was soon to happen in a big way on the coming day of judgment. The Temple was going to be destroyed.[4]

It is hard to know whether the Gospel accounts of Jesus' words during this episode should be accepted as authentic. In the earliest account, he quotes the prophet Jeremiah to indicate that the Temple cult had become corrupt, "a den of thieves" (Mark 11:17). Some scholars have thought that the charges of corruption in the Temple were a later Christianization of the tradition, a kind of incipient anti-Semitic attack on the worship of Judaism. And it's true that it has proved all too easy for Christians to stereotype the Jewish leaders of Jesus' day as greedy, power-hungry, self-serving hypocrites. But the charges themselves are scarcely anti-Semitic: they were taken from the Hebrew Bible itself, and reflect the kinds of accusations that some Jews occasionally made against others (i.e., they reflect *internal* Jewish disputes). In any event, the fact that Jesus himself leveled such charges is multiply attested in independent sources.

What he might have imagined could have been done to make things better is hard to say. That is, Jesus doesn't indicate how the Temple could function without people selling animals for the sacrifices that God commanded to be performed there, or whether he thought animals should be purchased with coins bearing Caesar's image. Nor does he say that the problem is that the money changers and animal sellers were overcharging. It may simply have been that as a country fellow from rural Galilee, who preached against wealth and power, the sheer opulence of the place made his blood boil on principle.

In any event, it's clear that Jesus was not alone in attacking the institution of the Temple. For we know of other Jews both during Jesus' day and before who thought that the Temple would soon be destroyed because it had grown corrupt. The prophet Jeremiah thought so (Jer. 7), as did the members of the Qumran community that left us the Dead Sea Scrolls (see the *Commentary on Habakkuk*). Similar views are found in other Jewish traditions, for example, an apocryphal book entitled *The Assumption of Moses*[5] and, possibly, the proclamation of Jesus' namesake, Jesus, son of Ananias, near the end of the first century (see chapter 9). Some Jews did think the Temple cult and the priests who ran it had become corrupt; there's nothing implausible in thinking that Jesus happened to agree.

How, though, did Jesus' prediction that the Temple would be destroyed fit into his broader apocalyptic message? Two possibilities suggest themselves. On the one hand, it is possible that he believed that in the new age there would be a new Temple, one totally sanctified for the worship of God. This at least was the view of the apocalyptically minded Essenes of the Dead Sea Scroll community, who were his contemporaries. Or it may be that Jesus believed that there would be no need for a temple at all in the Kingdom that was coming, since there would no longer be any evil or sin, and therefore no need for the cultic sacrifice of animals to bring atonement. This was the view later embraced by some of his own apocalyptic followers, such as the author of the book of Revelation (see Rev. 21:22). In either case, the implication of Jesus' actions would have been clear: for Jesus, the Temple cult and the officials in charge of it were a temporary measure at best, and a corruption of God's plan at worst. They would soon be done away with when the Kingdom arrived.

This message did not escape the notice of those in charge of the Temple, the chief priests who happened also to have jurisdiction over the local affairs of the people in Jerusalem. These priests were principally Sadducees, and they were the chief liaisons with the Roman officials, in particular with the Roman prefect Pilate. It is at this point in our earliest account, Mark, that Jesus begins to enter into serious disagreements with the Jewish authorities in Jerusalem, sometimes engaging in public arguments with them, and sometimes speaking ill of them to anyone who would gather around to listen (see, e.g., Mark 11:27–33; 12:1–12, 18–27; 14:1).

Jesus appears to have spent the week, then, teaching and engaging his opponents in the Temple. His most explicitly apocalyptic message, in fact, is said to have been delivered there, according to all three of the Synoptic Gospels—a message in which he predicted the coming destruction of the Temple, worldwide disaster, cosmic upheavals, and then the arrival of the Son of Man in glory in the presence of the holy angels. He assures his hearers that all these things will take place within their own generation (Matt. 24–25; Mark 13; Luke 21).

As the crowds began to swell, Jesus evidently started to attract more and more attention. The Jewish authorities in the Temple became concerned about an uprising. It had happened before and was to become a constant threat in the years to follow. For their part, the Roman authorities were armed and ready to act. It was decided to have Jesus arrested and taken out of the public eye by stealth, so as to avoid any problems.

Betrayal and Arrest

It is difficult to reconstruct the day-by-day activities of Jesus during the week before his death with any degree of historical accuracy. We do know that he engaged in his teaching in the Temple and confronted the Jewish authorities with his message. And we know that he was spending his nights outside the city, with friends in Bethany (Mark 11:11–12; John 12:1; this tradition appears to pass the criterion of dissimilarity, since Christians wouldn't really get any mileage out of it). We are better informed, though, concerning Jesus' final twenty-four hours. It's a story of betrayal and denial, abandonment and mockery. From the purely human perspective, it's not a pretty story.

According to our earliest narrative, Jesus celebrated the Passover meal with his disciples. We're not actually *told* that he had a lamb slaughtered in the Temple and cooked during the day for their evening meal. But since that's what Jews did in Jerusalem on the Passover, it would take special pleading to argue that he did something else.

Not only the Gospels but also an earlier source, Paul, indicates that Jesus instilled the symbolic foods of this meal with yet greater significance. According to these accounts, he told his disciples that the unleavened bread was (or represented) his body that would be broken, and the cup of wine was (or represented) his blood that would be shed (Mark 14:22–25; Matt. 26:26–29; Luke 22:15–20; 1 Cor. 11:23–26). It's very difficult to know whether this "institution" of the Lord's Supper is historical. On the one hand, it is multiply attested in independent sources, even though they disagree concerning the precise words that were spoken. And one of these sources, Paul, who claimed to know people who had been there at the time, was writing just twenty years after the event. On the other hand, the accounts seem so heavily "Christianized" with the doctrine of the saving effect of Jesus' death (a doctrine that developed, of course, after he had died), that it is hard to know what here is history and what is later theology.

It's not at all implausible, of course, to think that Jesus knew he was going to be arrested and possibly executed. One doesn't have to be the eternal Son of God to read the writing on the wall, provided it's written there clearly enough. Think again of Socrates and Martin Luther King Jr.! Jesus must have known that he had aroused not just the curiosity but also the animosity of some of the chief priests in the Temple, and he must have realized how the power structure in Jerusalem worked. All it would take was a word from someone in authority and he would be history. It had happened before and was destined to happen again and again.

What might have been less expected, though, was how it actually happened. One of Jesus' own, a member of the Twelve, Judas Iscariot, betrayed him to the authorities. This act of betrayal is about as historically certain as anything else in the tradition. For one thing, it is multiply attested (Mark 14:10–11, 43–45; John 18:2–3; Acts 1:16; possibly 1 Cor. 11:23). Moreover, it is not the sort of thing that a later Christian would probably make up (one of Jesus' *closest disciples* betrayed him? He had no more authority over his followers than *that*?). According to our accounts, Judas led a Jewish armed guard to Jesus after he and his disciples had left dinner to spend some time outside in the open. A number of details about the betrayal, however, are not clear historically, including such basic questions as what it was that Judas betrayed and why he did so.

Consider first what he betrayed. The matter is often thought to be quite simple: Judas told the authorities where they could locate Jesus apart from the crowds. That may in fact have been the case. But why would the authorities have needed to pay someone to tell them Jesus' whereabouts? Couldn't they simply have had him followed and saved themselves the bother and expense?

In this connection, it may be useful to see if there is some link between Jesus' betrayal and the explicit and punishable charges brought against him at his trial. These charges have to do with claims that Jesus allegedly made about himself—according to some accounts, that he was the Messiah, the Son of God, according to others that he was the King of the Jews (Mark 14:61, 15:2; John 18:33, 19:19). The problem is that in the public teachings of Jesus which we have established as historically authentic, Jesus never calls himself such things.

So where did the authorities get the idea that he did?

It's possible, in fact, that this is what Judas betrayed. We know that Jesus taught his disciples privately things that he didn't say in public. That, presumably, was one of the reasons for having an inner circle. Moreover, we know that he was charged at his trial(s) with making claims about himself that he is not recorded as having made publicly. And finally, we know that one of the inner circle divulged information to the authorities that led to Jesus' arrest and eventual execution. It seems plausible, then, that what Judas betrayed was not simply Jesus' whereabouts—information that the interested authorities could have secured with less trouble and expense, had they wanted—but Jesus' private teachings, which, as it turns out, involved a capital offense.

This matter requires some further reflection. What exactly did Jesus teach his disciples that proved so insidious? Unfortunately, we don't have the kinds of historical sources available to us to allow us to say anything definitive. But there are several hints that come at us from different directions, and we would do well to pay them serious heed.

Jesus' Punishable Offense

We will see momentarily that the charge leveled against Jesus by the Roman governor Pontius Pilate was that he considered himself to be the King of the Jews (Mark 15:2; John 18:33, 19:19). This is a curious charge, when you examine the historical record of Jesus' preaching. Jesus never calls himself this in any of our Gospels. Why would he be executed for a claim that he never made? Moreover, during his hearing before the Jewish authorities, who held a kind of preliminary investigation before turning him over for prosecution, he was evidently charged with calling himself the Messiah (Mark 14:62). As we have seen previously, the term "messiah" could mean a range of things to first-century Jews. Some expected a future cosmic judge of the earth to come in judgment, others hoped for a future priest who would give the authoritative interpretation of the Law of Moses, and others anticipated a future military leader who would overthrow the enemies opposed to God and establish a new Israel as a sovereign state in the land.

Jesus himself talked about the future cosmic judge, but he called him the Son of Man rather than the Messiah. He did teach, though, that after the judgment there would be a Kingdom on earth. If kingdoms, by their very nature, have kings, who would be the king of this kingdom? Ultimately, of course, it would be God—hence Jesus' common reference to the coming "Kingdom of God." But he probably didn't think that God himself would physically sit on the throne in Jerusalem. Who then would?

There are several indications in our earliest traditions that Jesus thought that he himself would be enthroned. Recall: Jesus maintained that people who heard his message and followed it would enter into the future Kingdom of God. Thus Jesus portrayed himself as the herald of this Kingdom, who knew when it was coming and how it would arrive. More than that, he evidently saw himself as having a special standing before God. After all, whoever accepted his message would enter God's Kingdom.

Would Jesus continue to be the special envoy of God once the Kingdom arrived? Recall that he told his disciples that they would be seated on twelve thrones ruling the twelve tribes of Israel. Who, though, would be over them? It was Jesus himself who called them to be the Twelve. Moreover, his disciples asked *him* for permission to sit at his right hand and his left in the coming Kingdom (e.g., Mark 10:37). They evidently understood that he would be the ruler in the Kingdom, just as he was their "ruler" now.

As a final piece of the puzzle, I should point out that it is almost certain that during Jesus' lifetime, some people, at least, believed that he would be the future ruler of Israel. Otherwise it's impossible to explain why they (his followers) thought he was the Messiah after he had died. You can't say that they started to think so only after they became convinced that he was raised from the dead, for the very simple reason that prior to Christianity, there weren't any Jews, so far as we know, who expected that the Messiah was *going* to be raised from the dead. In no surviving Jewish text—whether in the Hebrew Bible or later, up to the time of Christianity—is the Messiah said to die and be raised.[6] And so, if Jesus' followers called him Messiah later, after his death, they must have already thought of him as Messiah earlier, while he was alive. And yet in our earliest accounts Jesus doesn't teach that he's the Messiah and discourages his disciples from noising it about.

How does one make sense of all of these data? In my judgment, the best solution is to say that Jesus' teachings about himself were intimately related to his apocalyptic proclamation that the end of the age was coming soon, the arrival of the Son of Man was imminent, and the Kingdom was almost here. Those who heeded his words would enter into that Kingdom. This would be God's Kingdom, ruled by his chosen ones—the twelve disciples on twelve thrones. And Jesus himself would rule over them. He, in effect, would be the king of God's coming Kingdom.

In *that apocalyptic* sense (and I would say, only in that sense) did Jesus think of himself as the Messiah. He wasn't a cosmic judge, an authoritative priest, or a military leader. He was the one sent from God to proclaim the good news of the coming Kingdom, who would be the ultimate ruler when the end arrived.

What, then, did Judas betray to the authorities? This private teaching of Jesus. That's why they could level the charges against Jesus that he called himself the Messiah, the King of Israel. He meant it, of course, in the apocalyptic sense. They meant it in a this-worldly sense. But he couldn't deny it when accused. For that *was* how he understood himself, and the twelve disciples all knew it.

Why then, did Judas betray this information? Some people have thought that he did it for the money (see Matt. 26:14–15; John 12:4–6). This is possible, of course, but the "thirty pieces of silver" is a reference to a fulfilment of prophecy in the Hebrew Bible (Zech. 11:12), and so may not be historically accurate; that is, it doesn't pass the criterion of dissimilarity. Some have argued that Judas had grown disillusioned when he realized that Jesus had no intention of assuming the role of a political-military messiah. Others have reasoned that he wanted to force Jesus' hand, thinking that if he were arrested he would call out for support and start an uprising that would overthrow the Romans. Each of these explanations has some merit, but in the end, I'm afraid we'll never know.

Jesus was evidently arrested by Jewish authorities (multiply attested in Mark 14:43 and John 18:3), in the Garden of Gethsemane (Mark 14:32; John 18:1, 12). The disciples may have tried to defend him with swords (multiply attested: Mark 14:47–48; Luke 22:35–38 [L material]; and John 18:10–11; this doesn't seem like a tradition the later pacifist Christians would invent). But they then abandoned him, as all of our traditions suggest. In independent sources Peter is said to have denied knowing Jesus three times, another tradition that may pass the criterion of dissimilarity (Mark 14:66–72; John 18:15–18, 25–27).

What is abundantly clear is that at the end, no one stood up for or put his or her neck out for Jesus. He was tried and executed alone.

Jesus before the Jewish Authorities

The early sources are agreed that after his arrest Jesus faced some kind of preliminary investigation before the Jewish authorities, who had control not only over the religious practices of the Temple but over social and political life in Judea. In fact, the distinction that we ourselves tend to make today between the religious and political realms would have been quite foreign in the ancient world—especially in Palestine, where the Law of Moses included civil and criminal legislation and the leaders of the Temple were accorded the rulership of the people. The Romans, who ultimately controlled the affairs of Palestine, followed policies they had established elsewhere throughout their empire.[7] They allowed local aristocracies the right to control their own internal affairs. It is a mistake to think that Romans were involved in every detail of daily life in the provinces, with soldiers posted on every street corner in every town throughout the empire to enforce the will of Rome. The will of Rome was basically to collect revenues and protect its territory. Most inhabitants of the empire never even *saw* soldiers, who were for the most part stationed at the frontiers to defend the borders. There were no Roman legions housed in Palestine itself (though there were some in nearby Syria). Even the Roman governor had just a relatively small contingent for his own private use and to ward off any difficulties that might arise. Difficulties were particularly likely to arise at certain key times, such as Passover in Jerusalem, when the governor would come to town with troops in order to keep the peace.

When the governor was not around, though, the local authorities had both the privilege and responsibility of ruling the populace and maintaining control. Since the aristocracy in Judea was closely linked with the Temple, it was the Temple chief priests who were also the main civil authorities. They were headed by the high priest, who was chosen by the Roman overlords from among several of the most powerful aristocratic families of priests in Jerusalem. During the prefectorship of Pilate (26–36 CE), the high priest was Caiaphas. That he and Pilate had a solid working relationship and, probably, a mutual understanding is evident from our sources. When Pilate was deposed for mismanagement of Judean affairs in 36 CE, Caiaphas was removed as well.

And so it makes sense that a local offender would first be brought before the local authorities. In the case of Jesus, it was the high priest Caiaphas and his ruling "council," called the Sanhedrin (this also explains why it was *Jewish* police who arrested Jesus rather than Roman). Unfortunately, we have no reliable way of knowing what happened when Jesus appeared before Caiaphas. In part we are hampered by our sources: according to the accounts themselves, the only persons present were Jesus, who was to be executed the next morning, and the Jewish rulers. Where, then, did our sources get their information? There wasn't a court stenographer whose records could be consulted.

The real problem, though, is that it is difficult to understand the trial proceeding, if it actually happened as narrated. In our earliest account, the high priest asks Jesus if he is in fact the Messiah, the Son of the Blessed (Mark 14:61). So far so good. But when Jesus affirms that he is, and says that he, the high priest, will see the Son of Man coming on the clouds of heaven—sayings that in themselves coincide perfectly well with Jesus' teachings elsewhere—the high priest cries out "Blasphemy," and calls for his execution (Mark 14:62–64). The problem is that if this, in fact, is what Jesus said, he didn't commit any blasphemy.

It wasn't blasphemous to call oneself the Messiah—this simply meant that you understood yourself to be the deliverer/ruler of your people. Other Jews made this claim about themselves and about others both before Jesus and afterward, never with the charge of blasphemy. Nor was it blasphemous to say that the Son of Man was soon to arrive. This was simply to acknowledge that the book of Daniel had predicted something that would happen in your own day—something other apocalyptic prophets were saying as well, without being found blasphemous.

It seems unlikely, then, that the trial proceeded the way that it's described in Mark, our earliest source.[8] In addition, as scholars have long noted, the trial appears to be illegal on a large number of counts, when judged by the later descriptions in the Mishnah of how the Sanhedrin was to function. There could not be trials at night, for example, or on a festival; and a capital offense required two separate hearings. In light of these difficulties, and the fact that the Fourth Gospel doesn't narrate an actual trial before the Sanhedrin, perhaps it's best to conclude that Jesus must have appeared before some body of Jewish rulers, who decided to hand him over to Pilate after an initial questioning, but that we don't know exactly what happened at the proceeding.

Jesus' Trial before Pilate

That Jesus was turned over to Pilate, though, is certain. As we saw in an earlier chapter, not only is Pilate named in our early Christian sources (Mark, John, Gospel of Peter), but he is charged with the responsibility of Jesus' death in both Josephus and Tacitus as well.

I should say a word about Pilate's role and responsibility as governor of Judea before proceeding any further. Provincial governors were Roman aristocrats who were appointed to govern the various lands Rome had conquered. Pilate himself was not in the uppermost crust of the Roman aristocracy; he was of the equestrian, rather than senatorial, rank. As with all governors, he had two major responsibilities: to bring in the tribute and to keep the peace. The central imperial government in Rome was not overly concerned about how the governors achieved these two goals. That is to say, unlike today, where countries—even very large countries—have national laws that must be followed by local authorities, in the Roman Empire, governors were given virtually free rein to do whatever was necessary to rule. A governor could send out the troops, for example, to quell the riots, and if several thousand people were killed in the process, well, maybe next time the masses wouldn't be so quick to riot. And he had the power of life and death. If someone was perceived to be a troublemaker, there was no need to follow anything that would strike us as due process, at least for non-Roman citizens in the provinces—no requirement of a trial by jury, for example, or for a careful cross-examination of all witnesses. There were no appeal processes, no long delays in justice, and no long stints on death row. A governor could try an accused criminal, decide that he had been given a raw deal, and free him on the spot. Or the governor could decide that the accused was likely to cause more trouble and have him executed. The sentence was then carried out immediately. If it were a particularly problematic case, the execution might be ordered to be slow and painful.

Jesus was handed over to Pilate (Mark 15:1; John 18:28; cf. G.Pet. 1). It's not completely clear why the Jewish authorities didn't handle the problem themselves. It's possible that they simply wanted to show deference to the Roman prefect, who was after all in town precisely to take care of such problems during the Passover. And it's possible that the authorities really were concerned about the large following Jesus was acquiring (if in fact he was acquiring a large following; it's hard to know). If so, they may not have wanted to incur any animosity among the masses. It's also possible that they wanted Jesus completely taken out of the way—that is, that they wanted him executed. Most historians believe that even though the Romans allowed the local aristocracies to run their own affairs, they reserved the right of capital punishment for themselves.

Again we are in no position to say what exactly happened at Jesus' trial before Pilate. His followers who later told stories about it were not there, and the principal participants, Pilate and the chief priests, would not have made themselves available later for interviews. I should also point out that the Gospel accounts of the large crowds at the trial do not pass the criteria of contextual credibility or dissimilarity. We know from other sources, like Josephus, that Pilate was one brutal fellow who did not cater to the whim of the populace. And there would have been no reason to conduct a criminal investigation out in the open and ask for the crowds' opinions. Later Christians, however, may have wanted to emphasize the culpability of the Jewish people in the death of Jesus, as represented in the crowds amassed in Jerusalem for Passover. The stories that portray the Jewish masses screaming for his blood may reflect that Christian perspective (e.g., Matt. 27:25).

What is almost certain, though, is that the point at issue in Jesus' trial was again his own claims about himself. Pilate would not have cared one bit about whether Jesus kept the Sabbath, or told people to love one another, or urged his followers to give away their wealth. He *would* have cared about things that related to his rule as a representative of Rome. Moreover, it is independently attested that the ground of execution, as found, for example, on the title placed over Jesus' cross, was that Jesus called himself the King of the Jews (Mark 15:26; John 19:19). Not only is this tradition multiply attested and contextually credible, it also passes the criterion of dissimilarity. For this is not a title that Christians themselves used of Jesus, insofar as we can tell from our surviving sources. If they didn't use this title for Jesus, why do the accounts claim that he was executed for using the title about himself? Evidently because that's what came out at the trial.

Mark's account is not an eyewitness report, but it may not be far off in the essentials. Pilate, having heard from the Jewish chief priests that Jesus was known to speak of himself as the Messiah (= "king" in this context), queried him about it. Jesus either admitted to the charge or did little or nothing to defend himself against it. He *did*, after all, see himself as the king—at least of the Kingdom that soon was to be brought with the coming of the Son of Man. Pilate needed to hear no more. Jesus was a potential troublemaker who was stirring up the crowds and who thought of himself as a political usurper of the prerogatives of Rome. Without further ado, Pilate ordered him executed as an enemy of the state.

The trial itself may not have lasted more than a couple of minutes; it was probably one of several items on a crowded morning agenda. Two other persons were charged with sedition the same morning. All three were taken outside of the city gates to be crucified.

The Death of Jesus

In most Western societies today, it is thought that criminals should be punished out of the public eye. And if it involves a death sentence, the execution should be as humane and civilized as possible, so as to allow the person a modicum of human dignity and decency at the end. The Romans had a different point of view. Their idea was to make violent criminals suffer violent deaths, to make public offenders die in the public eye, to debase and humiliate troublemakers openly, to show what happens to those who opposed the power of Rome. If punishment was to be a deterrent of crime, it was to be as painful, prolonged, and humiliating as possible.

It's difficult to know which of these systems is more effective, but it's not difficult to see how they differ. If Romans had a problem with carjacking in New York, they'd crucify a bunch of car thieves around the outskirts of Central Park, and *then* see how many people wanted to run off with that BMW!

Crucifixion was one of the most horrible deaths used by the Romans. They didn't invent the practice, but they used it a lot, especially for people they considered to be lowlifes: slaves, common criminals, rabble-rousers, people causing sedition. Some Christians have evidently been raised to think that Jesus was the only person actually crucified. It is not, of course, true. When the Roman general Titus finally overthrew Jerusalem after a two-year siege in 70 CE, he crucified so many people that he ran out of lumber.

According to the Gospel traditions, before being led off to his execution, Jesus was flogged (Mark 15:15; John 19:1). This in itself was a horrific punishment; the Romans used leather thongs with little pieces of glass or bone tied to the ends to rip off the skin and, then, the inner muscle. It is hard to say whether the account of Jesus' flogging is a Christian addition to show how much he suffered or a historical account. Since public torture of criminals from the lower classes was the rule of the day, the accounts are in general terms completely plausible. In any event, Jesus and the others would have been taken by soldiers outside the city gates, carrying their cross beams to the upright stakes kept at the site of execution. The uprights were reused, possibly every day. There the condemned would have been nailed to the cross beams, or possibly to the uprights themselves, through the wrists and possibly the ankles. There may have been a small ledge attached to the upright on which they could sit to rest.

We know a bit more about crucifixion now than we used to, largely because of a significant archaeological discovery made some thirty years ago. It was the partial remains of a crucified man, his ankle bone still attached to a piece of olive wood through which a stake had been driven. The nail had been hammered into a knot in the wood. It apparently couldn't be removed when the man, named Yehochanan, was finally taken down for burial, a grim testimony to the realities of death by crucifixion. In this case, both ankles had been nailed to the upright, on either side. Yehochanan appears to have been tied to the cross by the arms, rather than nailed through the wrists.[9]

Death by crucifixion was slow and painful. It came not by loss of blood, but by suffocation. As the body hung on the cross, the lung cavity would distend so far that a person couldn't breathe. To relieve the pain on the chest, one had to raise the body up, either by pulling on the stakes through (or ropes around) the wrists, or by pushing on those through the feet, or both. Death came only when the victim lacked the strength to continue. Sometimes it took days.

In Jesus' case, death came within several hours, in the late afternoon, on a Friday during Passover week. His disciples were not there with him, though some of the women who had accompanied him from Galilee reportedly looked on from a distance (Mark 15:40). None was close enough, though, to hear what, if anything, he said at the end. By midafternoon, on the day before Sabbath, he was dead.

In several independent accounts we are told that Jesus' body was buried by an influential but secret follower, Joseph of Arimathea (Mark 15:42; John 19:38; G.Pet. 23). Some scholars have called this tradition into question on the grounds of contextual credibility. Crucified criminals were normally not allowed a decent burial, but were either left on their crosses to rot and be devoured by scavengers or tossed into a common grave. This was part of the humiliation. At least one recent scholar, otherwise known for his serious scholarship, has made a rather sensationalist suggestion that Jesus' body was in fact eaten by dogs.[10] One must admit that this is possible, but there is really no way, historically, to know.

In any event, it seems improbable that Jesus' corpse was simply left hanging on the cross. If it had been, his followers would presumably have seen it there later and been somewhat less inclined to maintain that it had been raised from the dead on the third day following. We can at least say, then, that Jesus' body was probably buried somewhere by someone, either by the soldiers in a common tomb or, as the tradition itself says, by someone other than his family and closest followers. The really important thing, of course, is what his followers came to claim happened next.

thirteen

from apocalyptic prophet to lord of all: the afterlife of jesus

FROM THE VERY BEGINNING, CHRISTIAN THEOLOGY HAS MAINTAINED THAT JESUS TRULY DIED, WAS TRULY BURIED, AND WAS TRULY RAISED FROM THE DEAD. THE EARLIEST AUTHOR OF THE New Testament already makes this confession in a fixed formula that he claims he inherited from those who were apostles before him: "For I gave to you as of first importance what I also received, that Christ died for our sins in accordance with the Scriptures, that he was buried, and that he was raised on the third day in accordance with the Scriptures, and that he appeared to Cephas and then to the twelve" (1 Cor. 15:3–5). Indeed, the reality of Jesus' actual, physical resurrection is attested by all of our earliest narrative Gospels, including the Gospel of Peter. Did it, then, really happen?

The Resurrection of Jesus from a Historical Perspective

Here I must stress even more strongly than before the problem confronting the historian when it comes to discussing miracles. Even if a miracle did happen, there is no way we can demonstrate it, by the very nature of the case (see my longer reflections in chapter 11). Historians try to determine what happened in the past. Since they can't *prove* the past, they can only establish what *probably* happened. But by their very nature, miracles are highly *improbable* occurrences. That is to say, the chances of a miracle happening are infinitesimally remote, as opposed to other weird things that happen in our world that are not in and of themselves so highly improbable that we'd call them "impossible." Thus, even if Jesus was raised from the dead—and many Christian historians personally believe he was, just as most other historians think he wasn't—there is no way we can demonstrate it using historical methods.

We can, of course, say something about the historical reports of Jesus' resurrection. Unfortunately, when we examine them, the results are not encouraging. All of our sources agree that Jesus was dead and buried, and that on the third day his tomb was empty. But they differ in detail on almost every level. Who were the women who discovered his tomb? What did they find there? Was the stone still before the tomb or rolled away? Did a man appear to them? Or was it two men? Or two angels? Was it two angels and Jesus himself? What were the women told to do? Did they do it?

Read the accounts for yourself (it is interesting to include the Gospel of Peter, which not only shows Jesus himself emerging from the tomb—an event never described in the canonical accounts—but also describes the cross walking out behind him and talking to the heavens!). They in fact differ at almost every point. And it isn't just a matter of one account adding some detail not found in another, or giving a slightly different spin to the story. Sometimes the differences seem nearly impossible to reconcile.

Even *assuming* that all of these accounts are accurate, some of the differences make it impossible to piece together a composite picture, even leaving the Gospel of Peter out of the equation. For example, in the earliest account we're told that the women learn that Jesus is raised and are instructed to go tell his disciples; but they flee the tomb and don't say anything to anyone because they are afraid (Mark 16:8). In the later accounts, however, they don't keep silent but immediately do as they're told. Well, which was it? If they *later* told the disciples (as in the other Gospels), then it's simply not true that they didn't tell anyone (as in Mark).

Even more striking, in Matthew's account the disciples are instructed to leave Jerusalem and go to Galilee, where they'll meet up again with Jesus. They do so, and meet him there, where he gives his final instructions to them. In Luke's account, however, they are instructed—quite explicitly—*not* to leave Jerusalem until they "receive the power from on high" (i.e., the Holy Spirit, who was to come to them over a month later on the Day of Pentecost, in Acts 2). They meet up with Jesus then in Jerusalem (never having left), who gives them his final instructions before ascending into heaven. Hence the problem: did they leave Jerusalem right away (Matthew) or not at all (Luke)?

My point is that even though there is some essential agreement in these accounts, there is massive confusion in the details.

Given the nature of these sources, then, what can we say for sure happened? It might be easiest to begin by pointing out what we *cannot* say. If we are relying on the historical methods, as I've just explained, we cannot say that Jesus was actually raised from the dead, that the women visiting the tomb saw divine angels who told them all about it, and that they, and the disciples, then saw Jesus alive, well, and bound for heaven. You are free to affirm these things, of course, if you happen to be a believer and think they are true. But your grounds for thinking so are theological or personal, not historical (since they defy historical probabilities).

Moreover, we cannot be completely certain, historically, that Jesus' tomb was actually empty. The problem is the one I alluded to at the end of the previous chapter. It is very difficult to establish that Jesus was actually buried in a private tomb that people could visit if they wanted (the claimants for the tombs in modern-day Jerusalem notwithstanding!). It would have been more common for the body of a crucified criminal to be tossed into a common grave, where within days it would have deteriorated beyond the point of recognition.

Nor can we say for certain that Jesus' followers began to proclaim his resurrection three days later. Our earliest account of this belief comes from Paul, for example, in the verses cited at the beginning of this chapter. And he was writing well over twenty *years* later. It's possible of course that the disciples came to believe in Jesus' resurrection that very weekend. But it's also possible that they came to this conclusion only later—say weeks or months later—and that having come to believe that Jesus was still alive, they turned to the Scriptures (like Hos. 6:2 and Jon. 1:17) and saw there references to the dead coming back to life on the "third day," and began saying, then, that that's when Jesus' body was reanimated by God.

What I think we *can* say with some confidence is that Jesus actually did die, he probably was buried, and that some of his disciples (all of them? some of them?) claimed to have seen him alive afterward. Among those who made this claim, interestingly enough, was Jesus' own brother James, who came to believe in Jesus and soon thereafter became one of the principal leaders of the early Christian church. The apostle Paul knew James and passed along this information about his vision of Jesus (1 Cor. 15:7). Moreover, Paul claims that he himself saw Jesus after his death (1 Cor. 15:8), although there is nothing to indicate that he knew what Jesus looked like beforehand. Furthermore, he does not come out and say that he actually saw Jesus in the flesh. It's unclear, in other words, whether Paul had a "vision" of Jesus or actually ran into him on the road.

And so even though we can't say with any assurance that Jesus was raised from the dead, when speaking as historians rather than believers or unbelievers, or that his disciples *immediately* claimed that he was, or that they could point to an empty tomb as proof (Paul, interestingly, never speaks of the evidence of the tomb), we can say with complete certainty that some of his disciples at some later time insisted that (a) women from their group went to anoint Jesus' body for burial and found it missing, and (b) he soon appeared to them, convincing them that he had been raised from the dead.

Their conviction on this matter eventually turned the world on its ear. Things have never been the same since.

The Belief in the Resurrection and the Beginnings of Christianity

I would like to prompt some further reflections on this issue by asking a simple question. Christianity, of course, has been the dominant religion throughout the history of Western Civilization, whether considered socially, politically, economically, or in just about any other way. Hypothetically speaking, every religious and philosophical movement has a point of origin. When did Christianity begin?[1]

Did it begin with Jesus' ministry? There is obviously something right about thinking so, in that without the words and deeds of Jesus, there would have been no religion based on him. At the same time, Christianity has traditionally been much more than a religion that espouses Jesus' teachings. Indeed, if Jesus was the apocalyptic prophet that he appears to have been, then the Christianity that emerged after his death represents a somewhat different religion from that which he himself proclaimed. To put the matter in its simplest terms, Christianity is a religion rooted in a belief in the death of Jesus for sin and in his resurrection from the dead. This, however, does not appear to have been the religion that Jesus preached to the Jews of Galilee and Judea. To use a formulation that scholars have tossed about for years, Christianity is not so much the religion *of* Jesus (i.e., the religion that he himself proclaimed) as the religion *about* Jesus (i.e., the religion that is based on his death and resurrection).

Should we say then that Christianity began with Jesus' death? This too may contain some element of truth, but it also is problematic. For if Jesus had died and no one had come to believe that he had been raised from the dead, then his death would perhaps have been seen as yet another tragic incident in a long history of tragedies experienced by the Jewish people, as the death of yet another prophet of God, another holy man dedicated to proclaiming God's will to his people. But it would not have been recognized as an act of God for the salvation of the world, and a new religion would probably not have emerged as a result.

Did Christianity begin then with Jesus' resurrection? I have already shown why historians would have difficulty making this judgment— since it would require them to subscribe to faith in the miraculous working of God. Yet even if historians were able to speak of the resurrection as a historically probable event, it could not, in and of itself, be considered the beginning of Christianity. For Christianity is not the resurrection of Jesus, but the belief in the resurrection of Jesus. Historians, of course, have no difficulty whatsoever speaking about the belief in Jesus' resurrection, since this is a matter of public record. For it is a historical fact that some of Jesus' followers came to believe that he had been raised from the dead soon after his execution. We know some of these believers by name; one of them, the apostle Paul, claims quite plainly to have seen Jesus alive after his death. My point is that for the historian, Christianity begins after the death of Jesus, not with the resurrection itself, but with the belief in his resurrection.

Jesus' Resurrection from an Apocalyptic Perspective

Recognizing this historical reality puts us in a good position to bring closure to our study of the earliest accounts of Jesus' life and death. I began this quest for the historical Jesus in chapters 2 and 3 with a discussion of the nature of our Gospels and how, given the kinds of books they are, we can use them to reconstruct the life of Jesus. Now that we have more or less finished that task (or have at least begun to scratch the surface of it), we can put our question in reverse and come back full circuit, asking *not* how we can move from the Gospels to Jesus (the task of the preceding chapters), but how we can move from Jesus to the Gospels. That is to say, given what we now know about who Jesus was, how do we make sense of the kinds of traditions that began to be circulated about him throughout the Mediterranean after his death, traditions that eventually came to be recorded in our surviving sources? Or to put the matter somewhat differently, how does one understand the movement from Jesus the Jewish prophet, who proclaimed the imminent judgment of the world through the coming Son of Man, to the Christians who believed in him, who maintained that Jesus himself was the divine man whose death and resurrection represented God's ultimate act of salvation?

We might begin by revisiting the question of who the first believers in Jesus' resurrection actually were.

As I have already intimated, even though the Gospels provide somewhat different accounts about who discovered Jesus' empty tomb and about whom they encountered, what they learned, and how they reacted once they did so, all four canonical Gospels and the Gospel of Peter agree that the empty tomb was discovered by a woman or a group of women, the first of Jesus' followers to realize that he had been raised. It has struck some people as odd that Paul, our earliest author to discuss Jesus' resurrection, does not mention the circumstance that Jesus' tomb was empty nor name any women among those who first believed in Jesus' resurrection (1 Cor. 15:3–8). On one important point, however, Paul does stand in agreement with our early Gospel accounts: those who initially came to understand that God had raised Jesus from the dead were some of Jesus' closest followers, who had associated with him during his lifetime.

It is probably safe to say that all of these people, both the women and the men, had accepted Jesus' basic apocalyptic message while he was still alive. Otherwise they scarcely would have been following him. This means, then, that the first persons to believe in Jesus' resurrection would have been apocalyptically minded Jews. And now the million-dollar question: What would Jewish apocalypticists think if they came to believe that a great man of God had been raised from the dead? Recall: Jesus' resurrection was not thought to be a miracle that some other holy person performed on his behalf. Jesus' followers believed that God had raised him from the dead.

Moreover, he was not raised for a brief period of time, only to die a second time. Jesus had been raised from the dead never to die again. What conclusions would be drawn by these Jewish apocalypticists, the earliest Christians?

We have already seen that apocalypticists believed that at the end of this age the powers of evil would be destroyed—powers including the devil, his demons, and the cosmic forces aligned with them, the forces of sin and death. When these powers were destroyed, there would be a resurrection of the dead, in which the good would receive an eternal reward and the evil would face eternal punishment. Many Jewish apocalypticists, including Jesus himself, believed that this end would be brought by one specially chosen by God and sent from heaven as a cosmic judge of the earth. Given this basic apocalyptic scenario, there should be little doubt concerning how the first persons who believed in Jesus' resurrection would have interpreted the event. Since the resurrection of the dead was to come at the end of the age and since somebody had now been raised (as they believed), then the end must have already begun. And it had begun with the resurrection of a particular person, the great teacher and holy man Jesus, who had overcome death, the greatest of the cosmic powers aligned against God. Thus Jesus was the personal agent through whom God decided to defeat the forces of evil. And he had been exalted to heaven, where he now lives until he returns to finish the job. For this reason, people were to repent and await his return. For Jesus would soon come again.

Sometime after Jesus' resurrection—it is impossible to say how soon (remember, our sources were written decades later)—these earliest apocalyptic believers began to say things about Jesus that reflected their belief in who he was, now that he had been raised. These early reflections on Jesus' significance proved to be of paramount importance for the beliefs that came to be discussed, developed, and modified for centuries to follow, principally among people who were not apocalyptic Jews to begin with. For example, these earliest Christians believed that Jesus had been exalted to heaven. That is to say, God had bestowed a unique position upon him. Even during his lifetime, they knew, Jesus had addressed God as Father, teaching his disciples that they should trust God as a kindly parent. Those who came to believe in his resurrection realized that he must have had a relationship with God that was truly unique. In a distinctive way, for them, he was the Son of God.

Moreover, these Christians knew that Jesus had spent a good deal of time talking about one who was soon to come from heaven in judgment over the earth. For them, he was himself now exalted to heaven; clearly, then, he must be the judge about whom he had spoken. Therefore, in their view, Jesus was soon to return in judgment as the Son of Man.

Jesus also spoke of the Kingdom of God that was to arrive with the coming of the Son of Man. As we have seen, he may have thought that he would be given a position of prominence in that Kingdom. For these early Christians, that was precisely what would happen: Jesus would reign over the Kingdom that was soon to appear. For them, he was the king to come, the king of the Jews, the Messiah.

Jesus also taught that in some sense, this Kingdom that was soon to arrive had already been inaugurated. He therefore taught his followers to implement the values of the Kingdom and adopt its ways in the here and now, loving one another as themselves. Those who believed in his resurrection maintained that the Kingdom proclaimed by Jesus had indeed already begun. As the exalted one, he was already its ruler. Indeed, he was exalted above all of creation; for them, Jesus was the Lord of all that is, in heaven and on earth.

Thus a variety of important ways to understand Jesus came into prominence quickly and naturally. Within several years after his death he was proclaimed in small communities scattered throughout the eastern Mediterranean as the unique Son of God, the coming Son of Man, the Jewish Messiah, and the Lord of all. Christians who understood Jesus in these ways naturally told stories about him in light of their understanding. And so, for example, when they mentioned Jesus' teaching about the Son of Man, they sometimes changed what he said so that instead of speaking about this other one to come, he was said to be speaking of himself, using the first-person singular: "Whoever acknowledges me before others, I will acknowledge before my Father who is in heaven" (Matt. 10:32; contrast Mark 8:38: "whoever is ashamed of me... of him will the Son of Man be ashamed"). So, too, when he spoke about himself, they sometimes changed words given in the first-person singular ("I") to the title "Son of Man." Thus Matthew's form of Jesus' question to his disciples, "Who do people say that the Son of Man is?" (Matt. 16:13; contrast Mark 8:27: "who do people say that I am?").

Jesus' Death, "According to the Scriptures"

The earliest Christians had an obvious problem when they tried to convince their fellow Jews that Jesus was the one upon whom God had shown his special favor, his Son, the Messiah. For non-Christian Jews who were anticipating a Messiah figure were not looking for anyone remotely like Jesus. We have seen that the messianic expectations reflected in our surviving sources are quite disparate. But they all had one thing in common: they all expected the Messiah to be a powerful figure who would command the respect of friend and foe alike, one who would lead the Jewish people into a new world that overcame the injustices of the old. Who, though, was Jesus? A relatively obscure teacher who was crucified for sedition against the empire. A convicted criminal was God's Messiah? Jesus never overthrew the state; he was mocked, beaten, and executed by the state. For most Jews, to call Jesus the Messiah—let alone Lord of the universe—was preposterous, even blasphemous. To our knowledge, prior to the advent of Christianity, there were no Jews who believed that the Messiah to come would suffer and die for the sins of the world and then return again in glory.

Christians today of course believe that this is precisely what the Messiah was supposed to do. The reason they think so, however, is that the earliest Christians came to believe that the Jewish Bible anticipated the coming of a suffering Messiah. It is important to remember that these earliest Christians were Jews who believed that God spoke to them through their sacred writings. For them, the Scriptures were not simply the records of past events. They were the very words of God, directed to them, in their own situation. This was true not only of the earliest Christians; most Jews that we know about from this period understood the Scriptures in a personal way, as a revelation of meaning for their own times. Thus, even though the Hebrew Bible never specifically speaks of the "Messiah" as one who is to suffer, there are passages—in the Psalms, for example—that speak of a righteous man who suffers at the hands of God's enemies, a man who comes to be vindicated by God.

Originally, these "Psalms of Lament" may have been written by Jews who were undergoing particularly difficult times of oppression and who found relief in airing their complaints against the evil persons who attacked them and expressing their hopes that God would intervene on their behalf (see, e.g., Pss. 22, 35, and 69). Christians who read such Psalms, however, saw in them not the expressions of oppressed, righteous Jews from the distant past but the embodiments of the pain, suffering, and ultimate vindication of the one truly righteous Jew who had recently been unjustly condemned and executed.

As they reflected on what had happened to Jesus, these Jewish Christians saw in his suffering and death a fulfilment of the words of the righteous sufferer described in the Psalms. In turn these words shaped the ways Christians understood and described the events of Jesus' own Passion. They took the words of Psalm 22, for example, as expressive of the events surrounding Jesus' execution:

"My God, my God, why have you forsaken me" (v. 1); "All who see me mock at me, they make mouths at me, they shake their heads" (v. 7); "I am poured out like water, and all my bones are out of joint ...my mouth is dried up like a potsherd, and my tongue sticks to my jaws" (vv. 14–15); "A company of evildoers encircles me. My hands and feet have shriveled; I can count all my bones—they stare and gloat over me; they divide my garments among them, and for my clothing they cast lots" (vv. 16–18).

For the early Christians, the sufferings of the righteous Jesus were foreshadowed by the sufferings of the righteous Jew of the Psalms. His sufferings were therefore no mere miscarriage of justice; they were the plan of God.

Yet other portions of Scripture explained why this was God's plan. These were again passages that did not mention the Messiah, but Christians nonetheless took them to refer to Jesus, whom they believed to be the Messiah. Most important were passages found in the writings of the prophet Isaiah, who also speaks of the suffering of God's righteous one, whom he calls the "Servant of the Lord." According to the "Songs of the Suffering Servant"—as scholars have labeled four different passages in Isaiah, the most important of which is 52:13–53:12—this servant of God was one who suffered a heinous and shameful fate: he was despised and rejected (53:3), he was wounded and bruised (53:4–5), he was oppressed and afflicted, he suffered in silence and was eventually killed (53:7–8). This is one who suffered and died to atone for the sins of the people (53:4–5).

The interpretation of the original meaning of this passage is difficult, and I do not want to take time to justify the widely held view among scholars that it was originally speaking of the suffering of the nation of Israel during the Babylonian captivity (but see Isa. 49:3). What matters for our purposes is that we have no indication that any Jew, prior to Christianity, ever took the passage as a reference to the Jewish Messiah. You may notice in this connection that the author refers to the Servant's suffering as past but his vindication as future. Christians understood Jesus' own suffering similarly, in light of this and other passages. For them, these ancient words described well what Jesus went through. Moreover, for them, Jesus clearly was the chosen one, given his resurrection and exaltation. Their conclusion: God's Messiah had to suffer. For what reason? As a sacrifice for the sins of the world.

The crucifixion, then, was turned from a stumbling block for Jews into a foundation stone for Christians (see 1 Cor. 1:23). In reflecting upon their Scriptures, the earliest Jewish Christians concluded that Jesus was meant to suffer and die. This was no mere miscarriage of justice; it was the eternal plan of God. Jesus faithfully carried out his mission, bringing salvation to the world. God therefore exalted him to heaven, making him the Lord of all and setting in motion the sequence of events that would lead to his return in fiery judgment on the earth.

The Emergence of Different Understandings of Jesus

This is not to say, of course, that all the Christian communities that sprang up around the Mediterranean were completely unified in the ways they understood their belief in Jesus as the one who had died for the sins of the world. On the contrary, numerous differences emerged among these groups, particularly as the religion spread from the small group of apocalyptically minded Jews who followed Jesus in Galilee and Jerusalem into other regions and among different types of people. This variety can be seen, on its most basic level, in the ways different believers in the first decades of Christianity would have understood the descriptions of Jesus that we have already examined.

Thus the term "Son of Man" might have made good sense to Jews familiar with the prediction of Daniel 7:13–14 that "one like a son of man" was to come on the clouds of heaven. For such an audience, the identification of Jesus as the Son of Man would have meant that he was destined to be the cosmic judge of the earth. But what would a pagan audience have made of the title? Either they would have to have been told about the book of Daniel, or, as also sometimes happened, they would have tried to understand the phrase as best they could, perhaps by taking it to mean that since Jesus was the son of a man, he was a real human being. As you may know, this is the way many Christians today continue to understand the term, even though it probably would not have meant this either to Jesus or to his apocalyptically minded followers.

So, too, the term "Son of God" would have meant something quite different to Jews, who could have taken it as a reference to the king of Israel (as in 2 Sam. 7:14 and Ps.2) than to Gentiles, for whom it would probably mean a "divine man" who was born of a god and a mortal and who could do great miraculous deeds. And a term like "Messiah" may have made no sense at all to Gentiles not familiar with its special significance in Jewish circles: literally it would designate someone who had been "anointed," that is, "oiled" (e.g., an athlete after a hard workout). Scarcely a term of reverence for a religious leader, let alone the Savior of the world!

Even communities that agreed on the basic meaning of these various titles may have conceived of their significance for Jesus differently. Take, for instance, the title "Son of God." If, in the general sense, the title refers to Jesus' unique standing before God, the question naturally arises, or at least it naturally did arise: When did Jesus receive this special status? Some early communities appear to have thought that he attained it at his resurrection when he was "begotten" by God as his Son, a belief reflected, for example, in the old traditions preserved still in some texts of the New Testament (e.g., Acts 13:33–34 and Rom. 1:3–4). Other communities, perhaps somewhat later, came to think that Jesus must have been God's special Son not only after his death but also during his entire ministry. For these believers, Jesus became the Son of God at his baptism, when a voice from heaven proclaimed, "You are my Son, today I have begotten you," as the story is told in the old traditions preserved in some manuscripts of the Gospel of Luke and in a noncanonical account known as the Gospel of the Ebionites. Others came to think that Jesus must have been the Son of God not only for his ministry but for his entire life. Thus, in some of our later Gospels, we have accounts that show that Jesus had no human father. In this sense, Jesus literally was the Son of God (see, e.g., Luke 1:35). Yet other Christians came to believe that Jesus must have been the Son of God not simply from his birth but from eternity past. Already by the end of the first century, Christians in some circles proclaimed that Jesus was himself divine, that he existed prior to his birth, that he created the world and all that is in it, and that he came into the world on a divine mission as God himself (as in the Gospel of John). This is a far cry from the humble beginnings of Jesus as an apocalyptic prophet. Perhaps these beginnings can be likened to a mustard seed, the smallest of all seeds....

The various notions of who Jesus was, and the diverse interpretations of the significance of what he had said and done, came to be embodied in the various written accounts of his life. This, in my judgment, is a certainty. Otherwise, there is no way to explain the radically different portrayals of Jesus that you find, for instance, in the Gospels of Mark, John, Thomas, and Peter. It was only later, when Christians decided to collect several of these Gospels into a canon of Scripture, that the differences came to be smoothed over. From that time on, Matthew, Mark, Luke, and John were all acclaimed as authoritative and interpreted in light of one another. For this reason, rather than illuminating the original emphases of each of these texts, their placement in the Christian canon led instead to a homogenization of their distinctive emphases, so that their subsequent interpreters maintained that they all told the *same* story, rather than slightly (or largely) different stories.

It is some form or other of this homogenized Gospel that most people in the Christian world today have come to know, rather than the distinctive story of Jesus found in one or another of our early sources—let alone the historical narrative of what really happened in Jesus' life, as it can be reconstructed only through a careful sifting of these early sources.

fourteen

jesus as the prophet of the new millennium: then and now

CHRISTIANS DID NOT STOP TELLING STORIES ABOUT JESUS ONCE THE EARLIEST GOSPELS WERE WRITTEN. TALES OF HIS WORDS AND DEEDS CIRCULATED WHEREVER CHRISTIANITY WAS spread, some of them based on the written texts that were becoming available, others passed along from beginning to end by word of mouth. As we have seen, this mode of transmission allowed the stories to be changed in smaller or greater ways, as they were told and retold year after year, decade after decade, among people who had not actually seen Jesus and who lived in other countries, came from other backgrounds, and spoke other languages.

Jesus from Different Perspectives

Throughout the Roman Empire, different Christians understood the significance of Jesus' life and the meaning of his person in radically different ways—for centuries. Take a couple of examples from just 120 years after his death.[1] We know of some people at that time who claimed to be the true Christians, who maintained that the God proclaimed by Jesus was not the same God who created the world and chose Israel to be his people. This Creator God, they said, was a harsh judge, who imposed an impossibly difficult Law on his people (through Moses) and then punished them with eternal judgment when they broke it—which they invariably did. Jesus, though, they maintained, proclaimed a kind and merciful God who was intent to save people from judgment. His was a God of love and forgiveness, not wrath and condemnation.

There were, in other words, two Gods—the God of the Jews and the God of Jesus. And the contrast between these Gods was quite evident, these Christians claimed, in the way each of them related to people. Whereas the God of the Jews instructed the children of Israel to enter into the Promised Land and take it for themselves by killing all of its inhabitants—for example, to slaughter every man, woman, and child in the city of Jericho, according to the book of Joshua—the God of Jesus said to love your enemies and pray for those who hate you, to turn the other cheek when anyone strikes you. These are clearly not the same God. Moreover, according to these people, since the God of Jesus did not create this world and had no connection with the God of the Old Testament, Jesus himself could not actually be part of this world. He was not really born, since that would make him a material creature like the rest of us, belonging to the God who made matter. Instead, he descended (full grown!) from heaven in the appearance of human flesh, to communicate his message of salvation before returning to his heavenly home.

These people understood themselves to be Christian, and maintained that their beliefs were the ones taught by Jesus himself.

And their view was by no means the most bizarre at the time, at least by our standards. There were other self-proclaimed Christians—lots of them, insofar as we can tell—who maintained that Jesus Christ himself was not a solitary being but, instead, two beings. On the one hand, there was the Christ, who, since he brought divine teachings from above, must have come from above as a divine being. If Christ was a divine being, though, he obviously could not have experienced the pain and suffering that we mortals must undergo. God is God! He's above the finitude, limitations, weaknesses, pain, and death that characterize our existence. How is it then that Jesus was crucified? According to these people, it was indeed Jesus who was crucified, not the Christ—because for them, Jesus and the Christ were not the same person. Jesus was the man—a full flesh-and-blood human being, born like everyone else—into whom the Christ entered after having come to earth from above.

This indwelling of the Christ began, they said, when Jesus was baptized, for we're told in the earliest accounts that the Spirit of God descended from heaven and entered into him. Once within Jesus, the Christ empowered him to do miracles and gave him the words that would bring eternal life. And then, at the end, when Jesus was about to be crucified, the Christ left him to return to his heavenly home. That was why, these people maintained, Jesus cried out in anguish on the cross, "My God, my God, why have you forsaken me?" It was because the divine element within had left him to die alone.

Still other Christians thought that something even stranger happened at the crucifixion. In their view, Jesus himself was divine, and so was not able to suffer. Moreover, they pointed out that Jesus was able to change his appearance at will. For example, after his resurrection Mary mistook him as the gardener (John 20:14–15), and the two disciples on the road to Emmaus didn't know who he was (Luke 24:13–27). According to these Christians, Jesus used his remarkable powers of transfiguration at the end of his life, so that he transformed himself to look like Simon of Cyrene, the man who had been compelled to carry his cross, and changed Simon to look like him. As a result, the Romans crucified the wrong fellow. According to some of these people, Jesus looked on the scene from a hill nearby, laughing at his enemies for thinking that they could kill him. Presumably Simon didn't find it so funny.[2]

None of these views—or any of the dozens of others that may seem equally peculiar—became the official line taken by Christianity. But even the official line—that is, the one that ended up winning over the most adherents and so became the standard interpretation—didn't spring up out of the ground overnight. Nor was it *directly* tied to the actual words and deeds of the historical Jesus, which were known by this time (the second century and following) only through sources that had been produced decades after the events they narrate. The official line, to some extent, emerged in opposition to views that many leaders of the church found objectionable, including some of the ones I've just summarized. For the sake of simplicity, I'll call these leaders "proto-orthodox" Christians, since the views that they developed in response to "heretical" views eventually became accepted as true (i.e., "orthodox") throughout most of the church.

These proto-orthodox leaders knew about the Christians, for example, who claimed that Jesus was so completely divine that he couldn't suffer. But for the proto-orthodox, if Jesus didn't really shed blood and die, then he couldn't have shed blood and died for the sins of the world. As a result, they insisted that Jesus was a man—completely human, just like the rest of us. At the same time, they knew of other Christians who agreed that Jesus was a man, but who said that he was nothing more than a man—a righteous man, to be sure, whom God favored above all others, but a man nonetheless, and nothing more. This view also struck the proto-orthodox as problematic, since they believed that the things that Jesus said and did were themselves divine, and (in their view) divine words and deeds require a divine character. Jesus, then, must have himself been God. But how could he be God if he was a man? The proto-orthodox rejected the view held by a large number of Christians, that Jesus Christ was two beings, one human and one divine—a view that did allow him to be both man and God—because for them this kind of disunity was a violation of the oneness of God. These proto-orthodox believers celebrated unity. There is only one God, one creation, one Son of God. So Jesus Christ was one being, not two. Yet he was both human and divine.

As a result of these debates, there emerged an orthodox view of Jesus that, by the time these debates and others like them were resolved in the fourth century, came to be embodied in the Christian creeds that continue to be recited in churches today. For example, in the Nicene Creed, Christians throughout the world still affirm that Christ is

> the only Son of God, eternally begotten of the Father, God from God, Light from Light, true God from true God, begotten, not made, of one Being with the Father. Through him all things were made...

At the same time, they continue to confess that

> he came down from heaven; by the power of the Holy Spirit he became incarnate from the Virgin Mary, and was made man. For our sake he was crucified under Pontius Pilate; he suffered death and was buried.

Jesus, then, is fully God and fully man. But how can he be both? In traditional Christian theology, the answer—as with most answers to the really interesting questions—remains a mystery. And it is *supposed* to remain a mystery. That's part of the power of the affirmation for those who make it.

Given everything we have seen so far, it should be clear that the concerns that drove these debates over who Christ was were far removed from the concerns of Jesus himself. The debates are ultimately rooted in the belief that Jesus' death had brought salvation to the world, as evidenced in his resurrection from the dead. That is to say, they relate more to what happened after his life than to the life itself. Or, to put the matter a bit differently, Christians appealed to their beliefs about the significance of Jesus' death in order to interpret his life—both the words he spoke and the deeds he performed. And that's what most people continue to do today. Those who subscribe to the orthodox notion that Christ was actually divine and human interpret what he said and did in that light. Rather than trying to understand what a first-century Palestinian Jew might have meant in first-century Palestine, they see Jesus' words and deeds in the light of their own beliefs about him. In other words, Christians tend to interpret Jesus' life from a dogmatic, rather than a historical, perspective.

Jesus in Historical Perspective

Even in the earliest stages of these debates over Christ's identity—that is, way back in the second century—Christians were collecting into a canon of Scripture certain texts that were thought to be authoritative for what they should believe and how they should live. Among these texts were some of the earliest accounts of Jesus' life. This is what has made a *historical* study of Jesus, such as we've engaged in here, possible in the first place. For not only did these texts embody the beliefs of their authors and their communities, and not only did they provide fuel for the fires of later theological controversies, they also contained genuine historical reminiscences of Jesus, the first-century apocalyptic prophet.

Once the historical sciences started to develop during the Enlightenment, historians could begin to approach these texts in a new way, looking not for their dogmatic content but for their historical testimony. The irony, of course, is that the historical value of these texts was there from the outset—available, on one level, even to those involved in theological debates that Jesus himself had no knowledge of or interest in. I call this an irony because one of the strands of Christianity that has been consistently marginalized throughout the course of the past 1,900 years has been one that took the authentic words of Jesus seriously (as opposed to the other words later placed on his lips). The historical Jesus did not teach about his own divinity or pass on to his disciples the doctrines that later came to be embodied in the Nicene Creed. His concerns were those of a first-century Jewish apocalypticist. Jesus anticipated that the end of the age was coming within his own generation. God would soon send a cosmic judge from heaven to right all the wrongs of this world, to overthrow the wicked and oppressive powers that opposed both God and his people, to bring in a perfect kingdom in which there would be no more hatred, war, disease, calamity, despair, sin, or death. People needed to repent in view of this coming day of judgment, for it was almost here.

Ever since Jesus pronounced this message of imminent judgment and salvation, he has had followers who agreed—even though the church at large has argued, sometimes vociferously, that Jesus must not have been speaking these words literally but figuratively. In this later Christian view, Jesus' proclamation must not have referred to an actual judgment of the earth and the appearance of an actual Kingdom, but possibly of judgment that people faced at the time of death, or of the kingdom that came in the community of Jesus' disciples who formed the church, a place of love, healing, and hope.

It's no wonder that a figurative construal of Jesus' words became so popular so soon and achieved such dominance for so long. If Jesus were to be taken literally—that is, if he really meant that the Son of Man was to arrive in the lifetime of his disciples—he was obviously wrong.

Some people, possibly lots of people, would claim that if Jesus was wrong, he can no longer be relevant. That claim can probably be disputed on theological grounds. But that is a different project from the one I've undertaken in this book. From the historical perspective that I've tried to maintain here, what is clear is that the apocalyptic Jesus we've uncovered is a far cry from the Jesus many people in our society today know. The Jesus of history, contrary to a modern "common sense" (at least in large chunks of American Christianity), was not a proponent of "family values." He urged his followers to abandon their homes and forsake families for the sake of the Kingdom that was soon to arrive. He didn't encourage people to pursue fulfilling careers, make a good living, and work for a just society for the long haul; for him, there wasn't going to be a long haul. The end of the world as we know it was already at hand. The Son of Man would soon arrive, bringing condemnation and judgment against those who prospered in this age, but salvation and justice to the poor, downtrodden, and oppressed. People should sacrifice everything for his coming, lest they be caught unawares and cast out of the Kingdom that was soon to arrive.

This message has not, for the most part, been overwhelmingly popular among people who call themselves Jesus' followers, even though, as we saw in the opening chapter, there have been individuals and groups on the fringes of Christianity since Jesus' day who have continued to proclaim it in a variety of different ways, from the apostle Paul in the first century to the Montanists in the second to Joachim of Fiore in the thirteenth to the Millerites in the nineteenth to the evangelical doomsayers in the present, including Hal Lindsey and loads of others of his ilk.

These later interpreters did not embrace the full message of Jesus with all its rich texture and nuance. They did not pay heed to his historical context or understand how his apocalyptic conviction about the coming of the Kingdom of God profoundly affected all of his words and deeds. Indeed, like most other Christian interpreters over the years, they opted to pick and choose from among the surviving words of Jesus, selecting the elements of his message that they found to be personally palatable. But their decision to focus on a central component of Jesus' actual message has led to particularly significant irony. Everyone who has predicted the end of their world has intuited one aspect of Jesus' teaching that appears to be historically accurate—the more popular strands of Christianity and the outspoken protests of numerous theologians notwithstanding. For those anticipating the imminent end of their own world have been able to base their expectations on the words of the historical Jesus, a first-century apocalyptic prophet who expected the imminent end of his.

notes

Chapter 1

1 Among the many intriguing accounts of millennial expectations, both today and throughout history, see especially the following: Paul Boyer, *When Time Shall Be No More: Prophecy Belief in Modern American Culture* (Cambridge, Mass.: Harvard University Press, 1992); Norman Cohn, *The Pursuit of the Millennium: Revolutionary Millenarians and Mystical Anarchists of the Middle Ages*, 2nd ed. (New York: Oxford University Press, 1970); Bernard McGinn, *Visions of the End: Apocalyptic Traditions in the Middle Ages* (New York: Columbia University Press, 1979); Stephen D. O'Leary, *Arguing the Apocalypse: A Theory of Millennial Rhetoric* (New York: Oxford University Press, 1994); Christopher Rowland, *The Open Heaven: A Study of Apocalyptic in Judaism and Early Christianity* (New York: Crossroad, 1982); and Timothy P. Weber, *Living in the Shadow of the Second Coming: American Premillennialism 1875–1982*, enlarged ed. (Grand Rapids, Mich.: Zondervan, 1983).

2 Nashville: World Bible Society, 1988.

3 Throughout this book, I will be using the nomenclature for dates that has become standard for historians. This involves the abbreviations of BCE (= Before the Common Era) and CE (= Common Era); these correspond to the more familiar abbreviations BC (= Before Christ) and AD (anno Domini, Latin for Year of our Lord). Scholars have moved to the newer abbreviations in order to be more inclusive, since our Western calendar is used not only by Christians, for whom it makes sense to talk about Jesus as both Christ and Lord, but also by Jews, Muslims, and others.

4   Edgar Whisenant and Greg Brewer, *The Final Shout Rapture Report: 1989* (Nashville, Tenn.: World Bible Society, 1989).
5   Hal Lindsey, with C. C. Carlson, *The Late Great Planet Earth* (Grand Rapids, Mich.: Zondervan, 1970).
6   For this abbreviation, see note 3.
7   See Boyer, *When Time Shall Be No More*, 126.
8   New York: Bantam Books, 1980.
9   "Soviets Still Masters of Deceit," *Countdown* (1990), 1.
10 See Weber, *Living in the Shadow*, 218; quoting *1980s: Countdown to Armageddon*, 146.
11 See the terrific little book by Stephen Jay Gould: *Questioning the Millennium: A Rationalist's Guide to a Precisely Arbitrary Countdown* (New York: Harmony Books, 1997), esp. ch. 1.
12 Miller's memoirs make for some fascinating reading. See Sylvester Bliss, *Memoirs of William Miller* (Boston: Joshua V. Himes, 1853) and the terrifically entitled apology by Francis D. Nichol, *The Midnight Cry: A Defense of the Character and Conduct of William Miller and the Millerites, Who Mistakenly Believed that the Second Coming of Christ Would Take Place in the Year 1844* (Washington, D.C.: Review and Herald, 1944).
13 Nichol, *Midnight Cry*, 33.
14 See O'Leary, *Arguing the Apocalypse*, 264, n. 61.
15 The studies, again, seem endless. For nice introductions, see Cohn, *Pursuit of the Millennium*, 108–12; McGinn, *Visions of the End*, and his shorter piece, "Apocalyptic Traditions and Spiritual Identity in Thirteenth-Century Religious Life," in *Apocalypticism in the Western Tradition* (Variorum, 1994) 293–300. For full studies, see especially Bernard McGinn, *The Calabrian Abbot: Joachim of Fiore in the History of Western Thought* (New York: Macmillan, 1985) and Marjorie Reeves, *The Influence of Prophecy in the Later Middle Ages: A Study in Joachimism* (New York: Oxford University Press, 1969).
16 Quoted from the abbot's "Letter to All the Faithful," 138; see further McGinn, *The Calabrian Abbot*, 191.
17 See R. E. Heine, *The Montanist Oracles and Testimonies*, North American Patristic Society Monograph Series, 14 (Macon, Ga.: Mercer University Press, 1989).
18 As quoted by the fourth-century heresy-hunter, Epiphanius, in his work *The Medicine Chest*, book 48, ch. 11.

Chapter 2

1   See the following authors in the bibliography: S. G. F. Brandon (Jesus as a revolutionary), R. Horsley (Jesus as a proto-Marxist), E. Schüssler Fiorenza (Jesus as a proto-feminist), M. Smith (Jesus as a magician), G. Downing and J. D. Crossan (Jesus as a Cynic).

Chapter 3

1   Because our surviving Greek manuscripts provide such a wide variety of (different) titles for the Gospels, textual scholars have long realized that

their familiar names (e.g., "The Gospel according to Matthew") do not go back to a single "original" title, but were later added by scribes.

2 Eusebius, *Ecclesiastical History*, III, 39.

3 Papias's comments are quoted in Eusebius, *Ecclesiastical History*, III, 39. For the text of the quotations and a brief discussion, see Bart D. Ehrman, *The New Testament and Other Early Christian Writings: A Reader* (New York: Oxford University Press, 1998), 362–64.

4 For a fuller discussion of these beliefs, and the reaction to them by Christians who found them heretical, see Bart D. Ehrman, *The Orthodox Corruption of Scripture: The Effect of Early Christological Controversies on the Text of the New Testament* (New York: Oxford University Press, 1993), ch. 1.

5 As we will see, there *may* have been a few other early written accounts of Jesus' words and deeds. But even if such accounts did exist, there is no guarantee that they were based on direct testimony — since they too were probably based on oral tradition—or that they were widely known. It is striking, for example, that our earliest New Testament author, Paul, gives no indication that he has ever seen or heard about a written account of Jesus' life, as we'll see further in ch.5.

Chapter 4

1 For a fuller, more useful discussion, see John P. Meier, *A Marginal Jew: Rethinking the Historical Jesus*, vol. 1; The Anchor Bible Reference Library (New York: Doubleday, 1991), 56–69.

2 See further the discussion and bibliography in Meier, *A Marginal Jew*, 93–98 and the fuller discussions of R. Travers Herford, *Christianity in Talmud and Midrash* (New York: Ktav, 1903) and Morris Goldstein, *Jesus in the Jewish Tradition* (New York: Macmillan, 1950).

3 See especially *Sanhedrin* 43a.

Chapter 5

1 Perhaps like Hercules, who was fathered by Zeus, whose twin brother, Iphicles, was fathered by a mortal. For a humorous retelling of the myth, see the play by the famous Roman comic playwright, Plautus, called the *Amphitryon*.

2 Eusebius, *Ecclesiastical History*, VI, 12.

3 It is possible, however, that Paul is not referring here to Judas who "betrayed" Jesus, since the Greek word he uses literally means "handed over" and more commonly refers to God's action of handing Jesus over to his death, as in Rom. 4:25 and 8:32.

4 I have a chapter devoted to the issue in my book *The New Testament: A Historical Introduction to the Early Christian Writings* (New York: Oxford University Press, 1997), ch. 6. See also the bibliography I give there.

5 See the preceding footnote.

Chapter 6

1 The two stories are not alike verbally. The do not, therefore, appear to have derived from Q.

Chapter 7

1 I've taken most of this sketch from my textbook, *The New Testament: A Historical Introduction to the Early Christian Writings* (New York: Oxford University Press, 1997), ch. 15. I include some further bibliography there. For a particularly valuable treatment, see the extensive and authoritative discussion of E. P. Sanders, *Judaism: Practice and Belief* 63BCE–66CE (London: SCM; Philadelphia: Trinity Press International, 1992).

2 See, again, the books mentioned in note 1. My figures in this section are taken from Sanders, *Judaism: Practice and Belief*, ch. 9.

Chapter 8

1 Schweitzer's autobiography is still very much worth reading: *Out of My Life and Thought: An Autobiography*, trans. Antje Bultmann Lemke (New York: Henry Holt, 1990; original translation: 1933).

2 For one thing, the way scholarship proceeds is by taking a consensus, disputing it, and establishing a new consensus (which is then disputed, leading to a new consensus that is itself then disputed, and so on, ad infinitum). In part, this kind of back and forth occurs because, well, frankly, historians have to write about *something*, and if everyone agrees about a particular issue, then there's nothing more to write about it. Radical shifts in scholarly opinion occur throughout all the disciplines of all the humanities all the time; they are as natural as vine-ripened tomatoes.

For some of the more interesting among the recent studies that take a nonapocalyptic view of Jesus, see the following in the bibliography given at the end of the book: Marcus Borg, John Dominic Crossan, F. Gerald Downing, Robert Funk, Richard Horsley, Morton Smith, and N. T. Wright.

3 It was put forth initially by a person who is, in fact, a very fine scholar, John Kloppenborg. See his work cited in the bibliography.

4 Crossan made a major impact on New Testament scholarship with his large and significant study, *The Historical Jesus: The Life of a Mediterranean Peasant.* In terms of sales, though, far more significant have been his two more popular books, *Jesus: A Revolutionary Biography* and *Who Killed Jesus?*

5 Recall: this criterion posits that traditions about Jesus that do not promote or support a Christian agenda, or that go against such a Christian agenda (i.e., that are "dissimilar" to what Christians were saying or wanted to say about Jesus), are almost certainly authentic. These particular traditions are ones that Christians evidently did not make up!

6 Not even the book of James, in which justification by works is stressed, coincides with the portrayal of Matthew 25—for in James, salvation is by *faith and* works, not works alone.

Chapter 9

1 This may be from Q. Note that it passes the criterion of dissimilarity, since Judas is included among the "twelve" here as a ruler in God's kingdom—not something a later follower of Jesus would probably make up!

2 This is Q, but Matthew has made the expected change from "son of man" to

"me," since Matthew, as most other Christians, understood Jesus himself to be the Son of Man.

3 See the discussion above, pp. 135–36.

4 For a fuller and convincing discussion of these points, see E. P. Sanders, *Jesus and Judaism*, 174–211.

5 E. P. Sanders, *Jesus and Judaism*, 200–11.

6 For fuller description of the Temple, with documentation, see Sanders, *Judaism, Practice and Belief*, 51–72, on whom I depend here.

Chapter 10

1 Compare G.Thom., 47: "No one is able to mount two horses or to stretch two bows; and no servant can serve two masters; for he will honor the one and treat the other with contempt."

2 I assume that the stronger term "hate" is original to Jesus, rather than "love more than," as in Matt. 10:37; and that the latter represents a change by Christians who recounted these words of Jesus and were taken aback by its harshness.

3 It is difficult to know whether these particular quotations go back to Jesus himself or were generated by Christian storytellers in Matthew's community after the destruction of the Temple in 70 CE. The thrust of the sayings, at least—with their minimizing of the importance of the Temple sacrificial cult—appears to derive from Jesus. Note, for example, the independent attestation of this theme, as I have observed.

4 See J. D. Crossan, *The Historical Jesus: The Life of a Mediterranean Jewish Peasant* (San Francisco: HarperSanFrancisco, 1991), 275–79.

5 I should emphasize that none of the parables gives a *complete* picture of all of Jesus' views about the Kingdom; instead, different parables stress different aspects of his teaching. In the present case, the parables of growth stress the contrast between the present—when the Kingdom was experiencing its rather inauspicious beginnings—and the future—when it will engulf the earth. These particular parables do not, however, illustrate Jesus' teaching about the cataclysmic break that will occur when the Son of Man comes in power.

Chapter 11

1 The most compelling and influential treatment has been that of Elizabeth Schüssler Fiorenza, *In Memory of Her: A Feminist Theological Reconstruction of Christian Origins* (New York: Crossroad, 1983).

2 Much of this excursus is taken from my textbook, *The New Testament: A Historical Introduction to the Early Christian Writings* (New York: Oxford University Press, 1997), ch. 14.

3 See, for example, J. D. Crossan, *The Historical Jesus: The Life of a Mediterranean Jewish Peasant* (San Francsco: HarperSanFrancisco, 1991), 313–20.

4 See, for example, Bruce Kapferer, *A Celebration of Demons: Exorcism and the Aesthetics of Healing in Sri Lanka* (Bloomington: Indiana University Press, 1983).

5 It might be noted that the stories I've just summarized occur in the same sequence in the Hebrew Bible and Mark. Did Christians model their accounts of Jesus on stories known from the Scriptures?

6 Recall the other antitheses, where Jesus also "radicalizes" a commandment of the Law; so Mark 10:2–9; cf. Matt. 5:31–32. See pp. 171–72.

7 Damascus Document, 11:13–14.

Chapter 12

1 Matthew's portrayal of the scene is particularly intriguing (Matt. 21:4–7). Evidently not realizing that the original wording of the Hebrew prophecy depicted a single animal, called both a donkey and a colt, Matthew thought there must have been two animals. And so he describes Jesus' straddling them both on his ride into Jerusalem!

2 See the fuller discussion in R. A. Horsley, *Jesus and the Spiral of Violence: Popular Jewish Resistance in Roman Palestine* (Minneapolis, Minn.: Fortress, 1987), 20–58.

3 For an interesting and controversial scholarly reconstruction of the event, its historical context, and its meaning, see E. P. Sanders, *Jesus and Judaism* (Philadelphia: Fortress, 1985), 61–76, on whom I'm largely dependent here (though see the following note).

4 This is, roughly, the conclusion reached by Sanders in the discussion cited in the previous note. I disagree, though, with Sanders when he insists that it is unlikely that Jesus was offended by the "corruption" of the Temple. As we'll see, we know of other Jewish apocalypticists from about this time, as well as Jews in earlier periods, who objected to the Temple cult on just these grounds, and it's not at all implausible to think that the earliest Gospel sources are right in indicating that Jesus did as well.

5 In which "Moses" narrates the future history of Israel that will transpire after he leaves the scene, down to the end of time, when the injustice and avarice of the Temple priests of the Temple cult will lead to its destruction; *Assumption of Moses* 5–7.

6 As we'll see in ch.13, Christians later interpreted texts like Isaiah 53 and Psalm 22 in reference to the Messiah. But it should be noted that the term "messiah" never occurs in these texts, and that no Jew prior to Christianity, so far as we know, ever understood them to refer to the future Messiah.

7 For brief discussion of the Roman presence in Palestine, see E. P. Sanders, *Judaism: Practice and Belief 63BCE–66CE* (London: SCM/Philadelphia: Trinity Press International, 1992), 30–43.

8 One explanation for Mark's narrative is that since Mark understood that Jesus himself was the Son of Man, he assumed that the high priest inferred this as well, and so thought that Jesus was claiming to be the divine judge of the earth, a claim that he found blasphemous. If this is right, though, it's a view that makes sense in terms of Mark's Gospel, written many years later and from a Christian perspective. It makes less sense, historically, as something that actually happened when Jesus was confronted by the Jewish high priest.

9 See the fuller discussion in James H. Charlesworth, *Jesus Within Judaism: New Light from Exciting Archaeological Discoveries* (New York: Doubleday, 1988).

10 J. D. Crossan, *Jesus: A Revolutionary Biography* (San Francisco: HarperSanFrancisco, 1991), ch. 6, entitled, "The Dogs Beneath the Cross."

Chapter 13

1 Much of the following discussion is taken from my textbook, *The New Testament: A Historical Introduction to the Early Christian Writings* (New York: Oxford University Press, 1997), ch. 16.

Chapter 14

1 See further the discussion on pp. 44–45, 71–76 above, and, for a fuller sketch, my book, *The Orthodox Corruption of Scripture: The Effect of Early Christological Controversies on the Text of the New Testament* (New York: Oxford University Press, 1993), ch. 1.

2 This view can be found, for example, in one of the Gnostic treatises discovered at Nag Hammadi, called "The Second Treatise of the Great Seth."

bibliography

Studies of the Historical Jesus (and Related Topics)

The following list is highly selective. I've included only the works cited in the course of the book, along with a handful of other books that, in my opinion, are among the most important and interesting (and accessible to nonspecialists) studies of the historical Jesus published over the past twenty or thirty years. For a full annotated bibliography, see Craig A. Evans, *Life of Jesus Research: An Annotated Bibliography*, rev. ed., New Testament Tools and Studies; 24 Leiden/New York/Cologne: E. J. Brill, 1996). Evans's bibliography has 2,045 entries of significant books and articles—and even this is nowhere near exhaustive!

Borg, Marcus J. *Conflict, Holiness and Politics in the Teachings of Jesus*. New York: E. Mellen, 1984.

———. *Jesus, The New Vision: The Spirit, Culture, and the Life of Discipleship*. San Francisco: Harper & Row, 1987.

Brandon, S. G. F. *Jesus and the Zealots: A Study of the Political Factor in Primitive Christianity*. New York: Scribner, 1967.

Charlesworth, James. *Jesus Within Judaism: New Light from Exciting Archaeological Discoveries*. New York: Doubleday, 1988.

Crossan, John Dominic. *The Historical Jesus: The Life of a Mediterranean Jewish Peasant*. San Francisco: HarperSanFrancisco, 1991.

———. *Jesus: A Revolutionary Biography*. San Francisco: HarperSanFrancisco, 1994.

———. *Who Killed Jesus? Exposing the Roots of Anti-Semitism in the Gospel Story of the Death of Jesus.* San Francisco: HarperSanFrancisco, 1995.

Downing, F. Gerald. *Christ and the Cynics: Jesus and Other Radical Preachers in First-Century Tradition.* Sheffield: JSOT, 1988.

Ehrman, Bart D. *The New Testament: A Historical Introduction to the Early Christian Writings.* New York: Oxford University Press, 1997.

———. *The Orthodox Corruption of Scripture: The Effect of Early Christological Controversies on the Text of the New Testament.* New York: Oxford University Press, 1993.

Frederiksen, Paula. *From Jesus to Christ: Thr Origins of the New Testament Images of Jesus.* New Haven, Conn.: Yale University Press, 1988.

Funk, Robert W. *Honest to Jesus: Jesus for a New Millennium.* San Francisco: HarperSanFrancisco, 1996.

Funk, Robert W., Roy W. Hoover, and the Jesus Seminar. *The Five Gospels: The Search for the Authentic Words of Jesus.* New York: Macmillan, 1993.

Funk, Robert W., and the Jesus Seminar. *The Acts of Jesus: The Search for the Authentic Deeds of Jesus.* San Francisco: HarperSanFrancisco, 1998.

Goldstein, Morris. *Jesus in the Jewish Tradition.* New York: Macmillan, 1950.

Harvey, Anthony E. *Jesus and the Constraints of History.* London: Duckworth, 1982.

Herford, R. Travers. *Christianity in Talmud and Midrash.* New York: Ktav, 1903.

Horsley, Richard A. *Jesus and the Spiral of Violence: Popular Jewish Resistance in Roman Palestine.* Minneapolis, Minn.: Fortress, 1987.

Johnson, Luke Timothy. *The Real Jesus: The Misguided Quest for the Historical Jesus and the Truth of the Traditional Gospels.* San Francisco: HarperSanFrancisco, 1996.

Kloppenborg, John. *The Formation of Q: Trajectories in Ancient Wisdom Collections.* Philadelphia: Fortress, 1987.

Meier, John. *A Marginal Jew: Rethinking the Historical Jesus.* Vol. 1: *The Roots of the Problem and Person.* New York: Doubleday, 1991. Vol. 2: *Mentor, Message, and Miracles.* New York: Doubleday, 1994.

Paulus, Heinrich. *Das Leben Jesu als Grundlage einer reinen Geschichte des Urchristentums.* Heidelberg: C. F. Winder, 1828.

Sanders, E. P. *The Historical Figure of Jesus.* London: Allen Lane/Penguin, 1993.

———. *Jesus and Judaism.* Philadelphia: Fortress, 1985.

———. *Judaism: Practice and Belief 63BCE–66CE.* London: SCM/Philadelphia: Trinity Press International, 1992.

Schüssler Fiorenza, Elisabeth. *In Memory of Her: A Feminist Theological Reconstruction of Christian Origins.* New York: Crossroad, 1983.

Schweitzer, Albert. *The Quest of the Historical Jesus: A Critical Study of Its Progress from Reimarus to Wrede.* New York: Macmillan, 1978 (original German edition: 1906).

Smith, Morton. *Jesus the Magician.* San Francisco: Harper & Row, 1978.

Stanton, Graham. *The Gospels and Jesus.* Oxford: Oxford University Press, 1989.

Strauss, David Friedrich. *The Life of Jesus Critically Examined*. Philadelphia: Fortress, 1972 (original German edition: 1835–36).

Vermès, Géza. *Jesus the Jew: A Historian's Reading of the Gospels*. London: Collins, 1973.

Wright, N. T. *Jesus and the Victory of God*. Minneapolis: Fortress, 1996.

Millennial Movements and Apocalypticism

Again, I have restricted this list to books that I've cited and a few others that strike me as particularly interesting or significant. I've included several works that embrace particular millennial views and those that study the phenomena from a scholarly perspective.

Bliss, Sylvester. *Memoirs of William Miller*. Boston: Joshua V. Himes, 1853.

Boyer, Paul. *When Time Shall Be No More: Prophecy Belief in Modern American Culture*. Cambridge, Mass.: Harvard University Press, 1992.

Bull, Malcomb. *Apocalypse Theory and the Ends of the World*. Cambridge: Blackwell, 1995.

Cohn, Norman. *The Pursuit of the Millennium: Revolutionary Millenarians and Mystical Anarchists of the Middle Ages*, 2nd ed. New York: Oxford University Press, 1970.

Gould, Stephen Jay. *Questioning the Millennium: A Rationalist's Guide to a Precisely Arbitrary Countdown*. New York: Harmony Books, 1997.

Heine, R. E. *The Montanist Oracles and Testimonies*. North American Patristic Society Monograph Series, 14. Macon, Ga.: Mercer University Press, 1989.

Kapferer, Bruce. *A Celebration of Demons: Exorcism and the Aesthetics of Healing in Sri Lanka*. Bloomington: Indiana University Press, 1983.

Lindsey, Hal. *The 1980's: Countdown to Armageddon*. New York: Bantam, 1980.

Lindsey, Hall, with C. C. Carlson, *The Late Great Planet Earth*. Grand Rapids: Zondervan, 1970.

McGinn, Bernard. *Antichrist: Two Thousand Years of the Human Fascination with Evil*. San Francisco: HarperSanFrancisco, 1994.

———. *Apocalypticism in the Western Tradition*. Brookfield, Vt.: Variorum, 1994.

———. *The Calabrian Abbot: Joachim of Fiore in the History of Western Thought*. New York: Macmillan, 1985.

———. *Visions of the End: Apocalyptic Traditions in the Middle Ages*. New York: Columbia University Press, 1979.

Nichol, Francis D. *The Midnight Cry: A Defense of the Character and Conduct of William Miller and the Millerites, Who Mistakenly Believed that the Second Coming of Christ Would Take Place in the Year 1844*. Washington, D.C.: Review and Herald, 1944.

O'Brian, Conor Cruise. *On the Eve of the Millennium*: New York: The Free Press, 1994.

O'Leary, Stephen D. *Arguing the Apocalypse: A Theory of Millennial Rhetoric*. New York: Oxford University Press, 1994.

Reeves, Marjorie. *The Influence of Prophecy in the Later Middle Ages: A Study in Joachimism.* New York: Oxford University Press, 1969.

Robbins, Thomas, and Susan J. Palmer, eds. *Millennium, Messiahs, and Mayhem: Contemporary Apocalyptic Movements.* New York/London: Routledge, 1997.

Rowland, Christopher. *The Open Heaven: A Study of Apocalyptic in Judaism and Early Christianity.* New York: Crossroad, 1982.

Stozier, Charles D. *Apocalypse: On the Psychology of Fundamentalism in America.* Boston: Beacon, 1994.

Weber, Timothy P. *Living in the Shadow of the Second Coming: American Premillennialism 1875–1982.* Enlarged ed. Grand Rapids, Mich.: Zondervan, 1983.

Whisenant, Edgar. *88 Reasons Why the Rapture Will Be in 1988.* Nashville, Tenn.: World Bible Society, 1988.

Whisenant, Edgar, and Gary Brewer. *The Final Shout Rapture Report: 1989.* Nashville, Tenn.: World Bible Society, 1989.

Sources for Extracanonical Texts

The following sourcebooks provide the primary texts discussed in this book.

Ehrman, Bart D. *The New Testament and Other Early Christian Writings: A Reader.* New York: Oxford University Press, 1998.

Elliott, J. K. *The Apocryphal New Testament: A Collection of Apocryphal Christian Literature in an English Translation.* Oxford: Clarendon, 1993.

Robinson, James W., ed. *The Nag Hammadi Library in English.* Rev. ed. Leiden/New York: E. J. Brill, 1996.

Vermès, Géza, ed. *The Complete Dead Sea Scrolls in English.* Rev. ed. New York: Allen Lane/Penguin, 1997.

Wise, Michael, Martin Abegg, and Edward Cook, eds. *The Dead Sea Scrolls: A New Translation.* San Francisco: HarperSanFrancisco, 1996.

Index of Subjects

Creation/Creator, 10, 14–15, 44, 75–76

Criteria, for establishing historically reliable tradition, 85–96; Rules of thumb, 87–89, 128–31; Specific criteria, 89–96, 134–37

Crucifixion, 223–24. *See* Jesus, death of

Cumanus, 116

Cynics, 189, 19. *See also* Jesus as a cynic

Daniel, book of, 6, 12, 119, 134, 146–47, 220

David, King, 37–39

Dead Sea Scrolls, 59, 111–13, 119, 134–35. *See also* Essenes

De-apocalypticizing of the tradition, 130–32

Demiurge, 78

Demons. *See* Exorcisms and Satan

Disappointment, the Great, 12–14

Disciples of Jesus, 185–87, 217–18

Dissimilarity, criterion of, 91–94, 135–37, chs. 6–13 *passim*

Divorce, Jesus' teachings on, 172–73, 202

Ebionites, Gospel of, 238

Egerton Gospel, 133

Egypt, 8–9, 63

Egyptian, The, 117–18, 135, 138, 158

Elijah, 199

Enemies, love of, 174–75

Enlightenment, 24–27, 243

Epicureans, 189

Epiphanius, 248n.18

Essenes, 108, 111–13, 138, 166, 203–05, 208, 213–14. *See also* Dead Sea Scrolls

Ethics, Jesus' teaching of, 163–81

European Commonwealth, 8–9

Eusebius, 43, 67, 249nn.2 [ch. 3], 2 [ch. 5]

Exiguus, Dionysius, 11

Exodus, book of, 32–33

Exorcisms, Jesus' reputation of performing, 197–98

Eyewitnesses, 41–53, 86

Faith in God, in the teachings of Jesus, 178–79

Family values, in the teachings of Jesus, 170–71

Fig tree, 5–6

Food, kosher laws, 164, 204–5

Forgiveness, 173

Four-Source Hypothesis, 80–83, 90

Fourth Philosophy, 113–14, 138, 205

Franciscans, 15

Galilee, 191–92, 201–02, 209. *See also* Palestine; Nazareth

Garden of Gethsemane, 219

Gemara, 62–63

Genesis, book of, 10, 75

Gentiles, 159, 205, 237–38

Gnostics / Gnosticism, 68, 73–78, 253n.2

Good Samaritan, parable of, 91

Gorbachev, Mikhail, 10

Gospels as "true stories," 30–40; as historical sources (*See* Sources for the historical Jesus); as myths, 27–29; as natural histories, 24–28; as supernatural histories, 23–24, 28–29

Index of Passages

Index of Modern Authors